The psychology of growing old

RETHINKING AGEING SERIES

Series editor: Brian Gearing
               School of Health and Social Welfare
               The Open University

The rapid growth in ageing populations in Britain and other countries has led to a dramatic increase in academic and professional interest in the subject. Over the past decade this has led to the publication of many research studies which have stimulated new ideas and fresh approaches to understanding old age. At the same time, there has been concern about continued neglect of ageing and old age in the education and professional training of most workers in health and social services, and about inadequate dissemination of the new information and ideas about ageing to a wider public.

This series aims to fill a gap in the market for accessible, up-to-date studies of important issues in ageing. Each book will focus on a topic of current concern addressing two fundamental questions: what is known about this topic? And what are the policy, service and practice implications of our knowledge? Authors will be encouraged to develop their own ideas, drawing on case material, and their own research, professional or personal experience. The books will be interdisciplinary, and written in clear, non-technical language which will appeal to a broad range of students, academics and professionals with a common interest in ageing and age care.

Current and forthcoming titles:
Simon Biggs *et al.*: **Elder abuse in perspective**
Ken Blakemore and Margaret Boneham: **Age, race and ethnicity:**
    A comparative approach
Joanna Bornat (ed.): **Reminiscence reviewed: Evaluations,**
    achievements, perspectives
Joanna Bornat and Maureen Cooper: **Older learners**
Bill Bytheway: **Ageism**
Beverley Hughes: **Older people and community care**
Anne Jamieson: **Company policies of care for older people**
Sheila Peace *et al.*: **Re-evaluating residential care**
Moyra Sidell: **Health in old age: Myth, mystery and management**
Andrew Sixsmith: **Quality of life: Rethinking well-being in old age**
Robert Slater: **The psychology of growing old: Looking forward**

The psychology of growing old
Looking forward

ROBERT SLATER

OPEN UNIVERSITY PRESS
Buckingham · Philadelphia

Open University Press
Celtic Court
22 Ballmoor
Buckingham
MK18 1XW

and

1900 Frost Road, Suite 101
Bristol, PA 19007, USA

First Published 1995

A catalogue record of this book is available from the British Library

ISBN 0 335 19318 8 (pb)   0 335 19319 6 (hb)

Library of Congress Cataloging-in-Publication Data

Slater, Robert, 1945–
   The psychology of growing old: looking forward/Robert Slater.
      p.   cm. – (Rethinking ageing series)
   Includes bibliographical references and index.
   ISBN 0–335–19318–8 (pbk.)   ISBN 0–335–19319–6
   1. Aging – Psychological aspects.   2. Aged – Psychology.   3. Aging – Great Britain – Psychological aspects.   4. Aged – Great Britain – Psychology.
I. Title.   II. Series.
BF724.8.S54   1995
155.67–dc20   95–5368
                                                                        CIP

Typeset by Type Study, Scarborough
Printed in Great Britain by Biddles Limited, Guildford and Kings Lynn

*To Mary, Tom, Frank and Joel, who put up with my
usual shenanigans while this book was in preparation.
And for mum and dad, who fostered my interest in
ageing and later life, and gave me their reflections on it.*

Contents

Series editor's preface		ix
Acknowledgements		xii
	Introduction: Looking forward – the psychological challenge of later life	1
1	'Us' and 'them'	12
2	On being older	29
3	Coping and failing to cope	44
4	Speed of behaviour	56
5	Our changing brain – causes, effects and responses	77
6	Belonging – supportive relationships	97
7	Belonging – place and purpose	111
8	Looking back	120
9	Finding meaning	127
10	Reconstruing reality	137
	References	147
	Index	158

Series editor's preface

The original aim of the 'Rethinking Ageing' series was to fill the gap between what is now known about older people and ageing populations and the relatively limited amount of knowledge and information available in an accessible form to professional and voluntary workers and others who are involved in the care of older people. The series has therefore focused on topics of current concern or interest to this primary audience. However, the first four books in the series have also attracted a significant secondary readership among researchers and postgraduate students who want a critical overview of an important contemporary topic in gerontology.

A third audience we have always had in mind comprises people who, whether or not they have a professional or academic involvement in gerontology, are interested in their own and other people's ageing. This book, Robert Slater's *The psychology of growing old: Looking forward*, will be of interest to all these categories of reader. It is an immensely informative, up to date and integrated review of the literature on psychological ageing. As such, it should be of great value to practitioners and researchers. But what should be further emphasized is that *The psychology of growing old*, perhaps more than any other book published so far in this series, is about *all of us*: the reader is addressed as an ageing person, someone who, whatever his or her chronological age, is growing older and can therefore be assumed to be interested in learning about this life-long process. As Robert Slater says, ageing is a *personal* issue for us all. We all need to know more about ageing to understand the course of our own lives and those of other people. We all have a stake in how society treats present and future generations of older people.

Books about ageing reflect the times in which they are written. In 1966, the first edition of the *The Psychology of Human Ageing*, Denis Bromley's ground-breaking and influential textbook, was published. Like Robert Slater's,

Bromley's book also aimed to provide a non-technical general introduction to the subject of human adult ageing which would interest the intelligent lay person, as well as providing a description of psychology as a scientific discipline. But if their objectives are similar, it is interesting to note some significant differences in the content of these two books: differences which are partly a reflection of the way that in the intervening thirty years the study of the psychology of ageing has changed.

First, there has been a welcome broadening of what psychology as a discipline considers its rightful subject matter. Psychology is the scientific study of mental life and behaviour, but psychologists have increasingly become concerned to study the whole context within which the individual ages. In particular, there has been an increased appreciation that observable instances of decline in mental capacity may be wrongly attributed to the process of ageing itself, rather than to the effects of ill-health on some older individuals. In addition, more attention has been given to the influence of other people, and other aspects of the interpersonal context, on the psychological health and well-being of the older individual.

In his discussion of intelligence, memory and other cognitive processes, Robert Slater reflects these disciplinary changes by emphasizing the importance of considering the whole person in his or her environment. He considers the extent to which common physical and mental changes associated with ageing have any significant practical impact on the individual's everyday life and capacity to cope (Chapter 3); and assesses the consequences of ageism and age prejudice for the way older individuals think and behave. As well as chapters on speed of behaviour (4) and changes in the brain (5) – the traditional subject-matter of psychology – there are other chapters on the experience of being older (2), on coping and failing to cope (3), and on our psychological attachment to people and places (6 and 7).

Part of the maturing of psychology as a discipline has been its willingness to acknowledge that there are as many questions as there are certain answers. This has led to changes over the past thirty years in the way psychologists approach ageing. Their interests have broadened from studying observable and measurable behavioural traits to a concern with how people experience ageing and old age, and how they may find meaning and integrity in late life. As the subject matter has broadened, so the methods of study have also had to develop. Accordingly, the laboratory experiment has been supplemented by qualitative research 'tools', such as the psychological case study, the phenomenological interview and the life history. This book reflects this methodological progress and also deals with the less measurable, but hugely important, existential aspects of the individual's psychology – notably in Chapter 9, 'Finding meaning', and Chapter 10, 'Reconstruing reality'.

As 'Looking forward' (the sub-title of this book) implies, psychologists of ageing like Robert Slater have also been increasingly concerned to adopt a *life-span perspective*, which sees old age as a time which cannot be isolated from the rest of life. Cohorts of individuals have been studied as they age through time, revealing at least some potential for development in later life. There is also much more emphasis now on the positive features of the experience of old age – psychological ageing is no longer characterized by images of decline, by 'doom and gloom'. In his important contribution to the new Open University course, *An Ageing Society* (K256), Robert Slater speculates as to whether this sea-change in the discipline of psychology itself – in subject-matter and overall view of ageing as well as in research methods – is solely attributable to an increasingly sophisticated appreciation of the 'facts of ageing' as revealed by empirical research, or whether, at least in part, it reflects 'ageing psychologists perceiving their subject-matter from a different perspective' . . . 'For the first time, "ageing" can be seen from the perspective of psychologists who have not only spent much of their life studying the subject, but who now have first hand experience of it. Perhaps that is one reason why it no longer gets the negative and relatively simplistic treatment it did' (K256, Unit 8, p. 95). This change is mirrored in the career of James E. Birren, an eminent research psychologist and author of the first major text on the psychology of ageing written in the positivist tradition, who in his later years has turned his attention to the topics of wisdom and spiritual maturity. It would appear that it's not just that gerontology and psycho-gerontology have matured as subjects: their practitioners have grown older and along with this has come an increasing interest in existential and 'spiritual' issues in ageing – in what it is like to experience being old and in the search for meaning in old age. Along with these new foci of interests come new methods of study. Birren is far from alone among psychologists of ageing in turning to autobiography, biography and personal narratives in order to understand human development. It has been suggested that psychology's 'dark age of wisdom' is coming to an end with the recognition that there is room for evidence collected from outside the laboratory (Birren and Fisher, 1990). This book is both a reflection of and a contribution to that growing enlightenment.

Brian Gearing
School of Health and Social Welfare
The Open University

References

Birren, J.E. and Fisher, L.M. (1990) The elements of wisdom: overview and integration, in R.J. Sternberg (ed.) *Wisdom: Its Nature, Origins and Development*. Cambridge: Cambridge University Press.

Bromley, D.B. (1966) *The Psychology of Human Ageing*. Harmondsworth: Penguin Books. Third edition published as *Human Ageing: An Introduction to Gerontology*, 1988.

Slater, R. (1994) Psychological changes and challenges in later life, Unit 8, *An Ageing Society* (K256). Milton Keynes: Open University.

Acknowledgements

This book is in many ways the outcome of a three-year secondment to the Open University, from the University of Wales, Cardiff. During that period, while working on the course *An Ageing Society*, I had the opportunity to collect much of the material referred to in the book and study leave granted to me by the Open University enabled work to start on it. I am very grateful to my course team colleagues at the Open University – Sheila Peace, Brian Gearing, Julia Johnson – and to Malcolm Johnson who took me on board in the first place. And to our support staff – Caroline Malone and Antonet Roberts.

Working with such colleagues was a pleasure and a learning experience. It was in course team meetings that I became more fully aware of the need to appreciate the experience of ageing and the diverse perspectives of those who study it and are engaged in it.

Looking forward – the psychological challenge of later life

Age is opportunity no less
Than youth itself, though in another dress.

(Longfellow, *Morituri Salutamus*)

This book is about *you*, the reader. If you are not old now, you may be sooner than you think. Time really does seem to go faster the older you get; finding that one is 'old' catches most people by surprise. We generally don't *feel* old, so much as come to realize that that is how others see us. Ageing is a personal matter, for the writer and readers of this book alike.

> I could never imagine getting old. I still can't, although I'm old. I still don't feel that I've got to 73 yet, you know what I mean? I still don't realise I've got to 73 because I don't feel 73. I don't feel what I imagine 73 should be like – you know.
>
> (Thompson *et al.* 1991: 121)

But being old is relative, of course. Consider the headline in the *Evening Standard* – 'The shock of the old' – which suggested that the Queen, John Osborne, Mick Jagger and Cliff Richard were 'suddenly showing their age'. Someone of the same generation as these public figures might wonder if the 'shock' might equally apply to him or herself, and have a closer look in the mirror. But to a teenager they have probably always seemed old. And how might they seem to a centenarian? And are people equally 'old' if they are the same age?

A 55-year-old friend of mine recently decided she's done enough for her grown children and it was time she had some fun; she sold up in the country and bought a flat in London. The couple she bought it from explained they were getting on a bit now, and thought they'd better move to the country to be near their daughter. They, too, were exactly 55.

(Whitehorn 1991:47)

The results of an Age Concern (1992) survey suggest that 'old age' is thought to start later the older one is. On average, 16- to 24-year-olds suggested old age began at 63, while those aged 75 and over suggested it started at 76. Whereas 59 per cent of the younger group suggested old age started between the ages of 60 and 75, only 27 per cent of the older group did so. The younger respondents also seemed more readily able than the older ones to give a definite answer to the question of when old age starts.

In 1951, 271 individuals may have received royal congratulations on reaching 100 years of age, but the 1991 census of Great Britain recorded some 4000 centenarians. More individuals than ever before will experience growing old, as life expectancy at birth and at later ages increases. Even at a 100 you have a 50:50 chance of living to be 101. But, at that age, will some of us be suffering from 'chronic life syndrome'?:

A disease which already affects hundreds of thousands of Americans . . . was identified by medical researcher Neil Henderson at the American Association for the Advancement of Science this week. Dr. Henderson . . . says that people are being increasingly affected by 'chronic life syndrome' in which the good effects of prolonged life are negated by the ill-effects of the illnesses that go with it.

(Ince 1993:9)

Some light is thrown on the above question by Manton and Stallard (1991), who consider the notion of 'active life expectancy', which is the number of years a person can expect to live free from 'serious' disability. An average American male of 65, for example, has a life expectancy of over 14 more years, of which nearly 12 might be active. At age 85, he could expect to live 5 more years, of which 2.5 would be active. But the picture for women is somewhat different, as it is for many other aspects of later life. At age 65 an American woman might expect to live on average another 18–19 years (some 4–5 to five years more than a man), of which 13.6 might be active (just under 2 years more than a man). At age 85, women might expect to live another 6–7 years (over 1 year more than a man), of which more than 2 years would be active (somewhat *less* than for a man). As we shall see in Chapter 2, although women live longer than men, at later ages they are relatively more impaired.

Living longer

American data suggest that even during the period 1962–84, life expectancy at every age increased, but the predictability of longevity for any particular individual became less exact the older the person was. Rothenberg *et al.* (1991: S70) conclude:

> It is still conceivable that the current expansion of mortality faces the maximum human life span as its ultimate barrier, and that compression [of mortality, wherein deaths cluster around some fixed limit] will eventually take place against this biological limit. If the maximum human life span is in the region of 115–20 years, it is not yet possible to test this hypothesis.

Headlines such as the one in the Welsh morning newspaper, the *Western Mail*, announcing 'Golden oldies set to hit new record', increase public awareness that not only are there more older people around, but people are living longer. In this instance, figures showed a projected increase in Wales of the number of people over 90 rising from a 1989-based figure of 11,900 to 22,300 in 2006 – almost double. A *Guardian* headline, 'Not so young as we were', had a somewhat more panicky tone, noting that 'we're already feeling our age, but new census results reveal an unpredicted explosion in Britain's elderly population'. The numbers of pensioners will *soar* and *spurt*; the new estimates will *ratchet up* the future community care bill; the key change is a *sharp increase* in the projected numbers of people over 45; and *the especially bad news* is that 'not only will there be fewer workers supporting more dependants, but the workers will be no spring chickens'. Rather than promote discussion of how we might plan to meet the challenges of what is, after all, a success story – gains in health, nutrition and hygiene mean that fewer people are dying prematurely – the tone is unconstructively alarmist. No mention that older workers might be better workers, that retirement might be made flexible, that there could be more work-sharing, or that expenditure priorities and taxation strategies could be revised. But what demographic changes are occurring?

We have known that the UK population is ageing for many years. More or less all populations in the world are, or will be showing the effect. But the 'worry' voiced in the *Guardian* concerns a revision of the British figures estimating how many people over 75 there will be in 2031. An estimate made in 1989 was revised upwards by 18 per cent in 1991, to suggest that in England and Wales in 2031 there will be some 6.1 million individuals aged 75 or more, compared with the 3.6 million who were alive in 1991.

A comparison of the 1981 and 1991 census figures for Great Britain of residents age 60 and over shows an 8 per cent increase to 11.6 million. And this rise itself was almost entirely due to a large increase in those aged 75 and over, and especially of those aged 85 and over, of whom in 1991 there were 50 per cent more than in 1981. In 1991, of all people aged 60 and over, 58 per cent were women, but two out of three people aged over 85 were women. In 1991, 21.2 per cent of the residents of Great Britain were aged 60 and over, varying from 17.8 per cent in inner London to 24.2 per cent in the South West. As to be expected, the highest localized proportions of older people were to be found in coastal retirement districts such as Christchurch (Dorset), and Rother (East

Sussex), which each had 37 per cent. New towns, such as Milton Keynes (Bucks) and Bracknell (Berks), were the relatively 'youngest'.

Clearly, we are all part of an ageing society, and consequently have more of a personal future to consider than did previous generations. That future will be spent in a society comprising increasing proportions of very old people, among whom we may number. The challenge of having some influence on our own future is also a challenge to influence the future of others by articulating the potential that having more life to live presents, and by discovering ways of achieving it. As Silverman (1987) suggests, older people are the modern pioneers.

Being a pioneer in this sense raises several challenges. Our future will have constraints, some of which we discuss later in Chapters 2 and 6. But there is a potential for freedom too. When those aged 55 and over were asked, 'As you grow older do you find that you enjoy life more than you used to, less than you used to, or about the same?', only 27 per cent of 55- to 74-year-olds said 'less', as did only 38 per cent of those aged 75 or over. When those who said they enjoyed life 'more' were asked why, 83 per cent mentioned the greater freedom they had (British Gas 1991).

Such freedom might be from the demands of work, perhaps, or from children, or from 'being hag-ridden by sex' (Heim 1990: 84). When we consider sex in Chapter 1, as part of an examination of attitudes towards older people, we shall note, as elsewhere, that values influence our perceptions. The sexual activity of adolescence and adulthood, used as a baseline from which 'decline' is measured, may be less 'missed' as 'freed from', if it is seen as involuntary and hormone-driven. Is the 'extroversion' of youth to be valued more than the 'introversion' of old age? In Chapters 8, 9 and 10, we shall also look again at values which underpin our perceptions of behaviour and personality. In Chapter 8, we examine how for some, reminiscence may lead to a better understanding of one's life, while in Chapter 9 we explore religious and spiritual frameworks, and the development of wisdom, as enablers of understanding. Chapter 10 further examines the influence of religion and our approach to dying and death.

Changes ahead

Freedom, though, often brings with it fear, because managing freedom requires a certain creativeness, discipline, and sense of personal responsibility and effectiveness. The freedom of retirement, for example, can be understandably daunting for some individuals, and is one of the issues we examine in Chapter 7. We may respond to such circumstances as retirement with what Langer (1991) calls 'mindlessness' – taking things for granted, letting others make decisions for us, being controlled rather than controlling. We consider such aspects of coping and failing to cope in Chapter 3. On the basis of her research, Langer suggests that encouraging more 'mindful ageing' can lead to a variety of positive outcomes:

Perhaps most important, these elderly men were encouraged to take a good deal of control over their lives. Other research . . . suggests that this variable is indeed powerful. Making demands on the elderly, as we did here, may well have been a big factor in reversing many debilities of old age . . .

(Langer 1991: 119)

As well as facing up to the fear of freedom and the difficulties of being mindful, extended life also brings the challenge of what Sartre (1957), in his existentialist perspective, calls 'sincerity' or 'authentic being'. In the context of discussing quality of life in later life, Sixsmith (1993: 218) notes:

The idea of 'facing up to life', of struggling to transcend the contingencies of life, is at the core of the existentialist view of human being. While much of life might be structured by external factors, we do not have to live our lives according to a predetermined blueprint, but are free to make choices within available options. So how do we make choices in life? Arguably, the common way of being is governed by conformism, doing what others want you to do, a kind of socially-defined, unauthentic self. This amounts to self-deception, where we evade personal responsibility by acting in the ways that are expected of us or following the well-trodden paths of life.

Of course, the paths of later life are not well-trodden because only of late are substantial numbers of us looking forward to embarking upon them or helping to create new ones. Pioneers can help the rest of us by writing 'travel guides', which might be one reason why Stott (1981), for example, wrote the appropriately titled *Ageing for Beginners*.

Other forms of 'help' come in the shape of alternative role models for later life. As other recent headlines suggest, these may be 'Armed pensioners [who] plan to lobby parliament', or those TV personalities who are '50 and proud of it', or those residents of an old people's home who 'took on a local authority in a High Court battle', or those who wrote the book *Growing Old Disgracefully* (The Hen Co-op 1993).

With the increased visibility in the media of such 'active older people', especially those who are 'ordinary' and so not to be dismissed as the exceptions that prove the rule, we witness an assertiveness and sense of power that contradicts the image of later life as enfeeblement and passivity. Consider, for example, the 3000 or so students currently registered with the Open University who are 60 or over. 'An important point which emerged from the analysis of the data on academic performance was that the most generally successful of all age groups in the Open University was that of 60 to 64 year olds' (Older Students' Research Group 1993: 2). Or consider those older people who have set up and are members of branches of the University of the Third Age, or the individual who, having retired from teaching, registered for a bricklaying course. We consider such issues again in Chapter 7, but examples abound: 'Ramon Blanco, aged 60, a Venezuelan violin maker has become the oldest climber to reach the summit of the 29,028-ft Mount Everest' (Anon 1993).

We will return to images of older people when we consider 'us' and 'them' in Chapter 1. Here let us note that current ideas about the psychology of old age, which permit discussion of *development* in later life rather than cataloguing ubiquitous *decline*, now present the possibility and perhaps the challenge of 'successful ageing' (Baltes and Baltes 1990). We consider such changes in psychological perspective in more detail in Chapters 4 and 9. Rethinking ageing this way – that is, giving it a positive gloss – is increasingly in evidence. The respected psychotherapist and counsellor Carl Rogers titled a chapter reflecting on his own old age 'Growing old: Or older and growing'. The famous developmental psychologist Erik Erikson called his book *Vital Involvement in Old Age*. The charity Research into Ageing has a glossy publicity brochure called 'Age: The time of your life'. And the introduction to the *Directory of Services for Elderly People* is called 'Looking forward: A positive view of old age'.

Though to be welcomed, these reconceptualizations should also be treated with caution. In wanting to be positive about later life, in introducing notions of late-life development, of qualitative as well as quantitative change, there is a possibility of introducing an all-singing all-dancing sanitized view of a later life that *could be*. We might psychologize away the realities of unwanted change or circumstances, through either a sort of wish-fulfilment or by blaming the victim. We may assume that the determining power of the social, psychological and physiological context in which individuals grow old can be more easily changed than is the case. Nor would many want to justify some of the suffering that can go on in later life on the grounds that something positive might come out of it, although such notions are raised in Chapter 10. We must be careful not to replace an 'all doom and gloom' view of later life with one of old age as Shangri-la.

Certainly, the possibility of a new golden age for old age might be marred for many by – as one headline suggested – a '"Death sentence" screening [that] would blight 1m lives before onset of disease without hope of cure'. The screening, for at least one form of Alzheimer's disease, which can be given at any age with an allegedly 90 per cent accuracy, raises profound ethical and social questions, some of which we consider further in Chapter 5. Perhaps we should maintain an ambivalent view about later life:

> Ancient Egyptian writings reveal an ambivalence towards growing old. On the one hand, ageing is accompanied by a variety of undesirable degenerative changes; on the other, ageing has some compensations and rewards including those associated with increased wisdom and social status. These give rise to contrasting attitudes and ambivalent feelings that persist today.
>
> (Bromley 1988:34)

Does the following ring true?

> Grow old along with me!
> The best is yet to be,
> The last of life, for which the first was made:
> Our times are in His hand

> Who saith, 'A whole I planned,
> Youth shows but half; trust God: see all, nor be
> afraid!'
>
> (Robert Browning 1812–89, from *Rabbi ben Ezra, i*)

It would be nice if the best *was* yet to be, wouldn't it? A more suitable challenge may be to make it better than it is, something we return to in Chapter 10.

Individuals in context

Rethinking old age in a more positive light might also have something to do with the age of those who research it. It is only recently that those who study ageing gerontologists have themselves grown old in any numbers No-one likes to fulfil the stereotype of old age as unproductive and useless, psychologists included. So 'older' psychologists, like everyone else, have a vested interest in reconstruing later life in a more positive mould. 'Successful ageing' may be a shining beacon, but it could become a siren dragging us onto the rocks of unnecessary dissatisfaction. Just as models of 'glamorous grannies' will succeed in making some older women feel inferior about their looks, so too might models who have aged 'successfully' conspire to deject those who are worried that they haven't. 'Successful ageing' might provide another sort of blueprint that we feel we should follow, which leads to another form of 'inauthentic' old age.

As to the determining effects of the social context, some psychologists have been critical of the more traditional academic focus, which has tended to look for causes within individuals and has thus helped individuals accommodate to their circumstances rather than looking to change circumstances to help individuals. What proportion of old people who are depressed are depressed because their circumstances are depressing? We look at such questions in Chapter 3, but where *do* we look for the causes of such a phenomenon as depression? Wherein lies the *cause* of the following?

> The gusto or zest of pleasure . . . is not so keen in old age . . . but neither is the awareness of its absence so acute. And nothing of which you are not conscious of lacking causes you vexation.
>
> (Cicero, De Senectute, 45 BC, cited by Heim 1990: 108)

Do the experiences of life over many years modify our thoughts and feelings, and in turn affect the production of certain chemicals in the brain responsible for communications between nerve cells (neurotransmitters)? Or, are more intrinsic age-related physiological changes, perhaps with genetic underpinnings, responsible for such changes in chemical production, and if so are they subjectively experienced as, for example, a lack of gusto and changes in levels of awareness? Even something like altruism can be set in the false dichotomy of a 'nature–nurture' debate:

> It may be that there are even deeper roots in human evolution, associated with the genetics of altruism insofar as this may affect inter-generational

relationships. The question is, 'Is our concern for the elderly infirm socially and historically constructed or does it have a specific genetic basis?

(Bromley 1988: 31)

Perhaps it has both. But by looking within individuals, so to speak, for both causes and changes, psychology has been accused of supporting the *status quo*. To produce the futures we want, I believe we need a psychology which is at the service of social as well as individual change.

Psychology in context

In order to justify its claim to be a scientific discipline, academic psychology has tended to a world-view which, to use Salthouse's (1985:15) term, is predominantly mechanistic, rather than organic or contextual. He suggests that the root metaphor of mechanism is that of the machine, that of organicism the living organism, and that of contextualism the historical event. One may wonder, then, just how much of psychology's academic approach to ageing has contributed to what Simmons (1990) identifies as the three main clusters of cultural metaphors of ageing: ageing as physical [and mental] decline; ageing as aesthetic distance from youth; and ageing as failure of productivity? In furthering our understanding of later life, we shall assume that, especially for practitioners, a knowledge of individual biography, of life-history – an eclectic view of person-in-context – is needed. For policy-makers, the context provided by gender, race and ethnicity, class and education, as well as physical or mental impairment, and the influence of such factors on the experienced subjective and on the objective quality of life of older people, cannot be ignored.

I believe that our understanding of the psychological changes and challenges of ageing is not best served by attempting to reduce all our psychological experience to biological bases, nor to reduce such bases in turn to the more mechanistic behaviour of sub-atomic particles. There is more to the under-standing of dementia and the person who has 'got it' than just knowledge of molecular biology. Academic psychology, in looking for general 'laws' of behaviour or of mental life, has also tended to adopt a perspective where 'each person is like all other people', as one looks for basic laws. This approach may favour *reductionism*, where the ultimate explanation of a phenomenon concerns molecules and atoms and the laws of physics and chemistry. Gutmann (1987) calls this perspective Linton's level 1, after the anthropologist who articulated it. Level 2 is where 'each person is like some other people', and level 3 is where 'each person is like no other person'. Whereas scientific approaches attempt to achieve predictability and tend to level 1, they often lose sight of humanity. Artistic approaches, which tend to level 3, tend to bring humanity into focus, but at the expense of other than idiosyncratic knowledge. At level 1, uniformity masks diversity; at level 3, individuality masks generality. An understanding of growing older needs to be informed by approaches at all levels. Since practitioners, policy-makers and laymen alike have to act, have to make decisions, they are of necessity required to make many a creative leap in taking the findings of scientific psychology – hedged as they often necessarily are by 'ifs' and 'buts' and the need for further research – and applying them to a practical everyday understanding of ageing.

Uncontroversial, unambiguous, well-established psychological 'facts', whose interpretation is unproblematic, are as yet relatively few and far between. Inevitably, then, interpretations and generalizations which appear in this book are partial and personal, reflecting the author's interests and values. In that sense, the book does not aim to be a conventional, objective 'psychology of ageing', but rather an attempt to raise 'ageing consciousness' and to provoke reflective responses in the reader whose own ageing is thus more centre-stage.

As Bromley (1988: 33) notes, mankind has been trying to understand ageing since recorded history. 'The Egyptian hieroglyph "old" or "to grow old" appears in inscriptions dated about 2700 BC. It portrays a human figure holding a staff for support'. *Plus ça change et plus c'est la meme chose!* Scientific psychological studies of ageing, begun in the late 1940s and motivated by a shortage of labour, had their origins in attempts to study the performance of people in later life relevant to their capacity for industrial work. What – the question asked – was the potential of those who had reached retirement age for continued work (Welford 1992). Warr (1994), in a recent overview of occupational geronto-logy, notes that the application of the knowledge about ageing that has accumulated over the last 40 years presents both a challenge and a wide field of opportunity, but it is not unproblematic.

Research on ageing and later life poses several methodological problems that limit the validity and reliability of findings. We need, therefore, a healthy scepticism about findings presented as general truths. For example:

> One of the most difficult problems in designing research on aging is the question of how health status affects behavioral and other phenomena, and to what extent it is permissible to generalize findings from any study for which the health status of its participants has not been adequately characterized . . . [It] is virtually always necessary to include some measures of health in studies of older persons because substantial pro-portions of individual variances on any dependent variable will be attribu-table to health status differences. It is less clear, however, what kind of definition of health should be utilized and how such a definition might be operationalized in a given study.
>
> (Schaie 1988: 250)

Changing methods

Various forces such as the bio-medicalization of old age, as well as cultural ideologies concerning individualism, self-reliance and independence, have shaped the development of gerontology. Nevertheless, until fairly recently its psychological facet could be characterized by the development of valid and reliable quantitative measures of phenomena, such as verbal intelligence, or speed of reaction to a stimulus, or levels of social engagement or self-esteem, that might be expected to change 'with age'. These were drawn from, or used in attempting to test, various psychological and sociological theories. We should be aware, however, that the disciplines making up gerontology – whether biological, psychological, physiological or sociological – identify and study their own 'brand' of age (Bytheway 1990). Nor should we forget that 'with age' and 'with the passage of time' are not one and the same thing. Marital infidelity may peak at around age 30, but only because of the '7-year itch' of those average individuals who got married about age 23. Perhaps the 'itch' takes longer the older you are?

Of late, an increasing interest has been shown in 'qualitative' approaches to gerontology:

> Qualitative gerontology is concerned with describing patterns of be-
> haviour and processes of interaction, as well as revealing the meanings,
> values and intentionalities that pervade elderly people's experiences or
> the experience of others in relation to old age. In addition, qualitative
> gerontology seeks to identify patterns that underlie the lifeworlds of
> individuals, social groups, and large systems as they relate to old age. A
> primary focus is on understanding and conveying experience in its 'lived'
> form with as little *a priori* structuring as possible. Qualitative gerontology
> attempts to tap the *meaning* of experienced reality by presenting analyses
> based on empirically and theoretically grounded descriptions.
>
> (Reinharz and Rowles 1988: 6)

Qualitative methodology in gerontology presents some different sorts of problems to those of quantitative methodology. Both sorts are considered in detail in *Researching Social Gerontology* (Peace 1990). Psychology's contribution to an understanding of ageing needs supplementing with understanding gained from a variety of sources and which takes account of the values which permeate our perception and experience of growing older. As with some other disciplines, psychology often raises more questions than it supplies unequivo-cal, robust and 'relevant' answers.

As well as a *knowledge about* the mind, Claxton (1991) suggests we need a discipline concerned with the *wisdom of* the mind – a science of self-knowledge, or what he calls a 'psychosophy'. We need something which is 'a generic psychology that is as soundly based as current knowledge allows, but which is of practical use to ordinary folk in reflecting upon and ordering their daily lives' (p. 249). He considers that this would concern itself with aspects of *la condition humaine*; for example, what constitutes a 'good' death and how to prepare for it, and our attitudes to illness and to old age. We have quite some way to go to achieve this science of self-knowledge. In the meantime, however, we have to apply what knowledge there is – scientific or otherwise – to inform decisions we make for ourselves about our own ageing and that of others; or let others, perhaps less well-informed than they think they are, but yet who think they know best, make decisions for us. Inevitably, our world view or philosophy of life, our personal values, will fill some of the gaps in the creative leap from scientific findings to policy and practice applications.

Looking forward

In the chapters of this book we consider a variety of issues pertaining to salient questions individuals might ask as they view their own future. Many will wonder how they will cope with the death of a life partner or life-long friends. Some will worry about getting Alzheimer's disease or having to look after someone with it. Others will be concerned with changes in their felt attractiveness or their sex life. Some will look forward to contributing to society through active citizenship or voluntary activities. Those who have worked all their lives and not developed hobbies might wonder how they will occupy themselves with life in retirement. People with money might wonder about where to live in retirement: Bognor or Barcelona? Should they be learning Spanish now? Individuals who have spent a significant part of their lives unemployed might be more concerned about continuing to cope with the hassles of everyday life and wondering if they will join the ranks of those who get hypothermia in the winter. What if I go deaf or lose my sight? What if my children emigrate? Clearly, for many people, loss of independence or autonomy is a significant concern for later life (Age Concern 1992). Increasingly, we hope, individuals will be mindful of their own futures and those of others in order that such concerns can be ameliorated.

It is the author's belief that an understanding of the psychological challenges and changes of later life requires an approach that is both holistic and eclectic. Practitioners and policy-makers, like other ageing individuals, can exert some influence on their own ageing, and that of others. To do so, however, presents not only a challenge to be mindful and authentic; it requires a creative attempt to bring the information gained from both the laboratory and from personal experience into the service of individual and social change. It requires both education and training for an ageing society:

> In particular we note that skills which have been developed to a high level in youth may be maintained by practice at similarly satisfying levels, even to the late 70s and early 80s, and in spite of the normal loss in speed and accuracy of problem-solving generally observed at that time of life. This suggests that the integration of older people into the workforce may be an extraordinarily rewarding goal for ergonomists, systems engineers, and for social engineers during the 21st century.
>
> (Rabbitt 1991: 789)

As Chapters 6 and 7 suggest, we may want to be integrated into more than just the workforce.

1

'Us' and 'them'

One doesn't have to look very far for evidence of the destructive influence of our habit to divide the people in our environment into groups, into us and them. 'Is he one of us?' Margaret Thatcher is alleged to have said, wanting to know if a politician shared her basic beliefs, values, ideology and world view. The sorry history of Northern Ireland – and, as I write, the ongoing 'ethnic cleansing' in Bosnia – echo the evils of The Holocaust and the legacy of racial prejudice in both the USA and in South Africa. They attest to what powerful majorities are capable of inflicting on less powerful minorities. And the power of ideological conviction can provide a justification that this or that act of barbarism is necessary and appropriate. In these situations we witness three concepts in action: ethnocentrism, prejudice and discrimination.

> *Ethnocentrism*: The tendency to view one's own ethnic group and its social standards as the basis for evaluative judgements concerning the practices of others – with the implication that one views one's own standards as superior. Hence, ethnocentrism connotes a habitual disposition to look with disfavor on the practices of alien groups.
> *Prejudice*: A negative attitude toward a particular group of persons based on negative traits assumed to be uniformly displayed by all members of that group. A failure to react to a person as an individual with individual qualities but rather to treat him [or her] as possessing the presumed stereotypes of his [or her] socially or racially defined group.
> *Discrimination*: The unequal treatment of individuals or groups based on arbitrary characteristics such as race, sex, ethnicity, cultural background, etc.
>
> (Reber 1985: 252, 567, 205)

A prejudiced way of looking at others tends to ignore diversity, rendering 'them' as homogeneous. It highlights the differences between 'us' and 'them' while glossing over the similarities. Part of the process involves the perception of attributes and what has been termed the 'fundamental attribution error' (Brown 1986: 176). This is the tendency for an observer to overestimate dispositional causes and to underestimate situational causes for the behaviour observed. One might suggest that psychology itself has a tendency to make such errors.

A frowned-upon behaviour enacted by one of 'us' may be seen as situationally caused, but be taken as evidence of a disposition in one of 'them'. But what happens when we can see some of them as individuals like us? In writing about a course she taught on literature and ageing, Woodward (1991) remarked on the chasm between the way in which her 18- and 19-year-old students described their grandparents and great-grandparents and the way in which they described other older people. Because their relatives were their familiars, the students generally demonstrated a sympathetic understanding for them and their lives:

> As for the others, the *other* is telling. The others were truly *other*. In language that was predominantly stereotypical they were defined simply and reductively as old. 'Old' was understood to be only one of the many aspects of these students' relatives (and it was often not a particularly important aspect at that). But for the others, 'old' was the sole and subsuming feature . . . They 'split' the old into two categories: those whom they knew well and did not see exclusively in terms of age, and those whom they did not know well and defined categorically as old. In the latter case 'old' took precedence over other culturally defined markers – over gender, race, and ethnicity.
>
> (Woodward 1991: 167)

There is a large literature about stereotypes, prejudice and discrimination concerning race, gender and ethnicity. 'Age' makes a curious non-self-serving addition. By and large individuals don't move from social category 'male' to 'female', from 'black' to 'white', from Jew to Roman Catholic, or from Roman Catholic to Protestant. In using social categories, the whole point often seems to be to enable an us/them demarcation to be made. But age represents the one dimension along which we all travel, during which time we uniformly move from one category 'young', to another category 'old'. And may it not parodoxically be the case that: 'Gerontologists are dangerously inclined to live a double life . . . in which they simultaneously deplore ageism and build their "careers" upon the study of "elderly people"' (Bytheway 1990: 17)?

As we shall note shortly, having an 'other' to contrast ourselves with may serve a psychological function, enable us to bolster our self-esteem perhaps, or even give us a target on which we can release feelings of aggression. Since we are ultimately 'the other', perhaps the main 'purpose' of making old age 'the other' is the irrational one of denying ageing itself. Of course, we also make categorizations about social groups without a necessary purpose. Categorization, and its consequences, seems to be an intrinsic part of the way we process information. But at the end of the day, the consequences will affect *us*; our stereotypes and prejudices will come home to roost. As Levy and Langer (1994) suggest, negative stereotypes about ageing may even contribute to memory loss.

Whatever stereotypes we have in youth about 'the old', we have the chance to take such notions with us as we become 'them'. This is probably one reason why some of the stereotypes about 'the elderly' may be held as much by 'the elderly' themselves as by younger people. Indeed, some stereotypes of 'the elderly' may be endorsed even more by older people than by younger people, for example by some older people living in institutional settings. I well remember my father at the age of 75 telling me that 'Age is a bugger, and don't let anyone tell you that it isn't. Even Freddie [a very healthy and active 85-year-old] will tell you the same. Nobody wants to be old'. He may have been depressed at the time, but it does pose the problem of interpreting what those who are in the best position to 'know' have to say about old age. The point about stereotypes is that they may often have more than a kernel of truth in them, but that this may get over-generalized indiscriminately. Perhaps middle-age is in part a preferred phase of life precisely because it is particularly ill-defined and subject to much individual interpretation as to what personal characteristics one should use to define it.

The American National Council on the Aging (NCOA) suggested that some common stereotypes about old people suggested they were: all alike, poor, sick, depressed, a drag on everyone else, unable to function in society, and that they live alone, die in institutions and will become senile. A more recent survey (British Gas 1991), for example, showed that 82 per cent of a British sample of 764 retired individuals over the age of 55 agreed strongly or agreed a little with the statement that 'A lot of older people feel lonely these days', yet 67 per cent of the same sample said they themselves 'have enough company' and 'never feel lonely', a statement also endorsed by 59 per cent of those aged 75 and over. This illustrates the overestimation of loneliness in others, contrasted with self-perceptions.

When asked 'What do you think are the main problems facing older people in Britain today?', roughly similar proportions of people age 16–24 as those retired and over 55 said 'financial difficulties' (45 and 48 per cent, respectively); and 12 per cent said 'problems with pensions'. But 69 per cent of the older group considered themselves 'reasonably comfortable'. More of the younger group considered 'declining health/ mobility' to be a problem (36 per cent) than did those retired over 55 (25 per cent). Nevertheless, 78 per cent of the older group considered their own health to be very good or fairly good. Similarly, 20 per cent of the younger group considered 'loneliness/isolation/no family' to be the main problem facing older people, whereas only 12 per cent of the older group did (British Gas 1991). Both the older and younger groups may have somewhat erroneous notions, those of the younger ones being somewhat more out of line than the older ones. How do such notions arise?

Theoretical underpinnings

> I sometimes think that essays on aging and papers dealing with the aged
> . . . ought to begin with a statement of the author's age. Readers ought to
> have some idea whether the author exhorts us from the vigor of youth or
> with the serenity of age. Words like *old* or *elderly* also need careful
> definition, for their meaning varies with who is doing the calling and on
> how long, at the time the paper is written, most people live . . . As a
> 66-year-old, I take it that the aged about whom physicians are concerned
> are older than 75 and that the very old – the 'old-old', they have been
> called – are those older than 85. Because people age at different rates, I
> worry about any general categorization.
>
> (Spiro 1991: 387)

The social psychology of ethnocentrism, prejudice and discrimination has
produced a wealth of evidence to underpin a variety of theoretical approaches
to the topic, all of which can make a contribution to our understanding of how
and why we develop stereotypes about others (Stroebe and Insko 1989).

Realistic conflict theory suggests that prejudice is a common outcome of
inter-group competition for some scarce resource. A perception of 'the other'
as a threat provokes hostility and increases ethnocentrism. Only of late have
older people been presented as a distinct threat in this way, in discussions of
what has been termed 'inter-generational equity or justice'. The thrust of the
argument is that 'the elderly' pose an economic threat in that they consume
(pensions, health and social services) without being producers, and that the
cost to the rest of society is not 'fair'. In the USA, the cost of 'the elderly' has
been cast as a direct threat to the welfare of children. Walker (1990) has
produced a rebuttal to arguments that pose older people as a threat in this way.
Nevertheless, the more older people are cast as a threat, the more we can
anticipate prejudice against them.

Social identity theory suggests that individuals are motivated to achieve and
maintain a positive social identity. Prejudice and stereotypes can be used as
weapons in a fight over scarce social resources, such as status and prestige
within society. If 'to be young' presents a more positive social identity than 'to
be old', then it will be clung onto. This is perhaps one reason why a denial of
being old seems so pervasive.

Social learning theory suggests that observations of apparent differences
between groups derive from socially influential sources such as parents,
schools, peer groups and the mass media. One might just as well learn from
television, for example, that older people are active, independent and
respected as that they are moaning, nosy and interfering. However, demeaning
charity advertisements and fund-raising TV shows can present images that
depict 'the elderly as dependent, vulnerable and collective social victims'
(Hazan 1990). Although the media seems to have discovered older people of
late, as in TV shows like *The Golden Girls* and *One Foot in the Grave*, they are
nevertheless much under-represented. Now national BBC radio networks are
claimed to target different audiences identified in part on the basis of age. Now

we have magazines called *The Oldie* and *Goldlife* for 'the mature generation'. As advertisers appreciate the fact that the population is ageing, older consumers are more likely to be targeted. Traditionally, advertisers have not liked the older market for three reasons. Conventional ad wisdom says the old are poor, set in their ways and therefore unlikely to change brands and, crucially, not interested in being young and dynamic – which is an image most companies have been keen to foster.

Any views of later life gained from the media will inevitably be partial, however. This probably explains why older people often have difficulty identifying with TV images of old folk presented as happy, carefree and easy going. Stereotypes are also shaped by the social roles that group members occupy when inter-group contact occurs. If older people are cast into playing a more dependent role, it may become to be perceived as a personal trait. Thus trait attributions and stereotypes can arise from socially structured differences, as they have done with women as 'carers' and 'caring', which may continue into later life.

Psychodynamic theories suggest that certain features of childhood, concerning aggressive feelings towards parents that cannot be displayed, can carry over into an adult personality with authoritarian dispositions. Such aggressive feelings are displaced onto weaker members of society, with accompanying rationalizations. Perhaps some instances of the abuse of older people, whether as family members or within institutions, represents prejudice formed in this way.

Cognitive theories suggest that the way in which we normally process large amounts of complex information has several consequences, one of which is the production and maintenance of stereotypes. Because human information-processing capacity is limited, inherent constraints result in apparent break-downs in perception and cognition. *Belief congruence theory* suggests that outgroup members are rejected not so much because of their physical characteristics, but because of their dissimilar or incongruent beliefs. Also at the root cause of private rejection may be attributed behavioural character-istics: I might reject older people because (I believe) they go to church, have faith in God, behave conservatively, look to the past rather than to the future, want to look too much before they leap and so forth.

Accentuation theory suggests that differences between individuals falling into different categories are accentuated or overestimated, while differences within a category are underestimated. This would suggest that 'older people' become homogenized, whereas their differences from younger people become heightened. Such accentuation effects are not necessarily limited to the categorization of people, but in that sphere much evidence has accrued to demonstrate their power (Hamilton and Trolier 1986). The *theory of illusory correlation* suggests that two distinctive events co-occurring by chance can give rise to the illusion that the two events are correlated; that is, co-occurrence is perceived as evidence of a relationship. For example, if you are behind a very old, very frail man going through the check-out at the supermarket, this may be an infrequent experience and the circumstances become salient (i.e. they draw your attention more than usual). If the man then also displays an infrequently occurring behaviour, for example he decides he doesn't now want some of the items which have gone through the scanner, this too might become salient. The two co-occurrences might be processed as 'frail older men can't make their minds up'. Similarly, evidence of a slight correlation, say between experiencing loneliness and being age over 75, may become perceived as stronger than it is.

Cognitive theories of stereotyping and prejudice suggest that, like race and sex, age might be a 'basic' category which may be used so frequently that its application and consequent effects becomes automatic. Just as sexism has been called a non-conscious ideology, wherein the automatic use of sex as a social category has the effect of subordinating and objectifying women, the same line of argument might be taken with respect to age. Age, however, is a 'fuzzy' variable; it is continuous not categorical. Like such a fuzzy variable as social class, which has several components defining it, 'age' can be differentiated in terms of psychology (whether older people behave as we would expect them to), physiology (how efficiently does their metabolism function) and sociologically (in terms of the age expectations we have concerning the roles they play). Nevertheless, as we shall note later, age becomes 'transposed' into a category when we use terms such as 'the elderly' or 'the aged'.

Prototypes enable us to identify members of fuzzy categories, and consist of the attributes of what we perceive as the typical category member. Individuals working with older people in hospitals and social care settings may have their categories of older people frequently primed so that prototypes of 'dear old gran', 'poor old Nellie' and 'awkward Alice', for example, develop. The problem might be, however, that older people with whom they come into contact less often – those not in need of such services – also tend to be matched against a limited set of prototypes. Furthermore, we tend to seek out information that confirms our preconceptions, and often exceptions to the rule are anticipated in such a way that the rule, the stereotype, is not disconfirmed (Stroebe and Insko 1989:43). Thus expectations based on stereotypes may serve as simplifying mechanisms or heuristics to reduce information-processing demands. As noted in the Introduction, operating at Linton's level 3 (each person is like no other person) may be too demanding and operating at level 1 (each person is like all other people) may be too simplistic; so we function mainly at level 2, where 'each person is like some other people'.

As we have noted, expectancy–confirming sequences of behaviour can lead to apparent self-fulfilling prophecies. If you expect older people to be dependent, and consequently treat them as if they are dependent, and encourage them to respond as if they are dependent, eventually they may indeed become more dependent. This might be evident, for example, in the unnecessary 'wheelchairing' of residents to lounges or the dining room of residential homes, or in various beliefs that you shouldn't do this or that – learn a new language, perhaps – 'at our age'. Low expectations will necessarily lead to under-achievement:

> Thus we categorize individuals into groups as a means of reducing the amount of information we must contend with . . . we establish in our minds categories of persons that correspond to a variety of types of people.
>
> (Hamilton and Trolier 1986: 128, 129)

Although the term 'the elderly' is ubiquitous in both the non-academic and the gerontological literature, common sense suggests that we may hold a variety of prototypes for sub-classes of the category. Those that come to mind include active old people, frail old people, confused old people and dirty old men. This explains why traits commonly attributed to older people can be contradictory: 'serene' and 'irritable', for example; or 'suspicious' yet 'naively trusting'; or 'conservative' but 'eccentric'. Evidence suggests that individuals who are themselves closer to, or part of, the category will have more complex representations of the category than those less proximal. So older people should have more prototypes to access than younger people for later life categories, as might those working with older people. In one study, American college students appeared to be able to differentiate out from the 'senior citizen' (the stereotype of the isolated, inactive older person who is likely to live in a residential institution) those women who are 'grandmotherly' and those men who are 'elder statesmen' (Brewer *et al.* 1981). In another study they report that most older females, not surprisingly, identified themselves with the 'grandmotherly' category, and in general older people were more likely to make stereotypic associations to other older people than to themselves, in particular to older people identified as being in the 'senior citizen' category.

Research itself can provide some of the bases for refinement of prototypes, at least for those who read the relevant literature! For example, cluster analysis of a variety of life style data for a sample of 619 older people produced, among others, those called the 'elderly elite', the 'family shielded', the 'ill and unsupported', the 'psychologically fragile' and the 'poor souls' (Taylor 1988). And market researchers identify, among older people, 'the getby's', 'the contenteds', 'the adventurers', 'the cautious' and 'the restrained'. 'The survivors', for example, are characterized as tending to be over 75, as watching their money carefully and being wary of the financial world, as buying a lot of tinned and dried food (stemming from war-experiences?), as watching a lot of TV soaps, game shows and drama series, and listening to the radio a lot (the sound of a human voice perhaps warding off loneliness?). They take few holidays but do like an evening down the pub (Third Age International 1991).

What's in a phrase?

What words come to mind to complete a phrase starting with the word old? Old flame, old love, old age, old fart, old lag, old bag. How many positive connotations can you think of for the word old compared with negative ones? One part of Age Concern's campaign in 1993, 'How to avoid becoming an old codger', shows an image of someone who could be a doting grandmother or favourite aunt (notice the potential prototypes). Next to this homely image in bold stark lettering is **SILLY OLD MOO**. And underneath the message runs 'How long before people call you names? Fight ageism now'. My 14-year-old son seems to prefer the somewhat dated labels of fogey, biddy and buffer to the more modern wrinklies, coffin-dodgers or nearly-deads. If he calls me an old fogey, he knows the joke is partly on him because I could be referring to him as a young spottie. Instead, I call him a young fogey and ask him which is worse. But are we being oversensitive to such labels?

> Sir: [Your correspondent] found extremely offensive a description of some daily inhabitants of Southwold's beach huts as 'Toothless retirees . . . sucking potted beef rolls'. She thinks this is a fairly typical example of 'creeping ageism in our society; terms such as "wrinklies" or "blue-rinse and Crimplene brigade" are becoming common'.
>
> Others will deplore such an example of creeping 'political correctness'. Easily offended people, who fear brushes with realities, seek to impose this creeping *censorship* on our spoken and written language. Thus they cannot dispel the realities which, whether we like it or not, include prejudices, delusions, deceptions, misdescriptions and, no better, unwelcome truths . . . Cruel, malicious, even mocking communications reflect on the perpetrators, not the victims.
>
> (Rubinstein, 1992: 16)

Perhaps such communications *should* reflect on the perpetrators, but much of the social psychological literature suggests the reverse. This is one reason why the even fuzzier term 'older person' is used in this book. Perhaps academics are more prone to creeping political correctness, but others in the gerontological field also seem to be moving away from 'the elderly'.

Terminological changes like this do attract criticism, however. Islington Council, for example, got mocked in a London evening newspaper as 'Older but no wiser; the borough where elderly don't exist', after suggesting that 'residents of mature years' should be referred to as older people. One staunch critic was reported as saying, 'The elderly don't mind being called elderly'. This would not appear to be correct. Only 5 per cent of those retired and over 55 in the British Gas (1991) survey said they would like to be called that, presumably because such words produce a knee-jerk response about decrepitude. And what does the term 'pensioner' conjure up? 'Pensioner – has that dire sense of withdrawal, of taking a back seat, of being the pit-pony turned out to pasture for a brief valedictory spell' (British Gas 1991: 12). In fact, 36 per cent retired and over 55 said they liked the term 'senior citizens' and the same proportion said they liked the term 'retired'. Despite the fact that 'older people' was less preferred than 'the elderly' (only 4 per cent liked it), the literature on the consequences of categorization, on the influence of terminology, and on our everyday ways of conversing, reveals how our perceptions of later life are moulded, and suggests that a sensitivity to language is not inappropriate.

Henwood (1990), for example, shows how stereotypes are invoked in conversations between older and younger women in which painful self-disclosures are made. But the fact that there can be recognition within conversations and group discussions that stereotypes *are* being evoked, also may present an opportunity in which 'themes of stereotyping and inter-group conflict can be actively challenged. This is an important feature of discourse, pointing up the potential for transformation as well as reproduction in recursive relations between 'subject' and 'object' in human social life' (Henwood 1990: 15).

The sociolinguistic construction of ageing is considered in some detail by Giles (1991). He notes that, 'By the time we reach retirement-age, many of us will have been well-primed to accept the "reality" of decremental ageing' (p.104), and that:

> Perhaps we should consider carefully the cognitive and behavioural non-reactive stances most of us have taken traditionally to expressed ageism, as they can contribute to unhealthy personal consequences as well as the reproduction of ageist sentiments and policies more generally. Even as a researcher into matters gerontological, I sadly recall an instance when a senior scholar enquired what research I was currently pursuing. In response to my answer, 'intergenerational communication', he retorted dismissively yet amusingly, 'ah, Wrinkle-Comm'. I have to admit responding in turn, *almost mindlessly*, with laughter. Unfortunately many of us collude in propagating such myths through humour, accounting for others' and our own disappointments, failures, and so forth in age-related terms. This collusion is doubtless an important element in the construction of our physical and psychological decline.
>
> (Giles 1991: 105, emphasis added)

Discrimination

The ideas and beliefs which comprise stereotypes, fuelled perhaps by the motivational bases of some of our prejudices, often give rise to action. Ageism might well be defined as 'the offensive exercise of power through reference to age' (Johnson and Bytheway 1993: 205). An extreme end result, but all too apparent, can be the ultimate rejection of the individual as a full human being – as the Nazis portrayed Jewish people in the Second World War, for example. Then 'euthanasia' was seen as an appropriate line of action to take with selected groups. Is there any likelihood of older people being perceived and treated this way?

> Some aged infirm persons lose the behavioural attributes (mobility, autonomy, reactivity, power, and so on) that are normally regarded as essential *human* characteristics; they may differ markedly in appearance from the normal adult. Furthermore, the aged person's expressive and communicative behaviour are diminished, so that social interaction is more difficult. Unless we are given ample opportunity to interact with the elderly infirm and to deal with them as individuals with a personal identity and life-history, then we may be inclined to perceive them as less than human and treat them accordingly. Isolation and segregation can lead

eventually to social distance and professional detachment, and thence to ageism, dehumanisation, institutionalisation and rejection.

(Bromley 1988:31)

Large oaks from small acorns grow! One's first experience of prejudice and discrimination concerning age may occur in an employment context, as a glance at some job advertisements will illustrate. Age seems to be a more salient judgemental characteristic to men than it is to women, with men demonstrating a stronger youth bias. That might, in part, reflect selection bias in secretarial, media and airline flight attendant recruitment. As a female columnist in the *Guardian* notes:

The 'covergirl' on this week's *Radio Times* is Kate Adie. She will soon be 48 and she looks, well, about 47. What I've just told you should be totally irrelevant but unfortunately it's not. What matters about Kate Adie is what she does, not what she looks like. What matters is her authoritative and sometimes controversial reporting, her bravery, her stamina. So why does she say, then, 'the convention of television is that women are young, so whether this old bat will be tolerated in front of the cameras for much longer, I don't know'? Here is a woman who can obviously withstand enormous pressure, yet the pressure to keep up appearances is one she feels very strongly.

Adie, like every other woman, is acutely aware of her shelf-life, a time when she will be considered too old to do what she does, even if she is perfectly capable of doing it. I wonder what mine is.

(Moore 1993: 11)

But perhaps some employers are more enlightened?

I am a 73-year-old 'wrinkly' who, determined not to become a cabbage after retirement, took up the piano at the age of 70. So far I have obtained Grades 1 and 2 of the Guildhall School of Music, with merits, and am looking forward to Grade 3 this December. Three days a week I work for an international trading company. My shorthand is still 120-plus and touch-typing is second nature to me. I would like to take up other things, but time is too demanding at present. Yes, let's work for 'equal opportunities' to mean exactly that!

(Ross 1991: 46)

As McEwen's (1990) book, *Age: The Unrecognised Discrimination*, illustrates, the consequences of age discrimination are to be found in all walks of life. Women may find they are too old to be offered screening for cervical or breast cancer, for example. People with disabilities may find they are not entitled to invalidity benefits – you can be retired or incapacitated, but not both apparently. Mobility and severe disablement allowances, industrial injury, and board and lodging payments, may all be affected by one's age. Are 'concessions' a form of positive discrimination that ultimately are demeaning? And if you buy fewer or less, do you have to pay more? And what of video-controllers with fiddly small buttons and tiny print? Age discrimination even operates against volunteers for the charity sector and age discrimination in local government has now begun to make newspaper headlines (Donaldson 1993). What of being made redundant on covert age grounds, or having to stop working because you have reached somewhere between 60 and 65?

Age as a proxy for other judgements – appropriateness for having driving instruction, ability to decide about getting married, fitness for being a juror, for whether treatment should be given, or whether one should be sent to 'coronary care' rather than 'geriatrics' – seems increasingly inappropriate given that the one thing that does change with age is the *variability* demonstrated by most of the measures or indicators for which it is taken as a proxy:

> Studies which have continued over the last ten years, such as that at the University of Manchester Age and Cognitive Performance Research Centre, now force us to re-evaluate our concepts of mental ageing in relation to the duration and nature of the working lifespan. The most striking lessons are that a marked increase in average life expectancy and personal efficiency is characterized by an even more marked increase in individual diversity. The most direct implication is that the concept of a fixed age at which a diversity of talent is lost to the economy by compulsory retirement is a costly absurdity.
>
> (Rabbitt 1991: 787–8)

Should age be part of equal opportunity legislation? The United Nations has recommended that countries should consider the question of age discrimination, and both the USA and Canada have enacted legislation against it. It has been considered in Australia and elsewhere, as well as proposed in the UK.

Keeping up appearances

> Anthony Quinn's lust for life results in 11th child at age of 78.
>
> (Sharrock 1993: 1)

A glossy supplement to a woman's magazine is entitled 'Look younger, live longer'. The front cover has photos of glamorous 50-plus celebrities: Raquel Welsh, Tina Turner, Julie Andrews, to name but a few. Brigitte Bardot, now more famous for her wrinkles, is noticeably absent. The cover mentions 'hair and make-up tricks of youth', and 'great skin forever'. Inside, various potions are advertised: 'anti-time day care cream – past, present, future', which will 'correct the past and shape the future'; potions that will give you 'a younger-looking, more radiant complexion'; potions that 'as part of your daily skin care strategy delay the first signs of ageing'; potions that 'give strength to your skin's night-time renewal programme', needed because 'with age this process slows down'. Or how about 'de-aging with colour: discover techniques for looking younger instantly'. The supplement tells you that 'nothing ages you more quickly than sticking with an outdated look'. Of course, taking pride in being fashionable and the self-esteem it can engender is nothing new: 'these New England women [after the American Civil War] took great pride in what little they had and put great stock in a particular dress, bonnet, or tea service that enabled them to maintain a sense of dignity and decorum in the face of great adversity' (Keating 1991: 187). But we seem to equate being fashionable with looking younger. We seem to have a thirst to know how to 'take off 10 years in 10 minutes' and that 'it is possible to delay signs of ageing' and that 'you can now postpone the arrival of a wrinkle for five to 15 years'.

> The year's, possibly the decade's, buzz words in facial anti-ageing are Alpha Hydroxy acids, natural acids derived from fruits, potatoes, sugar cane and sour milk . . . 'Women prefer to buy an expensive cream', points out cosmetic surgeon Dev Basre, 'when they could get cheap fresh AHAs by putting fresh apple or orange juice on their face' . . . Men's cosmetics concentrate on selling coolness and comfort rather than rejuvenation. But 1992 saw the first product aimed at protecting 'man's youthful appearance' (Aramis Anti-ageing Supplement Plus, £29/50ml), an 'advanced blend of sunscreens, free radical scavengers and anti oxidants'.
>
> (Sudgrove 1993: 10)

As Macnair (1992:16) points out, even if certain cosmetic potions do 'work' and have to be redefined as 'medicines', the real issue is why are we so terrified of wrinkles in the first place. 'Sadly, youth and beauty have become the currency of our society, buying popularity and opportunity. The value of age and experience is denied, and women in particular feel the threat that the visible changes of ageing brings' (ibid.). Young as well as older adults tend to judge physically attractive middle-aged individuals in 'more socially desirable terms than they do unattractive middle-aged adults', and 'adult women of all ages tend to rate physically attractive older women as less attractive than they do younger women of comparable beauty' (Webb *et al.* 1989: 117). Older men tend to be evaluated on factors other than physical attraction. Macnair blames the media for continually portraying men of all ages alongside young, smooth-skinned women as a vision of success, and suggests that as long as this goes on 'women will go on investing in pots of worthless goop' or various forms of cosmetic surgery. Indeed, Gupta *et al.* (1990: 903) caution that even 'Dermatologists should acknowledge their own philosophies and feelings about aging . . . and should take great care that their attitudes do not perpetuate the negative stereotypes that are often associated with growing old'.

What Macnair (1992: 16) wants us to see is 'more mature, wrinkled women in attractive, successful, happy roles and let's see men fighting to be with them'. But clearly, given prevailing pressures, it takes a certain amount of courage, self-confidence and perhaps status to be proud to look one's age and accept one's wrinkles, as Bardot seems to have. Is it true that:

> The misery of the middle-aged woman is a grey and hopeless thing, born of having nothing to live for, of disappointment and resentment at having

been gypped by the consumer society and surviving merely to be the butt of its unthinking scorn.

(Greer 1991: 9)

If so, then 'finding their full spiritual and intellectual range on the other side of 50' must indeed be a challenge to many women. Greer goes on to suggest that the object of facing up to the climacteric is to acquire serenity and power, but that calm and poise have to be fought for:

There have always been women who ignored the eternal-youth band-wagon, and agreed to grow up, who negotiated the climacteric with a degree of independence and dignity, and changed their lives to give their new adulthood space to function and flower.

In a childish world, this behaviour is seen as threatening. Nobody knows what to do with a woman who is not perpetually smiling and fawning. Calm, grave, stern women drive most men to desperation. Women who refuse even to try and empower the penis are old bats and old bags, crones, mothers-in-law, castrating women and so forth.

(Greer 1991: 10)

And a quick glance at the covers of current women's magazines demonstrates the popularity of matters sexual. Of fifteen displayed in one of my local newsagents, twelve mentioned a sex-related article on the front cover. The desire to look young, and the association of youth with sexual activity, both conspire to make sexual activity in later life the subject of humour, if not disgust and ridicule.

Sex as a case in point

Given the cultural obsession with youth and sex, and the reversing potencies of men and women as they grow older, it is little wonder that we may feel uncomfortable with the idea of sexuality in later life and at the same time, as with the young, feel guilty that we are engaged in 'it' too much or too little. In *Ourselves Growing Older: Women Ageing with Knowledge and Power* (Shapiro 1989: 131–3), five myths about women, sex and ageing are identified:

- *Myth 1*: Older people are no longer interested in sex and sexuality and no longer engage in sexual activity. Sex is for the young.
- *Myth 2*: Changes in hormone levels which occur during and after the menopause create a 'deficiency disease' that causes women to find sex uncomfortable and unpleasant.
- *Myth 3*: Women who are beyond their childbearing years lose their desire and their desirability.
- *Myth 4*: In order to have a full and complete sex life, a woman must have a male partner.

- *Myth 5*: The only truly satisfying sex is through intercourse culminating in mutual orgasm.

In a chapter on sex education for older people, Gibson (1992) suggests we should strive towards a new concept of sexuality; away from the 'whip it in, whip it out and wipe it' mentality (a phrase I remember being uttered by our biology teacher in sex education lessons, along with memories of a rabbit's reproductive innards in a tank reeking of formaldehyde), to something more broadly conceived:

> To most people, sex means copulation with the goal of the male orgasm, conceived of as the ejaculation of semen. Although most intercourse is engaged in not for procreation but for recreation, this goal is over-emphasised . . . One of the greatest benefits a counsellor can confer on an ageing man is to get him to realize that his masculinity does not depend wholly on his phallic prowess, and that an experienced lover will be able to give and receive sensual pleasure and emotional satisfaction through the wide range of love-making techniques that are generally known by sex therapists as 'pleasuring'.
>
> (Gibson 1992: 173–4)

Here, though, we come dangerously close to putting being 'an experienced lover' on a pedestal and giving ourselves another measurement yardstick by which we may feel relatively unsuccessful. As Rykken (1987) points out, we presume too often that older people aren't interested in sex, and that if they are, they shouldn't be. Should a 71-year-old couple who find they still like to have sex once a day feel there is something unnatural or abnormal about it? Or do you hope you feel the same?

> Sometimes lack of sexual activity is not a problem. Ours is a sex-obsessed society, and it is assumed that young people, especially males, are going to be extremely interested in sex. But people do not come out of factories built to uniform standards. Many people of both sexes welcome old age if only because it gives them an excuse to give up something they were never terribly interested in . . . It is also an error to impose inflated standards of the young on the elderly. It is no help to drop the stereotype of the sexless old, if 'normality' demands that they must perform marathon feats of eroticism to feel adequate.
>
> (Rykken 1987: 172)

We can now learn 'Why sex gets better as *he* gets older; no, we haven't got it wrong', which headlined a women's magazine feature article on 'How to make love with the same man for the rest of your life'. Airing some of the details of changes in sexual response with age, as this article did, must help dispel ignorance. But we should beware lest the expectancy that older people shouldn't have sex is replaced by one that demands that they should and holds up performance targets. Although a sex instruction video for 'third-agers' has yet to come on to the market, when it does will the responses to it be akin to that for line drawings of sexual positions older people might find more comfortable, which appeared in a nursing journal? The following issue of the journal brought forth comments both of praise and of outright disgust. Ambivalence is also demonstrated in our response to cartoons to be found in the likes of *The Geriatric Sex Guide*, where the old man's erection poking up the bed sheet is due either to rigor mortis (his wife's reaction in one cartoon) or to be taken as a sign he's ready for discharge (the nurse's reaction in another cartoon). There seems to be a double-bind in that sexual activity, or its absence, results in a sort of amused distaste either way.

Although age is no bar to sexually acquired infection, expectations about the sexual behaviour of older people may, for example, lead to the symptoms of AIDS going undetected. Already the headline 'Aids affects all age groups and perceptions of risk can be misleading' has appeared.

Any distaste over sexual activity in later life may be compounded when the sexual activities involved are themselves frowned upon. For older homosexual men and women, prejudice concerning age may supplement prejudice concerning sexual orientation. A subculture where masculine youthfulness is a major criterion for socio-sexual success, and where one can consequently be perceived as 'older' sooner, nicely illustrates the common difference between 'what you think' and 'what you think others think'. While homosexual men considered middle age beginning around 41 and old age at 63, they thought, on average, that other gay men saw middle age at beginning around 39 and old age at 54. 'With the exception of respondents 25 years and under, all age groups saw themselves as younger than they believe others in the gay community saw them' (Bennet and Thompson 1991: 73). Like older gays, older lesbians also experience age discrimination:

> Yet these women, along with their nongay peers, also know discrimination because of their age, even from those in their own lesbian community. One attempted to explain it by writing, 'Almost all known younger lesbians feel they will become aged and do not want to face it'. Others expressed their disappointment differently: 'I would like to see younger women working to change negative images of old age among other young women and more effort given to older women running older women's programs'; 'Younger lesbians talk a good deal about how bad ageism is, but *socially* they want nothing to do with older women'; 'There is a degree of ageism in the lesbian community here – a certain amount of patronizing'. One woman summed it up: 'The lesbian community thinks young'.
>
> (Kehoe 1988: 59)

Nurturing change

To change stereotypes we need to change our beliefs; to change our prejudices we need to change our feelings as well; and to change discriminatory practices we need to change our behaviour. None of these are easy, as continuing inter-group hostilities in the world attest, but change *is* possible, as Israeli–Palestinian dialogue bears witness as I write. Overt behaviour can be changed through legislation, and age discrimination could be brought within the anti-sex and anti-race discrimination equal opportunities legislation, perhaps. On the one hand this might have the effect of making some discrimination more covert, but on the other it might give individuals cause to question their beliefs, so that beliefs become more congruent with actions. In the employment sphere, for example, it might provide more opportunity for people to have the first-hand experience of working with those who could have been 'retired'.

Contact *with* individuals on an equal basis, so that they are known *as* individuals with a personal biography, provides grounds for the realization that the category 'the elderly' is a collection of individuals. Integration, then, rather than segregation should be encouraged, and personal experience of children with older adults, through ongoing contact in local history schemes at school, or through teachers' aide schemes that encourage older individuals to contribute, could be fostered. If 'community care' results in higher visibility of, and interaction with, older people who would otherwise have been 'put away', it gives us more opportunity to witness the evidence of being older for ourselves. This might be increasingly happening as leisure centres burgeon, where we can see older people swimming, playing squash or badminton, weight-training, or doing aerobics or circuit training – people who would simply not have had the opportunity even just a generation ago. The City of Cardiff's *Leisure Times* brochure for autumn/winter 1992, for example, has a front cover photo of five older people in a swimming pool, and a centre feature on being '50+, fighting fit and full of fun!'

Reflecting on the known cognitive consequences of categorizing, being 'mindful' and questioning in our choice of words, and sensitive to the effects on us of their use by others, should help stop us processing apparently age-associated information in a sort of unconscious automatic mode which leads to unwarranted indiscriminate dispositional attributions. Providing evidence of expectancy–disconfirming behaviour can help, since this often sticks in the mind and is more easily recalled. For example, a video of life in the retirement community for older people, 'Sun City USA', was well remembered years after viewing by a group of my students, because of its images of residents as gun-toting, motorbike-riding cops, and sex being more fun when you didn't have to worry about getting pregnant, among others. Expectancy–disconfirming behaviour still tends to be presented as the exception that proves the rule. Of late, the tabloids have reported one centenarian who was going 'bungee-jumping' and a 93-year-old who finished the New York Marathon and, dissatisfied with his time, increased his training schedule in anticipation of winning the $100,000 prize for the first centenarian to run it. Perhaps less exceptional and therefore less easily dismissed are the older people whose behaviour prompted headlines like:

Sit-in by geriatric 'terrorists' leaves Danish authorities in a quandary.

Greys protest over threat to activity scheme in Ely.

France's pensioners are no longer willing to be treated as if they are on the scrapheap. Michel Chemin reports on a generation that is still full of fight.

So glad to be grey.

On course to be a brickie – age is no barrier to learning new skills and building a new interest in life.

Elderly in demo cuts.

When will newspaper and magazine reports about 74-year-olds passing their grade 6 piano exam, or those such as the following, disappear because they no longer surprise?

> Police had to be called to Highwood Court old people's social club at Uttoxeter, Staffs, after neighbours had complained about the noise coming from a karaoke session. One of the organisers, 78-year-old Ossie Tortoise-shell denied the noise was excessive. 'We were all just singing along to Jim Reeves and The Seekers and joining in with Danny Boy and On the Sunny Side of the Street. It was not even 10 o'clock', he said.
>
> (Anon 1992: 20)

> A friend's father began the assault on my own stereotyped ideas about life after 80 when he arrived on his 84th birthday carrying surfboards. It was actually *he* who had to persuade *us* to go into the sea. I then met an 87-year-old lady who spent her day doing yoga and walking into the waves in blistering hot sun that had sent many younger local people into the shade. I was beginning to suspect that there might be a lot more to old age than I might previously have imagined. Last week I knew I was right. A friend's grandfather, aged 90, astounded his osteopath by arriving on a brand-new racing bike. Let's have more positive images of the later years of life please.
>
> (Rankin 1991: 15)

Visibility of older people on TV could also be improved, with more proportionate representation of the real demographic profile (i.e. one in four people appearing on TV might be in the retirement 60+ range). But, of course, since they are 'retired', they are not on our TV screens. Despite that, many TV celebrities such as Cliff Michelmore and David Jacobs have come out of the 'age closet' to front TV programmes aimed at older viewers. But couldn't they front children's programmes too? Having programmes targeting older people reflects the market segmentalization that has occurred within the field of advertising which is more evident in the USA than the UK. But could that be construed as ageist? At least more 'prototypes' are better than fewer, or than ignored invisibility, even if targeting by age misleadingly suggests commonality rather than reflecting diversity.

Perhaps the best way of nurturing change, however, is to undermine the sense of in-group/out-group, of 'us' and 'them'. We need to deny the false dichotomy imposed on a multifaceted process of continuities and changes. We need to see ourselves in those who have already become what we shall in turn become. Then might we do unto 'others' as we would be done by.

2

On being older

Does each older generation tend to feel that the relative hardship of their youth nevertheless made for happier people and better human relationships? Or is it that youth has a 'rosier' view that in old age influences retrospections? Might not nostalgia for the past lead to dissatisfaction with the present? What changes experienced over a lifetime are similar for each generation and which are relatively unique?

Experiencing ageing

In her retirement, Alice Heim, a psychologist specializing in individual differences and the designer of the famous AH5 intelligence test, wrote to many of her friends and ex-colleagues aged between 60 and 95 and asked them to describe their experiences of ageing. In note or consecutive prose form, at whatever length they chose, her respondents were asked to consider: (1) What do you personally consider to be the main snags of growing old; (2) What methods do you use to circumvent them?; (3) What are the nice things, if any, about growing old – the advantages, pleasures, compensations? Note the 'if any'.

Of her 180 contacts, 160 replied, and on the basis of their answers she wrote a witty and readable book, *Where Did I Put My Spectacles?* (Heim 1990), noting that it was too anecdotal, introspective, personal – and readable – to be a 'typical psychological book'. For example, she deliberately didn't write to friends whom she knew to be suffering from extreme forms of illness or who were in severe pain or incapacitated, because she thought this would be callous. Her sample, then, is biased. Nevertheless, *Spectacles* does provide some interesting personal insights.

Heim suggests that 30 years earlier she might have put all her respondents' answers together as representing what some of 'the elderly' (albeit a relatively well-educated and affluent 'elderly') thought about their experiences of ageing. But, in part spurred by incredulous friends who said that that would be just like lumping 30- to 50-year-olds together, she instead considered organizing her findings under the alliterative chapter headings of: the 'Sensible sixties', the 'Serene seventies', the 'Engaging eighties' and the 'Noteworthy nineties'. In the event, her scrutiny of the replies suggested that there were more differences *within* each decade than there were *between* them. As usual with studies of ageing, diversity is a major characteristic.

Some people clearly do feel old in their sixties, but many are genuinely able to say 'I don't feel old' at almost any age (Thompson *et al.* 1991). Heim herself identified nine main areas of what, at first glance, appeared to be conflicting views concerning the experience of ageing. The correctness or otherwise of the viewpoints her respondents expressed is not the issue, since given the diversity of ageing there may *be* no correct viewpoint. More important is an understanding of how these apparent contradictions arise.

First was the question of whether self-confidence grows or shrinks with the years. Heim suggests physical confidence tends to decrease through old age, whereas mental and social confidence tend to increase. Given that hearing, vision and sense of balance deteriorate, and speed of movement decreases, it makes sense to be cautious crossing roads and to drive cars more carefully. But 'we no longer mind if we are inappropriately dressed at a party; and we have no difficulty in declining invitations that do not attract us' (Heim 1990: 139). In part, she suggests, this stems from an awareness that people make allowances – 'she is nearly eighty after all'. Such playing of 'ageism' to one's own advantage, however, might well reinforce it. Also with age comes a sense of 'So what?' This, she suggests, relates to the second pair of conflicting views: that things matter less versus a sense of enhanced emotional impact because the time remaining is so limited. If things matter less, this may itself be confidence inspiring. But it is the disagreeable experiences which tend to matter less, she suggests, whereas it is the pleasant experiences that become heightened because they cannot be taken so much for granted. By and large, though, the emotional 'highs' are not as high and the emotional 'lows' are not as low as they once were, which Heim suggests may be a biological defence mechanism to protect the body from extreme physiological changes with which it might have more difficulty coping.

Her third contradiction concerned a resigned or even welcoming attitude to death versus increased apprehension as the prospect of it drew closer. Those believing that life on earth was preparation for better things to come seemed more accepting and less apprehensive of death, yet for some this was tinged with guilt. And some non-believers saw death as a kind of rest. Some were ready to go because they had had 'a good innings', while others wanted to avoid pain or potential senility. Heim suggests that on questions of death, as on most questions concerning living, few people are wholly rational or consistent, which might in part explain the fourth contradiction of increasing tolerance versus increasing rigidity and irritability. Perhaps some people do genuinely mellow with age while others fossilize, she suggests. Or perhaps individuals develop increasing tolerance for some things and less for others. Those who are more capable of learning from their experience, might consider that 'it pays to behave and talk tolerantly even when feeling irritable, and feelings sometime result from behaviour' (Heim 1990: 141). Clearly, toleration plays a part in inter-generational relationships and the attitudes one perceives another generation to have to one's own.

Heim's fifth contradiction concerns satisfaction in the respect accorded to white hair versus indignation at the casualness evinced by younger people. Those with the humility to expect a brush-off may be agreeably surprised when their advice is sought, whereas perhaps some other older people believe that old age should automatically command respect. Several of Heim's respondents said they got on better with their grandchildren and others of that generation than they did with the generation in between. Perhaps this is in part a consequence of a lack of mutual responsibility. But several of Heim's respondents suggested that they could only 'take' young children in small doses. Related to this was the sixth contradiction – the belief that the generation gap widens over the years versus the belief that older people have better relationships with children and teenagers than do the middle-aged. Stamina to cope with noisy, restless and potentially tiring children seemed to be a factor here relating to the seventh contradiction, over contentment at being able to fall asleep at any moment versus annoyance at 'dropping off'. Nearly all Heim's contributors commented on their decreased stamina – 'their tendency to feel physically and mentally tired "without cause"' (Heim 1990: 143). Having a doze was an example, for some, of the pleasure of being able to do what you liked when you liked. But those who were annoyed when 40 winks turned into 400 seemed to awake more tired than refreshed compared with those happy to oversleep.

Heim's eighth contradiction comes in the form of advice over how to manage declining memory: those who recommend not writing things down, in order to keep memory active and in good trim versus those who recommend keeping lists, diaries, memory-joggers, etc. Even those who believed that memory was like a muscle that needed exercising noted that often distant memories would appear vividly and unsought, while the name of the film you saw last week might have 'gone'. Even those who make lists might have to exercise their memories about consulting them and remembering where they are!

Heim's final contradiction concerns appraisal of the past and the present: social conditions have greatly improved versus 'fings ain't what they used to be'. Heim suggests that those who tend to moan about contemporary life do not deny the beneficial changes in health, nutrition, sanitation and hygiene, housing and living and working conditions, that have occurred in their lifetime. Rather, their complaints are about the spin-offs of technology, for example loud noise. Some seem to lump most technology together – computers, test-tube babies, nuclear power and bombs – and think 'we'd be better off without it'. Some are concerned at the increasing competitiveness and haste of society, which can leave older people feeling ignored, and pushed aside or down. Those in favour of technology, like people of any age, disagree as to where the priorities for its advancement should lie.

In the conclusion to her book, Heim (1990: 147) writes:

> . . . to live to a good age, with the certainty of surcease in due course, is found by many to be desirable in prospect and enjoyable in the event. An impressive number of nice points have been discovered and have been persuasively portrayed. Whilst they do not always outweigh the snags, they prove deeply satisfying and they offer new dimensions to life – which are positively not available to those who have not stayed the course!

Survivors

But could the same be concluded for those who seem to have stayed the course until the very, or should one write 'bitter' – end? What of people who have lived until they are 90? What is the experience of that age for them? In *Life After Ninety*, Bury and Holme (1991) achieved a response rate of 82 per cent from a representative sample of 222 people aged 90 or over they sought to interview. Seventeen of these individuals were centenarians, the oldest being 106. In their sample, women outnumbered men four to one. Bury and Holme noted that while objective circumstances played a central part in the quality of life of the people they studied, such factors did not always operate in an anticipated direction. For example, as an activity undertaken, 'engaging in chatting' was mentioned more often by those living alone than by those in communal settings with other folks 'on tap'. Health tended to be assessed subjectively as good when the objective evidence appeared contrary. Although good health and material circumstances were important components, they did not always appear essential to a sense of well-being, or for high levels of activity inside or outside the home, for example. Well-being often seemed more in evidence than circumstances led one to expect. Many of those interviewed had disengaged from former activities but remained content and even happy. 'Social relationships and a sense of fulfilment, or acceptance, often compensated for the losses which time had brought' (Bury and Holme 1991: 162). In their conclusion, the researchers remark that life after 90 can be compatible with a good quality of life, and that, as at any point in old age, it is characterized by diversity. As well as there being needs or problems that are in common, there is diversity in the process of reaching 90 and in the state of being 90. In drawing the threads of their study together, Bury and Holme remark that:

> The very old, however, are not simply an administrative or medical category, or a new problem group. They do not, on our evidence, threaten to overwhelm the health and welfare services with impossible demands for help. Nor should they run the risk of being blamed for the help they do need . . . We suggest that dependence be seen as intrinsic to the lives of everyone, regardless of age or sex, and that reciprocity, either immediate or delayed, is part of such dependence. Different kinds and degrees of dependency occur at different stages of the life course, and a realistic

recognition of its importance in very old age does not mean that it becomes its hallmark.

(Bury and Holme 1991: 164)

Grandparents

Thompson and co-workers' (1991) analysis of the experience of later life was based on the personal accounts of 55 grandparents. Like the other samples with which a more qualitative approach has been taken, the picture it draws is partial, but nevertheless illuminating of its particular subjects. The central theme of these accounts is highlighted in the title of the book in which they occur – *I Don't Feel Old.*

Thompson *et al.* draw attention to the fact that later life today is characterized by a relative inexperience of death, by a preponderance of women living alone, by socio-economic inequalities and by, at least in principle, a new degree of freedom and choice. On this latter point they suggest that later life is far from the stereotyped notion of a state of passivity. Rather, it is a time of many sharp changes which demand a special responsiveness and creative adaptability. It is such resourcefulness that they consider survivors to increasingly have in common: 'Those who make or seize their new chances are most likely to flourish on their purposefulness; those who cannot find meaning to their lives, to fade altogether' (Thompson *et al.* 1991: 244). Some survive against their will and 'have not succeeded in dying', whereas others maintain a meaningful focus and a sense of coherence and psychological integrity.

From their own evidence, Thompson *et al.* suggest that the search to find a personally meaningful way of life which connects the past with the present was conveyed to a greater or lesser extent in all the stories they recorded. The attempt to maintain, against the internal and external odds, a desired life-style, demonstrated the resilience with which people met the challenge of the losses of old age. Some have the strength and adaptability, others do not. A widow of 80 advises one who is 76:

'Don't give in' . . . 'This getting old is very trying, isn't it'. But the worst thing would be to become like the inmates of a home she has just visited, where 'the poor old things don't seem to have any inclination to *do* anything, they all sit around doing nothing . . . I am sure it is better to struggle on, than to give up your home, and have to submit to all sorts of rules and regulations.

(Thompson *et al.* 1991: 246)

An underlying message from many seemed to be not to feel that you can't start something new just because you are 'old', and the quarter of Thompson and colleagues' sample who had few leisure pursuits included some of the most discontented individuals. In contrast to this group were those who had taken up flower-arranging or sequence dancing, for example. Such new activities brought both meaning and pleasure into many lives. Those who attended church or political clubs seemed uplifted by the company, rather than the doctrine provided. Few, however, belonged to 'old people's clubs' – most were scornful of them. Perhaps that is where those who *do* feel old find themselves?

Not surprisingly among such a sample, a major sphere for the generation of fulfilment was grandparenting. Thompson *et al.* (1991: 248) suggest that:

> If the joy of becoming a grandparent is almost universal, the relationship which follows is one which needs to be positively created by winning a child's affection. Those who succeed feel that their role is easier and more pleasurable than parenthood, but in another way it is more difficult, because it cannot be taken for granted: grandparents cannot count on natural loyalty.

Just as relationships at any stage in life need to be repaired and cultivated, so too in later life do intimate relationships have continually to be rebuilt. Thompson *et al.* suggest that the most vulnerable are those men who have dedicated themselves to work and those women who have dedicated themselves to childrearing. The disappearance of these 'purposes' can diminish the meaning of one's life. Loss of intimate relationships requires the skill and determination to forge new ones: some of those who had remarried seemed the happiest of all – 'like honeymoon couples'. Women seemed to be better at filling the gaps left by lost intimates than were men, but even living alone was turned into something positive by one interviewee, Marjorie Dickens, who said:

> 'I like it that I can do as I please, go where I want to, and if I can afford it, buy what I want to, and eat what I want . . . I would never have dreamed of marrying again. I think if you've had one good man, you don't want to try again!'
>
> (Thompson *et al.* 1991: 249)

And what of those who have had one *bad* man? Would they want to try again? Clearly re-marriage does not have the same appeal for everyone.

Thompson *et al.* (1991) conclude that the myths of ageing which we are fed in youth and middle age just do not fit the actual experience of most older men and women, and that it is little wonder that the grandparents of their book do not recognize themselves in the unbalanced version of the realties of later life often presented in stereotypic images. Saying I don't feel old 'is a cry of protest against a myth which causes pain and fear: a call for the recognition of human individuality and resourcefulness at any age' (p. 250). Feeling old, they suggest, is feeling exhausted in spirit, and lacking the energy to find new responses as life changes:

> It is a giving up. Feeling ourselves means feeling the inner energy which has carried us thus far in life. It means accepting our own pasts as part of our present. It means feeling a whole person.
>
> (Thompson *et al.* 1991: 250)

'Feeling old', cast in this light, appears to have some similar symptoms to 'feeling depressed'. In the final paragraph of their book, Thompson *et al.* (1991: 252) note that:

Later life from the inside – like life at any age – is a story with its dark side, its pain and suffering. But the message that comes across most strongly from these accounts is of resilience in the face of twists of fate; of adaptability; and in some of these lives, of a powerfully continuing ability to seize or create chances for fulfilment, whether in work, leisure, or love.

Older women

Later life is a women's issue because there are more women to experience it, and relatively more so at increasing ages. Yet as Ford and Sinclair (1987: 8, 9) note in their presentation of the accounts of 13 older women:

> Even when women do recognise that their position is a consequence of wider social structures they are often at a point in their lives where their capacity to secure change is at its lowest . . . The experiences of old age are in fact mapped out at a much younger age and it is here that we need to begin to set the scene for a happier old age.

Many women still reach pension age after spending a life financially and emotionally dependent on others. Yet some of life's biggest challenges have to be faced from a base of inadequate income and the relative solitude of living alone. The women presented by Ford and Sinclair illustrate well the tension between seeking a balance between the need for security and the need for independence, and in this respect some were ambivalent towards accepting help, even from families from which they derived a lot of pleasure. Through various activities and relationships with others, they maintained their sense of status, self-respect and interests:

> Life's pleasures change as circumstances change. Mrs Patel still loves the noise and laughter her grandchildren bring, but Mrs Harman now prefers the company of people her own age who can talk about the same things. What becomes important is being able to go out and see others, being fit enough to join in activities that provide interest, companionship, and an opportunity to contribute and belong. Miss Moss enjoys the pleasure of not having to get up in the morning; Mrs Wates craves activities so she goes to the Ladies Circle, the Over 60s, a keep-fit class, plays bridge and goes to the library; Miss Stewart loves her telly, especially the afternoon soap operas. When talking about what it was they were seeking from old age the women used phrases such as, 'having some pleasure', 'peace', 'meeting people', 'enjoyment', 'pleasing myself', 'not having to fight'.
>
> (Ford and Sinclair 1987: 152)

But there was evidence that some feared going out alone, particularly at night, which curtailed their activities and increased their need for help from others. Ford and Sinclair (1987) suggest that attitudes that demean older people and threaten their sense of worth can be witnessed in the way in which everyday actions are interpreted to fit stereotypes. Thus 'stiff old women slowly crossing the road are seen as a nuisance, a danger to themselves and others' (p. 155).

And pensioners on a low income who have to take their time to shop carefully are seen as holding up busy modern workers who have a home, job and family to juggle. These older women, Ford and Sinclair suggest, are individuals who are keeping themselves active, caring for themselves and others, with every right to be out and about 'and in no sense making illegitimate or unreasonable demands' (p. 155).

Ford and Sinclair felt that their small sample of women responded towards younger people with a degree of generosity that they themselves did not receive to the same degree. They were fighting all the time to retain control and the initiative, yet had lives which for much of the time were pleasurable and satisfying. But the fighting was like a guerrilla war: 'unannounced, unacknowledged, small-scale and relentless', requiring inventiveness and creativity. As they note:

> This inventiveness and creativity can be seen in all the interviews recorded here. Although they are often in pain, the women go out to ensure they stay as mobile as possible. They cross roads, even if others do not stop and help them; they climb perilously steep bus steps, often watched by others, and risk falling, in order to go to town for a day out. They search for better places to live, and move house. They learn to drive to gain mobility. Many had taken up new activities as they aged – visiting places, joining a course – and several of the women explicitly said that activities were an important way of staving off further decline, both physical and social. There is an inevitable drawing in but a lot of evidence that it is fought. There are challenges against the acceptance of services for the old, and the expectations or wishes of kin. Some refused meals-on-wheels, preferring to cook for themselves; some refused to give up their homes and move in with relatives while they were able to care for themselves. Sometimes the challenges are less visible. Mrs. Hatter takes her water tablet from the orderly every morning and puts it down the sink because she doesn't need it.

> (Ford and Sinclair 1987: 157)

In their sociological analysis of the ways in which gender patterns the experience of later life in Britain, Arber and Ginn (1991) note how the domestic, caring and voluntary work in which women predominate has traditionally been devalued. One consequence of this is that older women are more likely to experience poverty than men; poverty has become almost 'feminized'. The same point is made by Gee and Kimball (1987) in their study of older women in Canada. There, as here, of those women who do enter the labour market, disproportionately more women than men work in peripheral sectors where pay and conditions of service such as pension rights tend to be poorer; they are to be found more in part-time jobs, where the same applies, and their working career is more likely to be discontinuous because of childbearing and child-care. In 1982, in Canada, data on people aged 65 or over suggested that 24.6 per cent of families with a female head were in poverty compared with 10.2 per cent with a male household head. And 60.4 per cent of unattached females aged 65 or over were in poverty compared with 48.9 per cent of males. While poverty among older people in Canada had generally been in decline, for families with a female head it had actually increased. Being poor may mean not being able to afford the things that help keep you mobile or make your home feel comfortable, safe and secure, and widows are particularly prone to having difficulties with home maintenance. While richer older people may be increasingly able to choose appropriate housing, for poor older women especially, the likelihood of this seems to be decreasing.

Though women live longer than men, they are disadvantaged by comparison in terms of their longer experience of poor health and disability. But as Arber and Ginn (1991) note, despite older people having left the labour market for a number of years, higher occupational class continues to be associated with better self-assessed health and lower levels of functional disability. This holds among all older age groups, although for women the gap between the socio-economic classes for self-assessed health seems to narrow with age. Previous occupational class seems to be a more important determinant of health among both elderly men and women than are current material resources, although the latter contribute significantly to a sense of well-being.

Gee and Kimball's (1987) Canadian data also suggest that older women appear to be 'sicker' than older men, especially in terms of milder forms of illness and disabilities. But both this and the mental health of older women need putting into a wider socio-economic and historical perspective. In many societies, women are expected to juggle several roles, which causes stress and tiredness that can be exacerbated at times of crisis or rapid social change. In Africa, for example, women produce 80 per cent of the food, by hoeing, planting and caring for livestock, and also search for water while still involved in child care. This may well be attempted while they are debilitated by chronic ill health. But as yet, women do not have much influence on health policy and are often the last beneficiaries of development schemes. Almost all societies value sons more than daughters – girls may be weaned sooner, fed less and receive less medical attention than boys. Such prejudice can result in women having a negative attitude to their own bodies, making them accept ill-health and pain as their lot in life.

Gee and Kimball (1987) suggest that women who are more 'integrated' into mainstream society have fewer health problems than those who have followed a traditional female role, and that as roles change – with women exercising more control over their lives and power generally – the high rates of morbidity among females may decline. But might mortality patterns not fall more into line with men's too?

If older women live in more impecunious circumstances and with greater levels of disability than older men, is this 'made up for' by appropriate informal and formal care? Arber and Ginn (1991) suggest not. They suggest that because of gender differences in living arrangements, older men are more likely to be provided with privileged and scarce caring resources. Older women are more likely to be perceived, and perceive themselves, as a burden than are older men. They also have less opportunity to purchase care services which could prevent institutionalization. Old women living alone are more dependent on the unpaid care-work of relatives or friends and neighbours than are men who receive proportionately more formal help. This may in part be due to the fact that today's generations of older women, despite their disadvantages in health and material resources, are more able to at least partially compensate for these by their better ability to make and maintain close friendships which afford some protection.

The roots of poverty among older women are put down earlier in life. For this reason, it is important to equalize the status of men and women throughout life, and in this respect Arber and Ginn (1991) suggest how the experience of future generations of older women might change. They may become more involved, as indeed older women in the USA have become, in campaigns around their own needs. In Britain, the Older Women's Project, set up in 1985, shows how older women are far from being 'gormless grannies whose sole interest is in knitting and bingo' (Quinn 1990: 19). The project has four job-share development workers and recognizes 'that issues of relevance to older women depend on their ethnic background, class, age, sexuality and physical and mental capacities'. At the Newham Older Women's Day in February 1990, 75 per cent of those present were Asian women.

With a longer education and more equal careers, women will have higher expectations. The values of mutual assistance, solidarity and reciprocity may then become more in evidence, tempering the male-dominated values of society. 'Wages for housework' and for the care-work that keeps society supported would be one means of enabling more people to contribute to more equitable pensions for their old age.

Gee and Kimball (1987) suggest that the 'public' anonymity, invisibility and vulnerability of many older women is counteracted by 'private' satisfactions and achievements often derived from rich relationships. Nevertheless, it is a strategy for maintaining well-being which has developed as a response to 'an alienating social structure that excludes women from full and equal participation in the wider society' (p. 112).

Ageing ethnic minorities

A Bangladeshi family were asked if they could take their mother home after a stroke had rendered her half paralysed and unable to speak. Much to the delight of the hospital staff, for whom it was a 'successful' discharge, they said they could. The old woman soon became confined to her bed and pressure sores rapidly developed. When asked if they could take their mother home, the family had taken the question literally – could they transport her from A to B? They had not been asked if they could look after her.

(Mathews 1992: 358)

As Fenton (1987) notes, many older south Asian parents came as the dependants of their children, and may not have become fluent in English:

'south Asian' itself covers differences of language and religion – Hindus, Muslims, Sikhs, Christians and numerous smaller groupings. Because there was a preponderance of men among the early immigrants, at the older ages men may outnumber women; something also noted among migrants to Canada. Many West Indians came to Britain with only a short stay in mind, but found themselves staying because of worries over changing rights to remain in Britain and because, working in poorly paid jobs, they couldn't save the money with which they had wanted to return home. Employment opportunities back home were also few. As a consequence, Fenton (1987: 3) suggests:

> Among all the *common* stresses of growing old, minority elderly also experience particular difficulties. Most of Britain's black elderly are earlier migrants, and it is when the settler reaches old age in the 'new country' that he or she feels most acutely the pain of separation from the country of birth. The more alien and hostile their present situation is, the more saddening it is to grow old in a cold climate, and the greater the yearning for 'home'.

Most people of Asian and of Caribbean ancestry place a very high value on the care of their older people, and to the extent that this is not fully realized and they are left with few family supports, this may be experienced as a source of great shock, disappointment, shame and a sense of loss. Fenton found many of the older Afro-Caribbean people he interviewed in Bristol spoke of their families being 'mostly separated', and it was from their attachment to church that many derived comfort. Among the older south Asians interviewed, a repeated theme was 'insecurity', which led to some feeling trapped in their own homes. Some worried that their children would be 'westernized' into uncaring individualistic attitudes towards older people.

Black people share disproportionately more of the class-associated inequalities in health we have mentioned before. Many of Fenton's (1987: 28) interviewees 'spoke about accidents at work and the effect on their health of many years of arduous employment, including unhealthy foundry work, building work, and, among the women, nursing and hospital domestic work'.

A lifetime of having to put up with social disadvantage and racial prejudice is bound to have some repercussions on physical and mental well-being. For some, old age will also bring with it the reliving of the traumatic experiences which drove them from their mother country; for others, a return to the mother-tongue may be a way of responding to stress. In addition, a lack of access to appropriate services, different cultural conceptions of ill-health and relevant responses, and difficulties with language will all place barriers in the way of older people from ethnic minority groups obtaining health and care services.

Although immigrants from the Indian subcontinent have significantly higher (and increasing) death rates from ischaemic heart disease and strokes than the indigenous UK population, and Caribbean-born immigrants also have a significantly higher death rate from cerebrovascular disease (but a significantly *lower* death rate from ischaemic heart disease) (Balarajan 1991), the majority of health-related problems are the same as those facing all older people. But for those from ethnic minorities health problems are compounded by isolation, poverty, racism and discrimination. In order to promote 'equal access to health care for everyone, regardless of their cultural background or country of origin', the government set up in the summer of 1993 an ethnic health unit. How much it will be able to foster equal access remains to be seen.

> Other works clearly show that community health services (like chiropody, speech therapy, occupational therapy) are consistently under-used by ethnic minority people and that a large proportion of this section of the community are unaware of the services available that they may need to use . . . With the current emphasis on care in the community it is obviously an issue of concern that community health services are not reaching minority elders, who are then often forced to use hospital based services and GP consultations inappropriately. This situation is obviously detrimental to the client but is also an inefficient use of NHS resources.
>
> (NAHAT, 1990: 2)

When an under-use of services is identified, the response often seems to be either that this is evidence that they aren't needed, or to 're-educate' black people through health education programmes which promote healthy, but *western*, lifestyles. Culturally appropriate residential accommodation has been provided in Jewish old people's homes for decades, but such supportive accommodation is marked by its relative absence for many ethnic minority groups. It is to be hoped that a 'clients first' perspective will help remedy the situation, but to get what you want in 'the market' requires effective purchasing power. Under the Community Care Act, black elders may be doubly penalized through their relative poverty, since social services departments' charges for services can eat into the income an individual has to pay for basic necessities.

Daily life in later life

In a paper on the use of time by older people in Great Britain, Abrams (1988) concludes that the patterns of activity for those aged 65 and over are surprisingly similar to those aged 45–64, given that older individuals face decrements in income, greater physical limitations, a greater prevalence of living alone, and that they have more time in which to engage in leisure. 'The general pattern of leisure life, at least for middle-aged and older people, is quite passive and homebound. The role of television in drawing attention to home-centred leisure and the consequences of a relatively low level of social and active leisure remains to be fully examined' (p. 40).On average, some 3.4 hours of daily 'free time' was spent by those aged 65 and over watching television. But Abrams suggests that TV programming designed for older people tends to drive them away from viewing! Radio was listened to on average for 1.2 hours, while 1.2 hours was spent reading, 1.5 hours resting or relaxing, and only 0.2 hours going for a walk.

For non-passive, non-home-based leisure activities to increase, they must be cheap in money terms, be provided in daylight hours and in relatively accessible places, give companionship, and be appropriate in terms of their physical demands. Where leisure facilities have been given some priority, the visibility of older people swimming or doing aerobics, for example, makes their presence increasingly taken for granted. Nevertheless, older people tend to go out less for meals, or to the cinema and theatre, or to sporting events, because of their associated costs. Women in later life tend to engage in social leisure activities somewhat more than men, but women's solitude increases significantly even when social interaction does too.

Daily life in later life for most people seems to involve a slight restructuring of previous lifestyles, where extra time is allocated across existing obligatory and leisure activities. For most there is no revolution in lifestyle and the uptake of new pursuits is as yet uncommon. But the physiological changes and ill health that appear to be age-associated can make some of the activities of our daily life feel more like daily hassles.

Daily hassles

Consider my close neighbour, Mrs Gwen Thomas, and her trip to the corner shop, which I make there and back – including my purchase – in less than five minutes on my bike. She has difficulty rising from her comfy but low armchair. She walks carefully across her sitting room floor in her slippers watching for the threadbare patch in the carpet with the loose bits in loops. She returns with her shoes which she sits down in the armchair to put on. She has trouble doing up the laces because of the arthritis in her hands. She gets her thick and heavy outdoor coat from the cupboard in the hall and has a bit of a struggle getting it on. She takes her bunch of keys from the hook nearby, and has a bit of trouble opening the front door, which only has a small circular lock knob, the serrated edge of which has worn smooth. She switches off the hall light to save electricity.

The path to the pavement is dark and wet and the autumn leaves on it are hard to see. Mrs Thomas is blind in one eye and her sight in the other is not good. The pavement, too, is wet and slippery with the leaves from the large trees nearby and, despite being relaid flat two years ago, the paving stones are now uneven again because of the new water pipes that have just been relaid under them. She knows if she falls she might break her arm, or her hip. She may not know that doing the latter, or breaking a femur, might lead to hospitalization and an increased mortality risk. She walks slowly and carefully to the shop, stooping somewhat because of a slight 'dowager's hump' caused by osteoporosis. With her vision and the poor street lighting she can't make out the details of people who approach on the pavement. The shop is brightly lit, but nevertheless she has trouble looking at the list of preservatives on the cans she is buying – she is trying to avoid one in particular. Because the print is small, she asks the young shopkeeper to read it to her. The background of Radio 1 makes it more difficult for her to hear – she has a typical high-frequency hearing loss which makes accurate speech perception harder. She really has to concentrate. She pays – is it a £20 or £10 or £5 pound note? Has she got the correct change? Her journey home is equally painstaking but this time she is frightened by a large dog that runs up and barks. She has trouble finding the right key for her front door, the front porch being very dark. Inside, after she has got her breath back and got warm again, she will have a bit of a struggle with the can opener.

Mrs Thomas is on eight prescribed medications. She is worried that her drowsiness in the late morning is due to some drug side-effect or drug interaction. Remembering which pill to have, when, is a bit of a bind. She's not supposed to have alcohol, but she likes a sherry in the evening from time to time, or even a bit of whisky in her tea. She wraps up well to keep warm, but tends to keep the same clothes on for quite a while to avoid going to the launderette too often. Sometimes she sleeps in her day clothes because she can't be bothered to get into her pyjamas in a rather cold bedroom. Every now and then she has a little 'accident' – but she doesn't seem to notice the slight smell of stale urine that is around. Often brushing her teeth seems more trouble than it's worth. The dentist suggested 'flossing' when she last went, several years ago, but 'it was too much of a faff'.

Most people create satisfactory lives for themselves in later life whatever their age, but this can require increasing effort or the acceptance of a certain amount of restriction – a 'drawing in'. The effort involved may tax diminishing resources which people draw upon to cope with the daily hassles that daily life in later life can bring. In particular, older women and those from ethnic minorities may be most disadvantaged. There is a need for increased awareness of, and sensitivity to, the things that we may take for granted when younger but which can represent a challenge to older people. People aged 65 and over comprise some 75 per cent of individuals who are disabled, and there is little doubt that they would benefit from legislation akin to the Americans with Disabilities Act, which came into force in the USA in January 1993. This makes 'access' a priority, whether it be 'laundromats or theatres, public libraries or buses'.

Access enables presence, and presence would lead, hopefully, to greater integration, toleration and understanding. But British attempts to bring in similar legislation have so far failed, perhaps because we have no direct equivalent, among our numbers of disabled people, of the returning and now middle-aged Vietnam war veteran. We should remember that many of us will be veterans of a more ordinary sort but with similar needs for equal access. But improving access is just one facet in removing unnecessary hassles from daily life.

Poorer vision requires better spectacles and poor hearing requires that hearing aids are not left in dressing-table drawers because appropriate counselling in their use was not provided. Should women in their 80s have to walk in the road on dark nights to avoid slippery uneven pavements? Do TV and video controllers have to be so fiddly and confusing? There is no doubt that the increasing availability of environmental aids now sold in chemists and other stores will lessen the stigma attached to design for 'the disabled'. Often good design for older people is better design for everyone. Information technology must also be brought to bear in increasing individual autonomy and independence — from teleshopping and telebanking, to 'smart houses' where servo-assisted motors can supplement weakened muscles.

EurolinkAge (1990) provides a European code of good practice for meeting the needs of older people who are disabled and suggests among other things that 'elderly disabled people should be afforded training on the nature of their disability, on how to cope with it, on how to develop self-confidence and self-advocacy, and on the skills of independence' (p. 3). It suggests that the principle be established of encouraging and supporting the most autonomous situation possible for, and most active life desired by, older people, whatever the nature or degree of their disability. The report also notes there has been a certain reluctance on the part of governments 'to afford to the problems of the elderly and disabled people the attention and priority they call for' (p. 15). Perhaps the activism and lobbying of those of us who are older *disabled* people might, in the future, encourage those of us who are disabled *older* people to be more militant in self-advocacy.

People's perception of their health often reflects how well they are managing the activities of daily life rather than the number of current health problems they might actually have. But policy to make activities of daily life easier needs promoting not only on the 'environmental obstacles' front, but also directly on the health front. An attempt to do this can be seen in the Welsh Health Planning Forum's (1992) protocol for investment in health gain on physical disability and discomfort. Here, an overall aim is to produce a measurable 15 per cent improvement in the quality of life of people with a physical disability between 1994 and 2002. More specific targets are to reduce by 50 per cent between 1995 and 2002 the number of people experiencing significant loss of mobility due to osteoarthritis of the hip and to reduce by the same amount the number of people developing significant contractures from reduced mobility. The protocol also considers some psychological health gains that need to be achieved, for example in reducing the levels of depression in the first year of recovery from a stroke.

As important as setting targets for health gain is the delineation of the means for achieving them. This the protocol seeks to do. Such gains in health, together with schemes of environmental improvement and thoughtfulness in the detailed design of everyday equipment, together with appropriate use of information and other high-technology, could clearly help many of us achieve a more hassle-free life in daily life as we grow older. Where there is a will, there may be a way to meet the challenges such targets provide. But if this is what we want for ourselves and others, we need to ensure it acquires sufficient political priority and appropriate funding.

— 3 —

Coping and failing to cope

Coping requires access to, and the appropriate use of, resources. Such resources might be external and physical, such as electric wheelchairs and better designed cutlery, or external but personal, such as help given by relatives and friends, or input of formal assistance such as that received from community nurses or home helps. Resources also include 'internal' ones, for example our problem-solving strategies and ability to resist stress and anxiety. In essence, *coping* refers to a person's attempts to manage (i.e. master, tolerate, reduce, minimize, etc.) internal and environmental demands and conflicts which tax or exceed his or her resources.

Personal support

For many individuals, apart from their own personal strengths, other people constitute the main resources in their lives and it is with good reason that Wenger (1984) titles her book on coping with old age as *The Supportive Network*

> This is a study of how a sample of the elderly manage their day-to-day lives. It looks at how they gain access to a range of services, what problems they face and how they overcome them. It is an optimistic book which demonstrates that the majority of the elderly are able people who, together with help from their families and friends, find solutions to most of the difficulties they encounter as they get older.
>
> (Wenger 1984: 3)

Wenger's older people living in rural communities in north Wales, whether they were indigenous or had retired there, were pretty self-sufficient for routine types of help. 'What is clear is that there are more elderly providing help than there are receiving help, and where help is given it comes predominantly from spouse, family, or friends and neighbours, while help from formal services is minimal!' (Wenger 1984: 134). Working-class older people were more likely to rely on help from the family compared with middle-class people, who were more likely to use friends, neighbours and professionals. Gender seemed to play an important part in the availability of help in that each sex was more likely to receive help in the opposite gender domain (e.g. men with cooking and women with household maintenance tasks). In crises, women tended to turn more to the family for instrumental support and men more so for emotional support. Wenger paints a picture of older people who are generally well-integrated and well-supported, with less than one in ten reporting they were very isolated or lonely or suffering from low morale. Even where loneliness and isolation existed, there were usually people in the immediate neighbourhood to whom a distressed individual could turn. Three-quarters of the older individuals in Wenger's sample had support networks of five or more people, although there was usually one individual who was the main source of support. If there was no 'obvious' person to take charge of providing support, such responsibility was often shared between other relatives, or by neighbours when more instrumental help was needed. Formal support from social services did not appear to undermine informal support. Wenger (1984: 180) concluded that:

. . . for the most part the elderly and their families respond to the challenges of ageing through adaptive and coping strategies and the majority make creative changes in life-style to accommodate the inevitable losses which are part of the ageing process. Two of the major components of the negative image of old age relate directly to the potential for adaptation – the reluctance of families to assume responsibility and the reluctance of the elderly to accept change.

Wenger argues that the evidence suggests neither of these propositions is true – quite the converse – and that:

. . . given the demonstrated capacity of the elderly for change and adaptation and the willingness of the family to help it seems that more attention could be given to public education on and preparation for the latter part of the life-cycle. The literature on both education and psychology emphasises the formative years of babyhood and youth to such a degree that most people assume that learning and growing are not for old people. Perhaps the time has come . . . for this perspective to be re-evaluated and for a greater emphasis on self-help and self-development throughout life. The elderly can adapt and they jealously guard their independence. In this context it would seem to be self-evident that they would welcome the knowledge and demonstrate the ability to take an active role in preventive and rehabilitative strategies with regard to their own physical and mental health.

(Wenger 1984: 190)

So important are relationships for coping and health, that the Royal College of Physicians has suggested that at least 90 per cent of 'the elderly' should be able to say that they speak to a friend at least once a week, and that a health target for the year 2000 should be that 95 per cent of 'the elderly' should be able to say they have one or more friends or relatives who cares about them (Brindle 1991).

Coping strategies

Coping involves more than having access to external resources; it requires an internal resourcefulness in order for external ones to be managed effectively. This implies 'active' coping by *doing*, which involves realizing there is a problem to be tackled, analysing the problem and bringing information and ideas to bear on formulating a solution; acting on those ideas, assessing the outcome, and modifying actions accordingly. There are, of course, other coping strategies. One can cope by re-conceptualizing the problem as not being a problem – a sort of cognitive coping; or one might choose to deny that there *is* a problem and try to ignore it – a form of denial or avoidance coping. Avoidance coping can include such behaviour as taking it out on others, refusing to believe something has happened, or eating and drinking to reduce tension. Older people experiencing high levels of stress may use avoidance coping if no other alternatives seem viable (Haldeman 1990), but so might younger ones.

The success and the appropriateness of the coping strategy might well depend on the nature of the 'problem' with which one is being challenged, and there may be no 'best way' for solving a particular problem for all individuals. How should one cope with the knowledge that one has a terminal illness or will go completely deaf or blind? How should you cope with the death of your life-long partner?

Comparing individuals in their sixties, eighties and hundreds, Martin *et al.* (1992) suggested that centenarians might cope with both health and family-related problems in a less behaviourally active manner than do the younger groups, and use cognitive coping for health problems somewhat more. Levels of avoidance coping seemed likely to be used to much the same extent by each age group. Although their study was cross-sectional and could not eliminate cohort effects, the authors remark that 'these patterns may indicate that in extreme old age individuals can be assertive and forceful' (pp. 27–8), which hardly fits our stereotypic notions. They continue:

> . . . centenarians tended to score higher on emotionality; high emotionality may primarily reflect the diminishing resources available to meet the challenges of the day. The same may be said for lower centenarian scores on active coping. The oldest-old may not have access to active support systems to help them with critical events, or they may not see the need to actively deal with every new problem. They may also be more accepting of their current situation, or coping may be an entirely different concept for the oldest-old.
>
> (Martin *et al.* 1992: 28)

If you hold the simplistic notion that most older people cope with all their problems in a similar way, a way different to that of younger people, the Bonn

Longitudinal Study of Aging (Rott and Thomae 1991) would quickly disabuse you of it. This study revealed just how diverse coping responses are. It suggested that there are situation- as well as person-specific response patterns to stress in later life. Although older individuals might respond to problems in, say, the *housing domain* differently from those in the *health domain*, and differently again from those in an *income* or a *family domain*, the Bonn study found that, by and large, their sample of older people were fairly consistent over a 15-year span in their response patterns to problems within the same domain.

The Bonn study used some 20–25 'response classes' to problems in the four domains mentioned above. The 'achievement-related behaviour' response, for example, would include the greater efforts it took respondents in their very old age to remain active and to take their daily walks and do exercises in order to remain healthy, and the response class 'adjustment to institutional aspects of the situation' would include steps taken to use any provisions and insurance that German society and health care systems offered to employed or retired women and men. Included in this category would be frequency of visits to a doctor, consumption of prescribed drugs and applications for financial help to go to a resort.

'Depressive reactions' to health problems changed over time from a very high to a very low rank for females, suggesting that 'surviving women learned how to cope better with their health problems in old age' (p.27). Rott and Thomae (1991: 27) also noted that:

> A learning process is also indicated in the change of 'Resistance' from high to lower ranks in the female sample, whereas this way of responding remains in the upper middle in the male sample. 'Resistance' includes all forms of non-compliance with the doctor's advice regarding smoking, drinking, diet and activity.

The consistency of response patterns to problems in a particular domain over a 15-year period suggests the influence of established habits, as well as perceived roles and norms, which regulate the daily lives of both younger and older people. But established response habits did not seem to be associated with standardized measures of personality. Having an extended time perspective was also associated with active forms of coping and achievement-related responses to health problems.

Responses that turn out to be useful in coping with a problem will tend to be retained, but if rigidly applied to all problems are likely to be incongruent with their demands, and indeed Rott and Thomae's data suggest that the response hierarchy to health problems differed markedly from that for family-related problems. With the former, 'adjustment to institutional aspects of the situation' responses rank very high, but very low for the latter. For family-related problems, 'adjustment to the needs and habits of others' and 'identification with the aims and fates of children' were among the most preferred responses.

The Bonn study found some clustering of individuals in their patterns of response to problems. For example, with regard to family matters, two groups were identified in terms of whether they used more, or less often, responses classified as: achievement-related behaviour; adjustment to needs and habits of others; revision of expectations; identification with the aims and fates of children and grandchildren; and cultivating social contacts.

With respect to housing-related problems, two different clusters of respondents emerged, who were characterized by whether they responded often or seldom by: adjustment to institutional aspects of the situation; adjustment to needs and habits of others; and in terms of less negative emotional responses such as depression, resignation and evasive reactions. With respect to health problems, the most significant difference in response clusters related to those individuals 'relying on others' and those not. But differences were also shown in their use of 'accepting the situation as it is' and in 'adjustment to institutional aspects of the situation' and in 'achievement-related behaviour'. In considering responses to income-related problems, Rott and Thomae (1991: 38) note:

> These findings point to a certain impact of personality variables on the ways of coping with stress, but the inconsistencies in the importance of the response classes at different measuring points [in the 15-year longitudinal study] suggests that situational factors have a greater influence on the selection of coping strategies.

The Bonn study suggests that preferences for specific ways of coping may be related to the degree to which older people believe in the unchangeability of unfavourable life conditions. Less flexible responses may be used if the situation is perceived as unchangeable. For those who perceive the situation as amenable to change, different coping strategies may be applied in an economic and flexible way according to the specific demands of the situation.

A sense of control

The unchangeability of unfavourable life conditions is an aspect of perceived sense of control, which in turn is likely to affect coping processes. Aldwin (1991) suggests that the literature does not sustain the notion that in general older individuals cope with problems in more passive ways and are less likely to try and master situations. Ill-health and problems of loss are more likely to evoke palliative or emotion-focused coping than instrumental action, which might explain some of the broad differences in coping strategies that have been suggested to exist between younger and older age groups. These might, however, be cohort effects, since younger generations tend to be better educated, and better education tends to be associated with a sense that more control is located within oneself. If some people learn from experience, one might expect that, as these people age, they become more adaptive – they have had more chance to learn which coping mechanisms are useful for which types of problems and in which sets of circumstances. Others, of course, might avoid problems by restricting their lifestyle (by 'drawing in'), while others may cling to ineffective means of coping with problems.

Aldwin (1991) points out that most studies suggest that older people use less escapist and fewer avoidance coping mechanisms, and similar levels of problem-focused ones, compared with younger people. But older individuals also tend to report less perceived control of events, which might lead one to expect them to use problem-focused coping less. Aldwin's own study to examine these issues found that while older adults were less likely to feel responsible for the management and solution of their problems – and, by implication, feel less control – this had no adverse effect on their coping strategies: 'Older individuals were less likely to report the use of escapist strategies that long experience may have shown them are ineffective techniques for coping with stress' (p. 179). She goes on to note:

> In addition, coping with health problems was apparently a source of efficacy for these older individuals. Having to cope with a problem that was, perhaps, all too familiar, was nonetheless a source of a sense of mastery for older individuals in this sample. Health problems may not be perceived as controllable, but nonetheless they may be manageable, and the process of managing the problem may give rise to feelings of efficacy.
>
> (Aldwin 1991: 179)

Aldwin's study did not include older people who were institutionalized, but Foy and Mitchell's (1991) review of factors contributing to learned helplessness in individuals who do live in institutions suggests where some differences may lie. Learned helplessness is a theoretical model which explains the pathological nature of declines in physical and psychological status beyond what appears to be warranted by actual physical problems. Within institutions, individuals may experience a loss of control and develop an expectancy of further inability to control relevant aspects of their environment. If a stressful outcome is perceived as uncontrollable, then there will be no attempt to try and control it, and frustration and depression may ensue. This can then undermine an individual's will to initiate efforts to control other events. One of the challenges that face us as we grow older is to overcome the physical and social losses we may encounter by using our residual capacities for resource management. Acceptance into an institution may be seen as acceptance of incompetence, and helplessness may be almost a prerequisite of nursing home residence. In institutions, incompetence, helplessness and sick role behaviour may be reinforced. Foy and Mitchell provide as an example toileting and bathing schedules, which are imposed on people irrespective of their individual needs:

> The aged person struggling to remain continent learns that toileting is not contingent upon his/her needs, but upon the imposed schedule or whim of caregivers. Attention comes not when the person needs and wants to be toileted, but randomly or when the person has already soiled himself/herself. The person's efforts to remain continent are ineffective in producing the desired outcome of getting to the toilet in time. Eventually

he/she gives up and becomes incontinent, a helpless behavior, which conforms to a picture of the institutionalized aged.

(Foy and Mitchell 1991: 8)

Clearly, a sense of powerlessness may contribute to learned helplessness and unsatisfactory coping. Certainly, staff in institutional settings often induce dependency by reinforcing and rewarding it. 'Helping' by others may be one of a number of seemingly benign contextual factors that can have a debilitating effect on coping. Control-enhancing interventions in institutional settings have been shown to produce improvements in cognitive, affective and functional deficits associated with learned helplessness (Foy and Mitchell 1991). Interventions which improve generalized feelings of competence also tend to have longer-lasting benefits than interventions which provide control over more momentary or specific events.

Failing to cope

An inability to cope is likely to result in a sense of undermined autonomy and individuality, and give rise to symptoms of anxiety or depression, or poor sleep for instance. Coping with a close relative with dementia, for example, can be particularly arduous and problematic, and an inability to cope can lead to crisis admission into an institution for the person with dementia. In a study of a carer support scheme, Milne *et al.* (1993) found that 'active cognitive coping' (i.e. giving conscious thought to the problem and its solution rather than responding in an habitual manner) was the most important strategy used. Furthermore, it was put into effect more by those who chose *not* to use the carer support scheme than by those who did. The outcome for both groups in terms of strain levels was similar. Milne *et al.* suggest that formal resources should be directed at enhancing the coping strategies of the less adaptive carers, while those with adequate coping skills may only require non-professional services and social support. Thus carers, like others, may need to be shown alternatives to avoidance strategies like increased smoking and alcohol consumption; alternatives such as realistic problem analysis, goal planning and choice of actions to reach the goal, as well as the monitoring of the efficacy of such actions.

Coping with the social and psychological difficulties that can arise from a deteriorating sensory acuity, or from speech loss or incipient dementia, or from acquired disability after a stroke or heart attack, brings additional challenges to those involved in coping with the physiological change itself. For example, coping with a high-frequency hearing loss that makes speech difficult to hear clearly, especially when other sounds are present, requires more than just the extra effort given to listening or lip-reading. In addition, hearing aids have to be coped with, one has to become assertive enough to find the best listening position in a room, to ask people to repeat themselves (especially on the telephone), and one may also have to cope with the attitudes of others which equate deafness with daftness.

As noted above, when one is not coping well, anxiety and depression, together with withdrawal, are common consequences. What is more, they have a knock-on effect, making coping even harder. Not surprisingly, people often turn to 'props' like alcohol. Some people drink to console themselves in bereavement or for other losses, others as a consolation or compensation for loneliness; some use alcohol to relieve pain, while others drink to help them sleep. In fact, increased alcohol consumption is a more risky business for older people; it can increase depression, lower brain function and impair coordination, make the absorption of vitamins from food harder, increase incontinence, and be dangerous when taken with certain drugs commonly prescribed to older people, such as sedatives, tranquillizers and sleeping pills. As with most people, alcohol consumption is better in moderation and taken to accompany food. Special celebrations can provide the excuse for having 'too much' once in a while, but the contribution of alcohol to coping is largely negative.

Some older individuals are acutely afraid of stigma and will avoid both labelling themselves as disabled and mixing with similar others and their associations. But in doing this they can cut themselves off from the most accessible and relevant sources of information and advice which they might urgently need – how to choose and obtain aids, for example, or how to approach service providers. Adjusting to new demands can be taxing at any time of life, but perhaps more so in later life. As a EurolinkAge (1990: 20–1) report notes:

> The sense that 'life has become a burden' may be particularly common among the new disabled, leading to self-neglect and even self-destruction, partly therefore accounting for the higher rate of suicide among elderly people. At the same time carers are subject to acute sensations of guilt whether in the face of sudden changes, for example as the result of stroke, or of more usually gradual but irremediable declines such as dementia.

Long-term stress, feeling distressed, being subject to unexpected unwanted events, sensing loss or threat, feeling humiliated, being uncertain about the future, having one's routine disrupted, and in particular experiencing a feeling that you are not in control, are some of the features of the crises that can occur when coping fails. People respond by failing to think clearly, partly through avoiding related thoughts, or become preoccupied by their thoughts which 'go round in circles'; or they may feel full of anger, shame and guilt; or they might show muscle tension, have disrupted eating and sleeping habits, or even have aches and pains, skin rashes and infections, that are responses to stress. Indeed, they may respond in a complex variety of ways. But because anxiety and depression are such common responses, we consider them in a little more detail below.

Anxiety and depression

Anxiety gets our physiological system ready for fight or flight – for a *physical* response. Often such physical responses are inappropriate, and the release given by fighting or fleeing doesn't occur. Over extended periods of weeks or months, individuals habituate to their levels of anxiety and fail to recognize, for example, that their muscles are tensed when they should be relaxed. Anxiety also produces more thoughts and mental images resulting in difficulties in getting to sleep, or waking up unrefreshed. People who are anxious often breathe fast and shallowly, which can have the physiological effect of making them feel edgy and jittery and giving them the psychological sense that something is wrong. Because physical illness is more common in older people, the confusion between anxiety symptoms and other symptoms may be easily made. For example, prolonged rapid breathing (hyperventilation) can cause dizziness and chest pain as well as being like the breathlessness which can result from heart and lung disease.

Depression of a severity that requires special help or treatment affects about 5 per cent of people over the age of 65. Less severe forms can often be helped by focusing on an individual's thoughts and feelings and ways of coping, perhaps through a counselling approach. As Short (1991: 13) notes:

> Counselling as a profession, in the next decade must pay attention to the different needs of the older couple and the older individual client. We must develop our own awareness examining our own unspoken assumptions about old age, challenging our own fears and anxieties. We must review the images that we present of our organisations and of counselling as a profession to ensure that they do nothing to deter the older client from seeking help which can be useful, constructive and supporting.

The most severe form of depression – clinical depression – may require treatment by increasingly sophisticated anti-depressant drugs, together with other forms of therapy aimed at undermining the negative thought processes which help characterize it. Common symptoms of a depressive disorder include feeling unhappy and tearful, feeling tired and apathetic, being slower in thought and action, worrying about the future, sleeping badly and losing an interest in food and the other pleasures of life. Feeling that 'the fizz has gone out of my pop' is common, and negative thoughts come more easily to mind as do negative memories.

Older people are probably more likely than younger ones to misconstrue the symptoms of depression as being symptoms of a physical illness. Also, older people with depression are more likely to feel that their memory is failing. Reassurance that there is no underlying physical illness or particular mental deterioration can itself be therapeutic. Not surprisingly, the likelihood of depression increases the more that negative life events occur simultaneously. Given the losses that can be experienced in later life, it is surprising that depression is not more common and its incidence relative to that of younger groups probably testifies to the coping skills which older people have developed with life's experiences.

Huppert and Garcia (1991), looking at psychiatric symptomatology among groups vulnerable to mental illness, which included 'elderly people with poor health', again found variation rather than uniformity characterizing patterns of response. Whereas anxiety and depression were significantly raised for most at-risk groups, older men in poor health did not show significant depressive symptoms but did show difficulty in coping, while older unemployed men and 'elderly women in poor health' did not show significant difficulty in coping. Symptoms of anxiety and depression were most common among single women with dependent children, but they had difficulty with coping only if they were also unemployed. Such findings, like those of the Bonn Longitudinal Study, illustrate the need to disaggregate data for supposedly homogeneous groups such as 'the elderly' or 'the unemployed', if one is to find any meaningful patterns in them.

Some people have a history of severe depressive episodes which carries over into later life, while for others the frequency and severity of such episodes decreases over time. While the bulk of depressions encountered in old age are the continuing story of depression at younger ages, a significant number do arise in later life for the first time (Gurland, 1992). These latter, though probably somewhat less severe, may be more persistent, complicated and harder to treat than those occurring earlier. It would also seem that physical illness can precipitate or prolong depressions that would otherwise clear up, and that depressions can aggravate, prolong or precipitate physical conditions. For most older people who have an episode of depression, recovery does take place, even though relapses do occur. Gurland suggests clinicians can take an optimistic therapeutic approach to depression, along with the realization that treatment may have to be flexible, tenacious, ingenious, extended and repeated.

When drug and other therapies seem ineffective, and where in particular depression takes a psychotic form where delusions are present, electroconvulsive therapy (ECT) may make a contribution. As Benbow (1991: 404) notes: 'ECT is a safe, effective treatment for a wide variety of depressive and other illnesses in later life and can be used despite extreme old age in the presence of dementia and cardiovascular disease or stroke'. In recent years, the use of ECT with older people has seen something of a resurgence, partly because promises of more effective and specific pharmacotherapy have not been fulfilled. But some might have qualms about what appears to be a drastic form of intervention, the precise mechanisms of which have yet to be delineated. Scrutton (1992) for one waves the flag for those who prefer a less medicalized and more 'complementary' approach to their health problems. One drawback of anti-depressants, for example, are their side-effects and as Scrutton (1992: 178) notes:

The other drawback of psychoactive drugs is social rather than medical, in that they help people to tolerate intolerable situations, reducing their capacity to come to terms with, and challenge, what is happening in their lives. This is often based on attitudes which suggest that older people should not feel emotional pain, should be protected from grief, and by doing so, removes from the individual an inviolable right to live and experience life as it is.

Of course, some people might prefer to swallow the pill and tolerate the intolerable rather than fight battles they feel they cannot win. But whatever one's views of medicine or 'alternative' medicine, informed choice requires the pros and cons of both approaches to be available for examination.

Suicide

If you do not have access to, or the ability to use, resources which help you tolerate the intolerable, or if you cannot find a way of coping with a life you find unbearable, ending your life might appear to be a solution. The incidence of suicide increases progressively with age and the rate for men is consistently higher than that for women, the differential between the two increasing with age from six men to every one woman at age 65, to more than twelve to one by the age of 85. Men also use more violent means of killing themselves and the highest age-specific rates are found among men aged 75 and over. In the UK in 1990, some 888 individuals aged 65 and over killed themselves and the rate for people aged 75 and over was some 43 per cent higher than the rate for the population as a whole. As many as 70 per cent of suicides are committed by people with depression, whereas some 30 per cent may be alcohol-related. For others, however, it may seem a rational response to uncontrollable circumstances, such as those produced by certain forms of terminal cancer. In the latter, suicide may be a reassertion of personal control in another form – a more dignified way of coping.

Older people seem to make fewer token attempts at suicide, communicate their intention to commit suicide less frequently, use more lethal methods, and are successful much more often than younger people. In America, suicide rates among older people appeared to increase dramatically in the 1980s, after falling for nearly half a century (Robinson 1990), a pattern which has been echoed, albeit less strikingly, in the UK since the 1970s. And now concern is also being voiced in some localities within the UK at the 'alarmingly high suicide rate among over 65-s' (Millar 1992: 10). The reasons for recent increases in suicide rates are unclear. More public awareness of Alzheimer's disease might be one factor, but more likely is a reduction in the resources which some older people can draw upon to help them cope with, or indeed change, the circumstances in which they find themselves. As can often be the case, the individuals most in need of help may be those who have most difficulty obtaining it.

Looking to our own futures, who knows which of us will need support – informal or formal – to help us cope with anxiety and depression, illness and pain, a poor physical environment, or the attitudes and values of others and the implications these have for the quality of our life in later life. In many ways, coping tends to be with what has come to pass, whereas prevention, as they say, is better than cure. Preventive coping involves looking forward, questioning whether the current state of affairs is inevitable, anticipating some problems, planning for change, and accepting that one has some responsibility for producing it. For some intolerable conditions, popping down to your local councillor or MP to apply pressure might be more effective in the long run, for others as well as yourself, than popping a pill.

4

Speed of behaviour

One common subjective experience about growing older, which by and large matches experimental evidence, concerns slowing down. Many of Heim's respondents mentioned it and she notes that had she embarked on her study of the experience of ageing earlier, 'I should have had the advantage of greater fluency and speed of thought, a more readily accessible vocabulary and the ability to hold more than one idea in mind at a time' (Heim 1990: 6). Whether experimental evidence about 'slowing' suggests it is a general factor, affecting performance on all tasks and all mental domains and processes in much the same way, or whether it suggests it is more task-specific or process- or domain-specific, is a matter of interpretation. Schulz (1994) introduces a four-paper debate on the issue, from which Fisk and Fisher (1994) conclude that all aspects of cognitive ageing cannot just be explained in terms of general slowing. The debate, however, is likely to continue until methodological, statistical and conceptual issues are clarifed.

In western society, speed would seem to be a positive attribute, but slowness can have its advantages too, as some of Heim's respondents mentioned. For example, it can afford the chance for a heightened appreciation of nature. In a similar vein, Gadow and Berg (1978: 85–6) suggest:

> It may be that with age we realise time has the dimensions of depth as well as duration . . . we slow ourselves then to explore experiences, not in their linear pattern of succeeding one another, but in their possibility of opening for us entire worlds in each situation and in each person encountered. We slow ourselves to be more gentle with these experiences, to take care to let their possibilities, their rich density emerge.

Drivers and pedestrians

Heim (1990) links deteriorating senses and the lack of the speed and vigour of youth to the older individual's physical slowness and immobility: 'we park our car in a small space more slowly and less accurately' (p. 22). With car driving (and being a pedestrian), it is both speed and slowness that contributes to accidents: speed of vehicles, and the relative slowness of our behavioural responses. Car driving provides a useful example of a complex integrated mental and physical activity, some of the components of which may slow down with age. We selectively look in the rear or side mirrors, or left and right at junctions; we change gears, brake and steer; listen to the weather forecast, talk to passengers; watch the car behind that is about to overtake; judge the speed of cars in front and approaching from behind as we think of overtaking; consider what we think the young man in the car in front (with condensation making his rear view impossible) will do at the next junction (he doesn't seem to use indicators for left turns); wonder about pedestrians – will that child step off the pavement, will that older person wait for the 'green man' to light? Driving demands a lot of visual attention. Whether this is sustained, divided or selectively utilized, the demands made on older individuals may be greater than those made on younger ones (Parasuraman and Nestor 1991).

A recent newspaper headline read 'Road safety plan targets the oldies' and noted that, as traffic densities increase, older people are having to cope with situations which are proving increasingly difficult. The same applies to people of any age, but when accidents occur we tend to make inferences according to the driver's age – was the younger person speeding or drunk, had the older person got good vision and health, were they 'mentally competent'? Another recent headline stated 'Elderly still driving with dementia' and reported doctors who had carried out a research study as saying that 'crashes are five times more likely amongst people with Alzheimer-type illnesses than amongst healthy drivers of the same age'. We shall return to this issue in the next chapter.

About half of all pedestrians killed on Britain's roads are over 60 years of age, as are over 20 per cent of all car drivers killed. Waller (1991) points out that although older drivers constitute the most rapidly growing segment of the American driving population – in terms of drivers licensed, miles driven and proportion of the driving population – the transportation system has not been designed with older drivers in mind. Are signs in the best place, with appropriately sized lettering in optimum foreground and background colours, and are they repeated often enough? There is an accelerating rate of crashes per mile driven, which begins around age 55, and when in a crash older people are more vulnerable to injury and have a higher fatality rate.

Are older individuals aware of their age-related sensory and cognitive deficits which have implications for road safety? Apart from a slowing of speed of complex decision making and behavioural response, several sensory changes are important. With respect to vision, older people take longer to adapt to darker lighting conditions and cannot see as well as younger people in dark conditions. Washout of vision from glare produced at night by oncoming car headlights on main beam, for example, takes longer to return to normal, and there is decreasing sensitivity to what is happening at the periphery of vision. To the extent that older drivers or pedestrians pick up cues from sound, then hearing difficulties may also inhibit optimum road safety. Distraction by listening to the radio, for example, may influence driving speed.

A study by Holland and Rabitt (1992a) suggests that those who are aware of deficits compensate for growing limitations by being more careful, driving with less haste, driving less altogether, avoiding driving in the dark and in bad weather or at the rush hour or in places known to be troublesome and which can be avoided. When the significant number of 'unaware' individuals in the study were made aware of their limitations, for example in their restricted night-time and peripheral vision, many modified their driving behaviour accordingly. This suggests a mechanism is needed to make individuals aware of their limitations. Perhaps as with MOT tests for vehicles, we should all re-take a driving test every five or so years, or more frequently if circumstances – like having an accident – suggest it. A recent motoring programme on TV found that seven out of a sample of ten 'ordinary motorists' failed when re-tested!

As Holland and Rabbitt (1992a) point out, the reduced information-processing capacity of older people tends to make them less efficient at monitoring their own performance, making them less aware of their mistakes and less able to remember making them. They also note that:

> Elderly people take in and process information more slowly (e.g. Salthouse, 1985). They are particularly impaired relative to younger adults when they have to deal with complex problem-solving situations . . . Older people even walk more slowly than younger people . . . and have difficulty taking in perceptual information (e.g. speed and distance of vehicles) at the same time as walking. The evidence that elderly drivers' accidents occur disproportionately at complex junctions . . . is evidence in itself that they find complex situations particularly difficult.
>
> (Holland and Rabitt 1992a: 299)

Of course, with time, poor driving habits can develop, and even 'normal' drivers may be worse than experts and novices at scanning actions such as mirror checking and at anticipating (e.g. braking at an intersection). Appropriate safety margins often get ignored; for example, the need for a suitable distance between you and the vehicle in front on a motorway. Unless accidents occur, people seldom get feedback on their deteriorating driving habits, which suggests that the greater experience of older drivers may not entirely compensate for other changes.

Having a car and being able to use it to get out and about preserves the mobility, independence and personal freedom of increasing numbers of older people, particularly so for those who live in our rural areas, or in the wide-open spaces of the USA or Australia. For them especially, the identity of 'being a driver' may be the main support of a sense that one has not yet grown 'old'. Eisenhandler (1990) suggests that resistance to giving up driving is strong, even as self-imposed limits curtail the kind of driving that is done. Driving can confer positive status and some individuals indeed learn to drive in later life to maintain dignity and independence. Driving may also contribute to a sense of continuity for those who learned to drive when young and on a practical level be the only feasible mode of transportation in some communities. Eisenhandler (1990: 7) notes its significance for women:

> Retaining a licence and driving were powerful ways to ward off an old age identity even if one limited driving to daytime, good weather, and short trips. Women without access to a car were more aware of old age as a prominent feature of identity precisely because their ability to get out was severely hampered. Several women made remarks similar to those made by this seventy-two-year-old widow who said she didn't feel old because 'I can work and take my car out and don't get that scary feeling "Oh, I don't want to drive anymore" [mimicking someone else] or give it up.' Later she added a bit dramatically, 'I'll die if I don't have a car.'

Given the variability in performance with age which has already been mentioned, it would clearly be discriminatory, inefficient and unfair that individuals should give up driving when reaching a specified age. Indeed, Ball and Owsley (1991) point out that in studies of age-group comparisons, a few debilitated individuals in the older group can significantly alter the group mean. This may erroneously lead to over-generalized conclusions about widespread age-related declines. What is needed, they suggest, are tests of functional ability that predict individual driving performance, given that group averages may not adequately characterize any single person's ability.

Their own predictive model used, among other measures, a composite appraisal of mental status and an assessment of 'useful field of view' – the visual field area over which information can be acquired during a brief glance. They conclude that more attention needs to be paid to identifying those who will *not* be involved in accidents, since their predictive research model classified many individuals as having been in an accident when in fact they had not been. On an optimistic note, Ball and Owsley suggest that 'useful field of view' can be improved by simple training. In the current absence of accurate predictive performance tests, perhaps re-taking the driving test might service a similar and useful purpose, because it might sensitize individuals – younger and older – to poor habits they have developed over time, or to changed sensory acuities. Perhaps a re-test would also be appropriate for all those who have shown they have been driving inappropriately; that is, those who get convicted for certain driving offences. But a road test cannot predict how someone will respond in an emergency, and affordable driving simulators which achieve good fidelity remain to be developed.

As suggested earlier, a variety of cognitive–motor activities are involved in driving. As Stelmach and Nahom (1992: 53) note in their review of experimental studies of age-associated changes in relevant parameters:

> Driving skill requires responding continuously to spatial and temporal information from the environment while coordinating head, neck, and

upper and lower limb movements. Vision provides the major sensory input through feedforward (anticipation) and feedback processes. Motor control is often of prime importance in emergencies involving braking, steering, turning, lane changing, recovering from a skid, and other actions.

Older drivers may well need longer to prepare an appropriate response and benefit from a longer exposure to stimuli, which suggests that the viewing time for signs should be increased by reducing the speed of driving and by placing signs further apart from each other. Situations where response choice is ambiguous may also disadvantage older drivers. Sometimes it is clear that braking is the necessary response, but in some situations it might be a decision between braking or accelerating and a lane change, for example when a lorry is bearing down on you on a motorway and the car in front has braked for some unknown reason. In other situations, older drivers might find it harder to inhibit quickly enough a conventional response which is inappropriate under particular circumstances. If the car in front brakes suddenly, there may be less overall damage, given the speed of the car behind, if you don't break suddenly but actually do hit the car in front. This weakening of inhibitory control might, then, cause problems. But since older individuals tend to trade-off speed for accurancy – a phenomenon which has been demonstrated in a variety of experiments (Stelmach and Nahom 1992) – older drivers under normal conditions may, on average, be 'better' drivers and less of a risk, up to a point, to insurance companies than are 'young men who drive red sports cars'.

If the circumstances are such that a trade-off of speed for accuracy is not the best tactic, the older person may well be disadvantaged. While driving more slowly will facilitate the intake of information, and may be anticipated by others, under emergency situations often both speed and accuracy are required. The actual movements and muscular effort necessary may be lessened by power-assisted mechanisms and, for example, by brake pedals, the power of which is pressure-sensitive rather than depression–distance related, and the skills needed in skid-breaking may be lessened by such things as anti-lock brakes. Muscular joint flexibility is an essential component of driving skill for such tasks as scanning side mirrors and turning the head to observe blind spots or to reverse, and may be problematical for some people with arthritis.

Although Stelmach and Nahom's review covered only cross-sectional studies, thus being suggestive of age (group) *differences* rather than age *change*, they concluded that:

All facets of movement initiation – including response preparation, response selection, response programming, and response complexity – showed this slowing, with response selection perhaps being the most age sensitive. Dimensions of movement execution revealed similar age-associated slowing. Collectively these data support Salthouse's (1985) hypothesis that nearly all cognitive motor processes are slowed by approximately the same proportional amount with increased age.

(Stelmach and Nahom 1992: 63)

As noted earlier, complex tasks are relatively more demanding of the information-processing capacities of the older person. Driving on fairly straight rural or semi-urban uncrowded roads may be untaxing because most aspects of driving are performed automatically in a satisfactory manner. But negotiating with ease and confidence an urban five-way crossroads, where the traffic signals are not working (but this fact isn't signposted ahead), the traffic is heavy and many pedestrians are trying to cross, may be difficult.

Given that almost all drivers of any age consider they are average or above average in their driving competence, we clearly need some mechanism for sensitizing ourselves to the fact that we are not as good as we think. And as we get older we need to consider constructively what compensatory measures we can take to lessen our vulnerability to accidents.

A general slowing?

Birren and Fisher (1992: 1) pose the question: 'Is the [generally observed] slowness a broad phenomenon reflecting other aspects of an organism's effective functioning and well-being, or is it a relatively minor feature of growing old, like greying of hair?' Speed of behaviour can be broadly defined as the time taken to perform any task which requires the processing resources of the central nervous system. This includes perception, attention, reasoning and memory, as well as simple or complex motor movements. Birren and Fisher prefer the term 'speed of behaviour' because it is more comprehensive than its forerunner, 'reaction time', which tended to be associated with peripheral nervous system processes (i.e. concerning incoming senory data and outgoing instructions to the muscles) rather than central processes (i.e. processes often assumed to be intrinsic to the higher brain centres). Because requisite information may dissipate during the processing required in a task, an unsatisfactory speed may mean one component may not get 'solved' in time for the outcome to be usefully fed into the overall process. If the arguments in a very long sentence are complex and cumulative, one may fail to understand the sentence immediately because the information contained early on has dissipated before it can be brought to bear to 'make sense' of what comes later.

After making the interesting aside that slowness may be more related to time future than to time past (i.e. the idea that in later life some phenomena are more 'time-to-death' related than they are to length of life already lived), Birren and Fisher (1992: 10) hypothesize that 'speed becomes more embedded within all types of behavior with age' and it may become a determining factor in optimum performance in increasingly resource-demanding circumstances. The effects of such slowing may be evident among younger people when they are required to produce maximum performance, which in real life may be seldom – when taking intelligence tests for example. For older people, maximum performance capacity on some tasks may be approached earlier and more often.

The time taken to put information into storage, manipulate and transform it, and to take it out of storage and select and execute a form of behavioural response, is a form of psychological power, indicative of the maximum rate at which psychological capacities or abilities can produce thought, information or movement. Adopting the computer metaphor of mind as an information-processing system (one of the dominant psychological metaphors of our time), Birren and Fisher conclude that some research suggests all components of processing slow to some degree (i.e. slowing is a general phenomenon), whereas other research suggests it better characterizes certain components of processing.

Slowing is an observable end-product. But the train might arrive late at its destination because it travelled the route more slowly, or because is was diverted onto a route which was more circuitous. By continuing with this crude journeying analogy, one might expect older, more experienced travellers to know the vagaries of various routes – those liable to flooding, those narrow lanes with heavy lorries at certain times. Birren and Fisher's (1992) review of electrophysiological measures of ageing concludes that the actual time taken for certain events at the neural level (specifically the P300 component of event-related electrical potential) may be longer in normal older adults, and the electrical events may themselves be less clearly defined. Signals may be weaker and increased random activity may blur the signals and lead to error. However, it is not clear to what extent these changes characterize 'central' or 'peripheral' processes, whose definitions, in any event, are not standardized.

In older individuals, brain activity may be more homogeneous and the shift towards a broader distribution and less well-defined pattern of electrical activity might reflect some 're-routing' or exploration of options. Some tasks may require this more than others. For example, solving one of life's problems – such as things to do with marital disharmony – may require a more searching and sophisticated cognitive journey than slamming on the brakes as soon as you see that the driver in the car in front has done the same. Birren and Fisher (1992) suggest that 'de-differentiation' may provide an appropriate metaphor for age-associated changes: the autonomy of various components of mental activity – emotions, intellectual abilities, information processing, and be-havioural responses – may be reduced. Capacities that were more clearly defined and separate in one's younger days become more interrelated in later life. In certain ways, these suggestions arising from experimental evidence mirror the subjective experience of some of Heim's (1990) respondents of the interconnectedness of life, for example a sense of being more 'at-one' with nature. Speculating further, perhaps such de-differentiation lends itself to the development of some facets of wisdom. As Birren and Fisher (1990) suggest, one facet of wisdom may be integrating affect and cognition (emotions and thought) and another may be the acceptance of contextuality, relativity and uncertainty.

Intellectual abilities

It is worth repeating that there tends to be an increase in the variability of task performance with age. A large part of this may be due to the variability in the extent of slowing that has taken place. Performance on some tests, however, such as those that measure 'crystallized' intelligence (i.e. one's storage of facts and ability to utilize them), change little enough with age for them to be used as an estimate of a baseline from which 'fluid' intelligence (i.e. the ability to solve novel problems creatively) has changed. When any speediness is removed from tests of crystallized intelligence, performance on them improves, and when speediness is removed from tests of fluid intelligence, the apparent decline in fluid abilities is lessened. Birren and Fisher (1992: 24) suggest that 'in the main, the results from these large studies using psychometric tests support the notion that the decline in speed of behavior is fundamental to the decline of higher-order intellectual abilities'. While such declines may not be solely due to slowing, nevertheless many of the components of the information-processing system alter with age, and this in turn may differentially affect how fast information can be processed within the different components. As Birren and Fisher (1992: 26) point out:

> . . . age (defined as chronological age) appears to have little effect on its own on the change in intellectual function over time. But age-related changes in speed accounted for a large proportion of the variance associated with changes in intellectual abilities. Although the results indicate that speed is fundamental to change of intellectual abilities with age, changes in speed of behavior presumably cannot explain all changes in abilities.

Can a change in speed of processing at least explain in part changes in such cognitive processes as memory? Much of the decline in performance on some memory tasks may be due to declines in verbal speed, as measured by tests in which, for example, one has to produce in a given time as many words beginning with a certain letter as possible. Perceptual speed, measured for example by tests where one has to cross out all the a's in a piece of prose, or detect differences between two similar drawings, may be influenced by such factors as life stress, and not necessarily in the direction that common sense might lead you to expect. Birren and Fisher (1992: 26) reviewed studies in which individuals who had had a greater number of stressful events in the past five years had *higher* perceptual speed scores than those who had experienced fewer stressful life events. Perhaps a certain amount of stress helps 'keep you on your toes'?

Both life stress and physical fitness seem to have a connection with aspects of speed of behaviour. For example, with regard to fitness, Birren and Fisher (1992) suggest that aerobic exercise can improve older individuals' performance on tests of speed of information processing such as the 'digit symbol' task. In such a task, a code transforming say the numbers 1 to 10 to particular symbols has to be used for a random series of numbers (e.g. when you see a number 2 you have to draw in a square, when you see a number 4 a triangle, and so on). The test is timed to see how quickly you do it, and clearly there is a measure of accuracy in the number of correct substitutions made. Similarly, improvements following aerobic exercise were shown on tasks of selective attention (e.g. you have to say the colour of a word which actually spells a different colour – the word might be presented in the colour red, but actually say 'yellow'), and in simple reaction time (e.g. where you have to press a button when you see a light come on) and in critical flicker fusion (e.g. if you slow down a film, at what speed to you stop seeing motion but individual frames instead?). Birren and Fisher suggest that selective attention and reaction time are closely tied to biological functioning from an evolutionary perspective – spot the tiger and run! But I don't suppose evolution had car drivers in mind! Exercise may result in more efficient metabolism of neurotransmitters, the chemicals which function as vehicles of communication between neurones, the basic cellular units of the nervous system. Thus exercise might help ameliorate some of the slowing in response speed with age, and it might also increase arousal – heightening a readiness for activity.

Health and illness

In looking at age-associated changes in psychological functioning, often the health status of the older individual has been overlooked. As Rabins (1992) points out, in the study of changes in intellect it is difficult to avoid including individuals with early dementia because the earliest signs and symptoms may only be identified and validated in retrospect. In distinguishing healthy age-associated changes from disease, he notes that:

> Clinical experience suggests that there are certain characteristics of memory difficulty that identify pathological memory impairment but there are few confirmatory data. Individuals with non-progressive, age-associated memory changes complain of memory loss during everyday activities such as producing the names of people or thinking of specific words. They report misplacing things. However, neither the patient nor other informants reports that important major events have been forgotten or that there are dramatic changes in function such as becoming lost while driving a familiar route or being unable to set a table or write a cheque.
>
> (Rabins 1992: 480)

Holland and Rabbitt (1991a) explore more fully the issue of taking into account health – or, rather, illness – factors in studying cognitive changes with advancing age. At the moment, it is not clear to what extent changes in average abilities are the result of a steadily increasing probability of the occurrence of a variety of pathologies and to what extent they are caused by 'involutional processes', which may in some sense be 'natural'. Here we are in murky waters, since even 'intrinsic' processes at a cellular level, such as the production of destructive free radicals thought to play a part in 'biological ageing', may be amenable to influence by interventions which mop them up directly, or assist the body's mopping-up processes. It is for this reason that authors such as Holland and Rabbitt put apostrophes around the word normal, and increasingly gerontologists refer to age-*associated* changes rather than age-*related* changes, since the nature of the actual relationship is hard to specify. If something is age-related, then *all* individuals should eventually have that attribute. Cerebrovascular disease, for example, may not be an inevitable, 'natural' and ubiquitous accompaniment to ageing, but something which happens to occur more often with advancing age for other reasons.

We have already suggested that people 'age' cognitively at very different rates. While a simple memory task like asking someone to repeat an increasingly long string of numbers immediately (a digit span test) will reveal an average decline with age in later life, some people show little or no such decline. As noted earlier, one way of estimating cognitive decline is by looking at the difference in performance on the 'crystallized' and the 'fluid' sub-tests of general intelligence tests. Studies by Holland and Rabbitt suggest that decline in performance with age tends to speed up during the eighth decade, but nevertheless up to 7 per cent of 70-year-olds still show no detectable loss on this measure. The question they raise concerns the extent to which cognitive decline reflects differences in pathology located elsewhere, differences which are themselves related to both genetic and socio-cultural factors.

One candidate in the 'underlying pathology' explanation is the cardiovascular system, in particular that supplying blood to the brain. Although the evidence implicates its involvement, even when individuals are screened for cerebral or vascular disorders, some slowing on reaction time tasks with age is still evident. But the picture is complicated, as Holland and Rabbitt (1991a: 85) note:

> Furthermore, it is certainly the case that a wide variety of illnesses are known directly to affect CNS [central nervous system] efficiency, and so may be expected to bring about cognitive changes directly. Other common diseases, such as arthritis, may have secondary effects on cognitive ability by reducing mobility – and thus general metabolism and well-being – or in respect of the side-effects of the prolonged medication they may require.

Some of the studies reviewed by Holland and Rabbitt (1991a) suggest that decline in cerebral blood flow may be more evident in the left hemisphere of the brain, which for most people is dominant over the right hemisphere in the control of bodily movement and speech. Other studies do not support this, however. More focused studies of decline in cerebral blood flow suggest that those areas of the brain responsible for fairly constant activity, such as speech and use of the dominant hand, show *less* decline, suggesting that sustained functional activity of parts of the brain may help protect against structural changes. Relative under-use may, perhaps, facilitate deterioration.

Since it is oxygen supply to the brain that is one of the key factors in brain sustenance, it is not surprising to find reports suggesting that diseases such as chronic bronchitis, which result in inefficient uptake of oxygen into the bloodstream, are associated with worsening cognitive abilities. In the main, the evidence suggests that it is the 'fluid' aspects of intelligence that are most likely to be affected.

It seems likely that improving health and fitness, in particular oxygen metabolism, can also improve aspects of cognitive functioning, and that physical ill-health can have deleterious effects on them. Armed with this information, one can begin to plan a realistic regime of fitness improvement which takes into account any constraints imposed by current illness. I remember well a pre-Christmas holiday in Benidorm a few years ago when I eavesdropped on some retired British holiday-makers sitting on a bench poking fun at a group of some twenty retired German holiday-makers exercising on the beach in front of them. I wonder who the 'joke' was really on?

High blood pressure, related as it is to cardiovascular disorders, has not been demonstrated in and of itself to influence unequivocally performance on cognitive tests, although some of the drugs administered in its treatment, such as propranolol, may produce mental slowness. Diabetes, also more common in later life, may be associated with poorer memory and fluid ability performance. Holland and Rabbitt (1991a: 90) suggest that 'cognitive losses associated with chronic conditions can prevent patients from following efficient treatment regimens and so initiate a spiral of increasing difficulty'. Certainly depression, which was considered in the last chapter, is one psychological condition which itself reduces cognitive efficiency and may become an important determinant of cognitive change. Indeed, complaints of memory loss and cognitive dysfunction can themselves be symptoms of depression (Rabins 1992). Subjective responses like felt stress, to chronic illnesses such as arthritis or diabetes, are mediated by one's personality and one's developed ways of coping. Stress, like depression and anxiety, *can* reduce cognitive performance. While it would be foolishly naive to say we should all 'get out there and lead healthy, stress-free lives', we must nevertheless make more informed decisions about whether or not to attempt to change patterns of behaviour which we can construe as being to some extent under our control.

A multivariate approach to cognitive change with age is provided by Jones *et al.* (1991) in a study of 100 healthy males aged between 30 and 80 years. Their conclusions echo Birren and Fisher's (1992) point referred to earlier, namely that age *per se* has little useful explanatory power. In Jones and co-workers' study, some 36 variables from eight domains – including the demographic, biosocial and psychosocial, as well as measures of brain structure and functioning – were used to examine interactive determinants of the variability in performance of individuals on several cognitive function measures. In their report, Jones *et al.* (1991: 227) remark that 'the direct effect of age on cognition is substantially reduced when social, life-style, physiological and brain-state variables are allowed to become intervening variables'. We must, therefore, increasingly question 'age' as any sort of reliable proxy for other changes that take place over time in individuals.

Psychological tests of intelligence may not originally have been formulated with assessing the perhaps different qualities of adult thought in later life in mind, for example the importance for adults of contextuality. They may appear to measure a decline which is partially misleading, because some of the underlying phenomena have changed qualitatively rather than quantitatively. However, while it might be comforting for those in middle-age and later life (psychologists and laymen alike) to construe 'intelligence' as changing in quality rather than in quantity, in all likelihood it does both. If one defines intelligence pragmatically as the ability to solve the problems encountered in everyday life, clearly older people tend to have a somewhat different set of problems to solve.

As Rabbitt (1993: 273) points out, 'lay people are as sophisticated in their appraisal of intelligence as most experts' and 'they quite rightly interpret intelligence as the *practical* manifestation of strikingly appropriate behaviour, and they are also enlightened in the sense that they understand that different kinds of behaviour may be appropriate at different points in the person's life cycle'. He suggests there is room, however, for other conceptions of intelligence than the strictly pragmatic; namely, intelligence as an ability to deal with novelty which is different from and cannot be expressed in any particular learned performance, and intelligence as something not embodied in any particular acquired skill or knowledge but which is 'a prerequisite for acquiring a high level of practical competence in any one of a number of different areas, which is seen as most characteristic of young people'. But with age, other facets of psychological functioning gain in relative importance to performance on tests of intelligence.

Staudinger *et al.* (1989) provide a convenient summary of the key findings concerning the potential and limits of intelligence in later life:

1 There are sizeable differences between individuals in intellectual ageing.
2 There is age-related decline in intellectual functioning involving demanding novel cognitive tasks which have to be performed at speed.
3 There is age-related stability and growth in intellectual functioning involving the solving of practical problems of everyday life, knowledge and verbal comprehension.
4 Many older persons have a sizeable reserve capacity and an ability to learn and improve performance where tasks are not maximally demanding of speed or functioning of their cognitive components.

A study by Maylor (1994) of 'Masterminds', from the TV programme, found that there was no age effect on performance in the 'specialized subject' round, and that older 'masterminds' did better than younger ones on the general knowledge component. While we are not all 'masterminds', this might suggest a 'limited' impact approach in theories of cognitive ageing, and some grounds for less pessimism. Maylor suggests that age-related declines in fluid intelligence may not necessarily affect everybody and everything.

Salthouse (1990), who authored a particularly influential paper suggesting 'slowing' as the key to understanding cognitive ageing, takes a somewhat less optimistic tone. If you 'learn from experience', then experience should moderate the effects of cognitive changes. The experimental evidence on this point is, at the very least, ambiguous he maintains. But then there is 'experience' and *experience*, and one has to consider the issue of just what implications differences in measures of cognitive performance made inside the psychological laboratory have for functioning outside it.

Taking the pragmatic facet of intelligence which reflects the mental ability involved in successfully adapting to one's environment, Staudinger *et al.* (1989) outline a model of 'successful ageing', a concept we shall return to in a later chapter. They suggest that a strategy which facilitates successful ageing is one where (a) a number of domains of functioning are *selected* for concentration upon, so as (b) to achieve *optimization* of performance through practice and systematic training, and complement (c) *compensation*, which requires special efforts to search for alternative substitute skills when one is unable to perform requisite components of a task sufficiently well. They review some experimental evidence to support this perhaps commonsense view that one should capitalize on one's strengths as well as finding ways to compensate for one's weaknesses, although the former may be more cost-effective than the latter.

Memory

While fluid intelligence may give some indication of the everyday competence of groups of older people, among those matched in fluid intelligence there will still be variation in aspects of memory competence. In particular, prospective memory tasks – that is, tasks where individuals have to remember to do something in the future – and tasks involving the recall of the gist of a passage of prose, may still reveal decline with age among individuals of equal 'test intelligence'.

It is in everyday tasks that individuals may first sense that their memory isn't quite what it was. A 'clinical entity' called 'age-associated memory impairment' has been reified and tests of everyday activities such as remembering names and faces, first and last names, and recognizing faces, have been devised to measure it. This is a form of memory decline said to be experienced by some healthy individuals after their fifties, which, while remaining within the bounds of 'normality' and unassociated with specific disease states, can be 'quite troublesome to many middle-aged and elderly adults enagaged in intellectually demanding activities' (Crook *et al.* 1990: 81).

Before rushing to the shops for a 'memory pill', we should raise the question of how accurate older individuals are at estimating changes in aspects of their cognitive performance. As always, the answer is not so straightforward. Older people answering self-rating questionnaires probing memory efficiency in everyday life reported fewer problems than younger people (Rabbitt and Abson 1990), but this might be due to the fact that conscious self-monitoring and the ability to remember errors improves with IQ but declines with age (Rabbitt 1990a). Thus those with higher IQs tended to report greater recent decline in memory efficiency and greater current frequency of loss of objects. Depression scores were also found to be correlated with reported cognitive failures. Individuals who are depressed may feel they are functioning at a lower cognitive level (Rabbitt and Abson 1990) and some may actually be functioning at a lower cognitive level. By and large, scores on self-completed questionnaires correlate poorly with performance on laboratory tasks, and it would seem that the accuracy of individuals' assessments of their own abilities changes with age-associated changes in fluid intelligence (Rabbitt and Abson 1991). Age-associated changes in self-regard and lifestyle probably help predict changes in accuracy of assessment of abilities. One's own understanding of aspects of one's cognitive performance – for example, knowledge of one's memory (i.e. 'metamemory') – is likely to be influenced by 'perceptions, beliefs, attitudes and expectations regarding performance in situations demanding cognitive skills' (Dixon 1989: 412). This is not to say, however, that 'memory complainers' should be treated lightly, since a legitimate basis for memory complaint is more likely to be found among them than it is among non-complainers.

As we grow older we should be open to discussion of change in our cognitive abilities, and perhaps, in particular, of our memory, since that is where change may occur that most of us will notice. But perhaps we should be less open to suggestion, since much of it may be based on stereotypical understanding of what is a complex and far from perfectly understood set of phenomena. For example, Erber and Rothberg (1991) found that the memory problems of both 'elderly' and 'unattractive' target subjects in a psychological experiment were judged to be due more to a lack of ability or mental difficulty, and to need evaluation, compared with the memory problems of young and attractive targets. The memory problems of young target subjects tended to be attributed to a lack of effort and lack of attention, while those of attractive targets were judged to be due to a lack of attention and task difficulty! With attractive subjects, we may prefer to see the 'cause' of poor performance partially externalized, beyond their control – as not their fault.

One common experience which involves a memory lapse is the 'tip-of-the-tongue' (TOT) phenomenon. We know that particular information is in memory, but we can't retrieve it immediately. TOTs seem to be a universal experience which occur on average about once a week, are frequently elicited by proper names, and are resolved during the experience about half of the time. Often one 'knows' the first letter of the 'forgotten' word. Furthermore, the frequency of the experience seems to increase with age, and older individuals tend to simply wait for the word to spring to mind, whereas younger ones are more active in trying to access it (Stuart-Hamilton 1991: 77).

Aspects of memory

Learning and memory are so closely linked that they are difficult to disentangle. Crudely, memory implies the retention of information, whereas learning is the process during which memories are acquired. Furthermore, there are different sorts of memory: for what you did ten minutes ago; for what you were doing when Kennedy was shot; for an incident that happened to you when you were 6 years old (I fell into a large deep bed of nettles); for smells; for 'atmospheres' (at the first night-club you went to); for emotions (how you felt when your friend died); and for other events in the past that had little direct concern for you. There is memory for what you intend to do (pick up a paper on the way home from work tonight); or for the plot of the book or film you saw recently; for how to conjugate the Latin word *mensa* or for Pythagoras's theorem; for what salt tastes like; or the fact that New Zealand comprises two islands in the southern hemisphere, south of Australia. There is also memory for the last word of each of the propositions which you had to decide were either true or false, that a psychologist gave you as a memory test. General theories of cognitive slowing, of changes in information-processing speed, do not seem able to explain all aspects of change in all aspects of memory (Nettlebeck and Rabbitt 1992).

Poorer memory for proper names (e.g. people's names) is something which older people tend to report and wish to improve. Indeed, experimental evidence shows that older people are less able than younger ones to recollect common proper names, although their knowledge as to whether they have come across the name before (i.e. familiarity with the name) may remain relatively unimpaired (Jones and Rabbitt 1994). As one 'accumulates' names over a lifetime of meeting people, it is likely that there is increasing 'proactive interference'. That is to say, so many previous names, many of which will be similar, make current discrimination and therefore recollection more difficult. Recollection of relatively rare names shows less deterioration, and Jones and Rabbitt's study suggests that the cue value of the surname for remembering the first name may be stronger than the other way around. Perhaps this is because the pool of first names is much smaller than that of surnames. In their study, these age-associated memory changes seemed independent of fluid intelligence.

Central to an understanding of many cognitive changes is the concept of 'working memory', the idea of a temporary workspace where material is held while performing tasks. An oft-cited example is repeating a string of digits backwards (i.e. in the exact reverse order to that in which they were read out to you). One has to hold the forward string in working memory as one works out the reverse order. Another example is the intermediate results one has to hold in mind when one works out in one's head something like 15×16. The example given earlier, of remembering the last word of a proposition one has to decide the truth value for, illustrates three concepts of importance: *speed*, in that one cannot control the rate of spoken input from the person reading out the propositions; *divided attention*, in that one has to understand the words and evaluate their logic *and* also to note the last words; and *working memory* may be stretched by holding the propositions and last words in mind. Such laboratory tasks give older people more trouble than younger ones.

Remote memory is memory for distant but non-autobiographical events that have occurred in a person's lifetime, but not ones that were so famous or generally well-known that they have passed into the domain of general public knowledge, that is into semantic memory. *Semantic* memory concerns the general knowledge or factual information that is available to an individual, while *autobiographical* memory is for past events of particular personal significance. The latter is considered to be a domain of *episodic* memory, which concerns events from a person's own life but which are less peculiar to it. Clearly, these concepts are intertwined and the distinctions between them are less than clear-cut. Stuart-Hamilton's (1991) review of how they change with age leads him to conclude that 'Ribot's hypothesis' – namely, that it is recent events that are more likely to be 'lost' with age – is not true; rather, it is remote memories that tend to get forgotten.

While semantic memory, like 'crystallized intelligence', seems to change relatively little, one's confidence in it may decline, perhaps through cultural expectations. Older individuals may be just as perceptive as younger ones in knowing whether their knowledge represents anything from being a complete guess to a certainty, but nevertheless consider that their semantic memory has declined when there is little evidence that that is the case. As for autobiographical memory, asking for recollection of the most vivid memories tends to produce ones culled from early life, and unpleasant rather than pleasant ones at that. But ordinary everyday memories are more likely to be from the recent past, since for most people they are more likely to be of help in dealing with what lies ahead. Recall of fine detail from your past may be more difficult the older you are, or the less processing capacity you have as determined by intelligence test scores (both fluid and crystallized, according to Holland and Rabbitt 1990).

For people resident in institutions, whose future may require little active anticipation or participation, memories from the more distant past may provide a more interesting mental life than those furnished by the sameness of the immediate surroundings. Here reminiscing may be a form of entertainment, induced by the environment, rather than a mechanism for understanding and making sense of one's past.

The examination of *prospective* memory has produced conflicting results. For some tasks, older people seem better than younger ones at remembering to carry out an activity in the future. Perhaps the key to the conflict is how well-rehearsed (and perhaps, therefore, crystallized) the tasks themselves are. Remembering to put the milk bottles out before the milkman comes, or to put the rubbish out on Fridays, or to switch the gas off after you've fried the egg – things you do habitually – may show little decline with 'normal' ageing, but when they are forgotten may be indicative, as noted earlier, of other, perhaps pathological changes. In a memory-test situation, remembering to do at the end of the session whatever the psychologist asked you at the beginning of the session to do at the end of the session, may be unusual and therefore less likely to be remembered. Prospective memory involves remembering that something has to be done, remembering what has to be done, doing it and remembering that it has been done, so it is not repeated. Maylor (1993) suggests that older people are disadvantaged on prospective memory tasks in different ways from those in which they may be disadvantaged in restrospective memory tasks. In the latter, initial performance decreases most across age groups, and subsequent performance decreases less, if at all; whereas with prospective memory, initial performance may be similar, with the decrease more noticeable thereafter.

Bringing together the results from 122 experimental studies of memory recall, Verhaeghen *et al.* (1993: 166) conclude that in studies set up to yield maximum age differences, 'age differences in memory performance are large, and – in the present sample of short-term and episodic memory tasks – are omnipresent'. But, they continue:

> However, it is extremely important to note that the findings reported here do not necessarily imply the breaking down of everyday memory functioning in old age . . . results from such research cannot be generalized automatically to everyday performance . . . from a functional point of view, decline must not be confounded with deficit . . . it may be not so much that the elderly have a bad memory as that the memory functioning of the young is truly excellent.
>
> (Verhaeghen *et al*. 1993: 168)

Language

Older people tend to use fewer subordinate clauses than younger ones ('Because I have been typing for so long, my wife has become impatient'). There is little doubt that, other things being equal, older individuals would have more difficulty than younger ones with Marcel Proust's *A la Recherche du Temps Perdu* if they were required to read and comprehend it at speed. It contains immensely long sentences, and multiple embedded clauses. As it is, for most people the book benefits from mulling over and re-reading. Convoluted speech, which comes at a speed you cannot control, provides more problems, particularly so for people who are deaf and who may be simul- taneously having to guess at words not heard properly. Thus the combined effects of a decline in speed of processing and limitations on working memory capacity may mean that implied but unstated meanings may be missed and the main details (the gist) may not be satisfactorily separated from the less important details. The moral of the story is to keep communication simple, clear of ambiguities and red-herrings and at an acceptable pace for the audience. Of course, some changes in language skills may be due to lack of practice. You may not be able to get to the library to get books out, or afford to buy them, and if you are less able to join in social situations you will have less opportunity to practise your conversational skills. As Stuart-Hamilton (1991: 96) notes:

> More interesting in this respect are the changes in reading habits – the elderly seem on the whole to prefer lightweight reading, such as newspaper or magazine articles, rather than heavyweight literature, such as 'classic' fiction or textbooks. It is tempting to conclude that this is because the elderly can no longer cope with the intellectual demands of the latter. However, there is no strong proof for this assertion, and equally

plausible is that old people cannot be bothered to wade through turgid fiction because they no longer have to prove to themselves how well read they are.

Thus what may appear to be information relating to cognitive performance may also be indicative of motivation or indeed of the influence of self-image and identity.

The scope for cognitive improvement

Never forget how easy it is to forget – from page 60 of a book titled 'Enjoy old age: a program of self management', by the famous behavioural psychologist B.F. Skinner.

(Skinner and Vaughan 1983).

We noted above how recall of detail, from both one's autobiographical memory and from, for example, written material, can be more of a problem for older people. An experiment by Holland and Rabbitt (1992b) suggested that more text details were remembered when subjects where instructed to process the text more elaborately (more 'deeply'). In the experiment, some subjects had to put some sentences in a correct order, in order to make up a passage which made sense. This was considered to encourage 'deep processing' or more 'thinking' about aspects of the task. Other subjects were given the correct passage but with seven vowels missing from each sentence, which they had to fill in. This guided them to focus on 'surface' aspects of the task. Deep processing helped recall of information from the passage.

A variation on this might be in the way in which one learns foreign vocabulary; for example, that *tobillo* is Spanish for ankle and *rodilla* is Spanish for knee. I learnt these words by thinking that the *to* at the beginning of *tobillo* was, like the toe, nearer the ankle, and ditto the *o* at the end. Whereas *r* might be rump and *a* might be arse, and the knee is nearer both of them (well almost). It may seem convoluted, but for me it works better than reciting '*tobillo* is ankle' a multitude of times until it 'sticks' – until tomorrow, that is! Don't learn material in meaningless lists, as we were taught our Spanish vocabulary, starting with a and working through to z. Chunking things into groups so they have something in common or can be remembered more as a unit, and then categorizing them (i.e. putting the kitchen utensils together, with sub-categories of those used on the stove or in the oven, those used in food preparation, etc.) and then perhaps listing them alphabetically in each sub-group, has been found to help. And giving yourself an overt incentive might not go amiss, since 'older people appear to have untapped retrieval skills that can be brought to bear if they are sufficiently motivated' (Storandt 1992: 59). Better encoding strategies (making sure the thing to be remembered has an optimum chance of 'going in'), such as categorizing, and better retrieval strategies (making sure one optimizes the ways of getting the memory 'out'), such as recollecting contexts, need to be taught and used more routinely. For long-term benefits, such devices should be incorporated into one's daily habits.

While these methods will probably benefit younger people just as much as older people, it is older people who are more likely to need to give them a try.

'Deep processing' is a way of forming connections or elaborations and the more the connections the better. Huppert's (1991a) review of age-related changes in memory suggests additional ways of helping oneself, some more easily said than done. Among older people, cognitive disadvantages associated with low education levels can be partially offset by participation in leisure activities – 'keep yourself busy and stimulated'. Don't rely on your memory but make sensible use of memory aids; notes and stickers as reminders left in attention-grabbing places prompting you for what is to be done. People who are more forgetful for some perverse reason seem less prone to initiating such self-cueing or prompting than those who are less so! Making some effort to remember, trying to think of other ways to bring something to mind – the context in which it happened or in which you first remembered it, the mood you were in – is likely to help re-establish connections that will also help bring the memory back again on subsequent occasions. Also, in line with the model of 'successful ageing' mentioned earlier, one might try to find ways of reducing demands, of not spreading oneself out too thinly over too many cognitive activities, but rather concentrating on one's strengths. Memory demands might be reduced by utilizing other memory aids, ranging from electronic organizers and reminders, through pocket dictating machines, to location devices (like key rings which whistle back when you whistle for them), telephone number diallers (put in the name and not the number, perhaps) and wristwatch alarms.

Rabbitt (1990b: 240) suggests that:

If we adopt this, admittedly crude and untested, framework we may extrapolate some important practical advice for the elderly: the mainten-ance of skills acquired throughout a lifetime's practice will probably require ever-increasing effort, since progressive loss of components and connectivity will affect even well-established optimum pathways and will be increasingly difficult to repair by new training. However, it may still be more cost-effective and rewarding to maintain existing skills at a high level than to spend time laboriously attaining mediocrity at entirely novel tasks. Elderly people may well find it more cost-effective, in terms of the time and effort involved, to adapt existing skills to new needs than to attempt to learn radically new ways of doing things.

Manage your (selective) attention so that you focus on 'one thing at a time' wherever possible (and sensible) and make a conscious effort to attend to the salient rather than the incidental aspects of the situation. We noted earlier that being fit and healthy also helps. So too does being able to relax. And don't assume that you can't learn – that your memory isn't up to that Spanish vocabulary. If you have the interest and motivation, your 'laborious effort to attain mediocrity' will service its purpose if it helps you get by when you are on holiday in Benidorm! As Huppert (1991a: 132) notes:

The important point is that even if there is age-related memory decline, the reserve capacity is such that older adults are far more capable of learning and remembering than has hitherto been realised. This tremendous human potential represents a largely untapped resource.

This view is also reflected by Rabbitt (1992: 476–7), in his review of memory changes in later life:

The present review . . . has also raised the issue that old age is not solely a degenerative condition of the central nervous system. Long life offers more opportunity for the acquisition of useful information and skills. There is accumulating evidence both that prolonged practice can have more radical effects on levels of attainment of particular skills than can gross individual differences in attainment on intelligence tests and that highly practised skills may be intensely domain-specific so that they represent isolated islands of competence which may not be predicted from general levels of performance on others tasks. The relevance of these issues for age comparisons was illustrated by evidence that patterns of relative accessibility of autobiographical memories from different parts of the life-span may be governed as much by social and personal uses to which these memories are put as by age-associated pathological changes in the central nervous system.

Perhaps fostering realistic positive beliefs about the scope for improvement in cognitive functioning, given an appropriately supportive environment, is one way to counteract the stereotypic 'ubiquitous irremediable decline' imagery which can undermine both morale and motivation. It is self-confidence that propels one outward and lack of it which inevitably leads to withdrawal, and 'if older persons adopt or internalise generalised beliefs about age-related intellectual decline, they may fail to maintain or optimise effective functioning in cognitively demanding situations, even when they are capable of adequate performance' (Grover and Herzog 1991: 109). Without considering the current situation in which individuals live, and therefore the *use* they are required to make of their memories, it is a little presumptuous to assume that differences between young and old are simply due to 'age' (Holland and Rabbit 1991b). Perhaps we should feel less self-conscious about declines in intellectual functions for which we have little practical use, even if they are pointed out to us by psychologists. Or perhaps we should engage, unself-consciously, in what Lachman (1991) calls 'memory aerobics' (workouts for the mind) as well as 'gerobics' (exercises for the older body). Several of these have been presented in the popular press; for example, in the *Daily Mail* (19–20 January 1993), readers were exhorted to 'give your brain its daily workout' and to 'develop a mental, exercise programme that will keep your mind younger for longer' (not that 'younger' is quite the right word). Try, it suggested as one among several exercises, reading your newspaper when it is upside down! Perhaps the reader can think of something more practical.

Self-management of behaviour change in order to maintain or enhance our cognitive repertoire is, like self-management of eating or smoking habits, difficult. No surprise, then, that we turn to the apparently easier option (but perhaps less effective and with more unwanted side-effects in the long-term) of popping a pill. Already headlines have appeared saying: 'Some doctors claim that smart drugs are good for you, can radically improve intelligence and are so safe that everybody ought to be taking them'. But O'Brien and Levy (1992) advise caution with respect to drug treatment for 'age-associated memory impairment'. Like 'benign senescent forgetfulness' (characterized as difficulty on some occasions in remembering names and dates from the past which are easily recalled at other times – suggesting a problem with retrieval), this proposed clinical entity has yet to be validated. Valid or not, the drug companies are proposing treatments.

In the next chapter, we shall look at what is known about alterations in the brain which may underlie the changes we experience – both normal and pathological – and those which psychologists can detect and which pharmaceutical manufacturers produce drugs to influence. But there are other ways to acheive cognitive improvement besides looking for drugs. As Rabbitt (1990b: 244–5) suggests:

> At the moment we can foresee that even hereditary differences may be controllable by genetic engineering, but this is a distant prospect, and we must not allow it to distract us from the many other factors which we can already profitably attack. Cognitive change will be slower; the old will live richer, socially more useful, and longer lives if we come to grips with the simple evils that have always devastated human existence, ignorance, poverty, hunger, and lack of compassion for the weak.

If they have 'always devastated human existence', one may wonder just how amenable to change they are. Perhaps it helps to reiterate that it is our own cognitive futures we are talking about.

5

Our changing brain – causes, effects and responses

Many changes in cognitive functioning currently tend to be explained in terms of computing metaphors, where the idea of 'information processing' is central. Four key concepts are: reduced processing capacity, reduced speed of processing, reduced working memory capacity and production deficiencies. The latter, which are somewhat like inefficient mental strategies, may be thought of as sub-optimal software programs (software programs, like the one my computer is now using to word-process this text, are written by people). They may in part be sub-optimal because an individual's previous learned habits, training, experiences and education fostered sub-optimal approaches. Clearly, some word-processing programs are more efficient and comprehensive than others. But changes in our thinking processes and behaviour may also be due in part to other 'reductions', which themselves are likely to be more hardware-related. Just as the hardware of some computers is more powerful than others (more memory capacity on the hard disk, for example), so too changes in the physical material that comprises the brain may reduce our memory power (reductions in the physical connections between brain cells, for example). This chapter looks more closely at some of the changes in our 'mental hardware', how they reveal themselves and how we respond to them. Such changes are often referred to as being either pathological (i.e. due to disease), or 'normal' (i.e. due to intrinsic ageing processes). As we shall see, such distinctions are not always easy to make.

Ageing or disease?

Rinn (1988), for example, after reviewing much evidence, suggests that observed mental decline is neither an artefact of motor or mental slowing, nor of educational disadvantage, nor a cohort effect, but rather is evidence of a 'sub-clinical' dementia – a dementia so slight that it would ordinarily go undetected. Such decline is not 'natural' but posited to be the product of minute pathological changes in the brain, gradually accumulating over the life-time. To say decline is 'normal' or 'natural' is really no explanation at all, since it fails to address the question of cause. Since some individuals show hardly any cognitive deterioration, and cognitive decline in others starts at substantially older ages, the intriguing questions, then, concern the factors that contribute to cognitive continuity and protection.

As noted in the previous chapter, research has attempted to detect 'psychological change with age' over and above that which might be related to age-associated disease, or to cohort factors. But the research methodologies used are not without their difficulties. As Rinn (1988) points out, longitudinal studies – in which the same individuals are studied over an extended period of time – often suffer from the problem that people fail to turn up for re-testing and it is those who did most poorly initially who do not come back. Many of them simply die. Those who do return tend to be the healthiest and brightest, and are therefore no longer representative of the original sample. Another problem is that treatable conditions go untreated, as Rinn (1988: 155) notes:

> Many of the medical conditions associated with the decline [in mental functioning] are treatable. Indeed, the greater severity of the age-related decline in the 1938 Wechsler [intelligence test] norms, as compared to the 1955 or 1981 norms may be attributable to less adequate health care in the Depression era. Post-war prosperity made good medical care more readily available. With the medical advances of the 1980s, many of the medical causes of mental deterioration can be arrested or even reversed. It behoves the clinician working with the elderly to attend closely to their complaints of failing memory and cognitive disorganization and not write off these symptoms as being 'normal for the person's age'.

What is 'normal' becomes immensely problematic. Brayne and Calloway (1988: 1265), for example, suggest that 'there is little evidence to support the view that senile dementia of the Alzheimer's type [which we examine in more detail later in this chapter] is distinct from the normal ageing process'. They consider that the changes in brain function found in normal ageing ('benign senescent forgetfulness') and Alzheimer's, can be seen as a continuum, and that this may reflect a single underlying process. If Alzheimer's is a distinct pathology, why have so few 'risk factors' for it been identified? If there is a single underlying process, would not those who seem to remain cognitively relatively intact eventually show signs of Alzheimer's if they didn't die of something else first?

In a seminal work, Gubrium (1986) also questioned the hiving off of Alzheimer's as a unified entity, in a category by itself, to be separated from ageing. Perhaps elucidating some of the causes of Alzheimer's will also illuminate some of the causes of what we call 'ageing'. For example, disturbances of the structure and/or functioning of the brain by the presence of certain proteins (e.g. beta-amyloid) may represent accelerated and intensified biological ageing phenomena or disease. At this level of examination, drawing a distinction between disease and normal ageing could be said to be like attempting to separate the undefined from the undefinable. The notion that 'ageing is not a disease' might, in the future, become a matter of demonstration rather than of rhetoric. But are 'diseases of intrinsic origin' part of 'biological ageing'? The definitional waters are murky.

Memory in 'normal' ageing and dementia

One common effect of brain changes concerns memory efficacy. If you take a sample of community resident older people, assess them on a battery of tests so as to be confident about who is showing signs of dementia and who is not (on other than memory-based criteria), and then examine differences in their performance on the memory tests, you will find those designated as 'having dementia' perform worse. Incidental memorizing appears to be a good discriminator. For example, if you conduct a naming test (e.g. you present objects to subjects and ask them to name them) and later ask the subjects to recall which objects you presented (something they were not asked to remember), those with dementia will fare relatively badly. Unlike some memory tests – which, through obvious test-failure, make it only too clear to testees that they have problems – 'incidental' tests may be more acceptable because poor performance can be attributed to the unexpectedness of the recall task.

Another acceptable test on which someone with dementia may do relatively badly (acceptable because it mimics ordinary memory problems) is recalling the name of a person in a photograph that he or she was asked to remember a few minutes earlier. People labelled as having dementia show difficulties of acquisition; they have more trouble getting information firmly embedded into memory in the first place. Once embedded, their rate of forgetting may not be markedly less than it is for older people whom one might label 'normal'. For example, Huppert and Kopelman (1989) found that normal ageing processes produce a mild acquisition deficit and somewhat faster forgetting of visuo-spatial material, whereas dementia gives rise to a more severe acquisition deficit. Their research led them to conclude 'that senile dementia is qualitatively, as well as quantitatively, different from normal senescent decline, is independent of it, and probably superimposed on it (p. 858).' Nevertheless, further research is needed to clarify the position. That such performance differences can be detected and that 'dementia' is being labelled earlier and earlier does not, of course, in and of itself mean that it is other than an early or more marked form of a variety of age-associated processes.

Rohling *et al.* (1991) suggest another difference between age-associated memory decline and that seen in dementia, namely that between memory processes thought to be 'automatic' and those which require effort. Effortful remembering is considered to be more difficult for people with dementia than for 'controls', whereas automatic encoding is not. Encoding information into memory storage automatically is presumed to require little or no attentional capacity and to occur without intention – to be, perhaps, genetically 'wired in'. Rohling *et al.* suggest that, for example, 'frequency of an event' and 'location' are stimulus characteristics which may be encoded automatically. They examined group differences for recall of a series of photographs with pictures occurring once or twice, and being located in one of four quadrants on a page. However, their results suggested that individuals with dementia performed worse on all aspects of the memory task. Thus, differences between automatic and effortful encoding performance, or between implicit and explicit memory tasks, cannot as yet be used to discriminate in a completely reliable way 'normal' older people from those with dementias. Perhaps they may do so in the future.

Differential diagnosis and detecting early dementia

The search, then, is on to find ways of discriminating between normal age-associated changes in cognitive performance and those that are indicative of dementia; both, of course, located to a substantial degree in changes in brain function. At the same time, increasing effort is also being put into detecting dementia earlier with a view to ultimately developing ways to slow down its progression and to plan appropriate forms of service provision and carer support. Early detection might, for example, contribute to accident reduction, since many people with dementia continue to drive. Such detection and discrimination at present rests on psychological rather than physiological tests.

For example, the Mini-Mental State Examination (MMSE), devised by Folstein *et al.* (1975), has become one of the most widely used of a variety of brief forms of appraisal of cognitive state used by clinicians as an initial part of the process of forming a diagnosis of dementia. Having a simple cut-off point on such a test to indicate a significant probability of dementia in individuals who score below it is, however, problematic. MMSE scores are associated not only with age, but also with socio-economic status and educational level, whereas only age has been found to be significantly related to the diagnosis of dementia. While useful as a screening device, a diagnosis that is as definitive as possible requires more effort. Even with more sophisticated research instruments, such as the cognitive sub-tests of the Cambridge Examination for Mental Disorders in the Elderly (CAMDEX: Roth *et al.* 1988), there is evidence that its scores are also affected by age, socio-cultural factors and visual and hearing deficits in addition to dementia, although in this case not by depression (Blessed *et al.* 1991). Clearly dementia, especially early dementia, cannot simply and infallibly be detected just by the administration of such tests. Diagnosis requires a full clinical examination, as well as the collection of much information from close friends and relatives. The importance of diagnostic accuracy is obvious, but as Byrne *et al.* (1991: 199) note:

> In clinical practice there is evidence that the diagnosis of dementia is very inaccurate. McCartney (1986) reviewed surveys of the ability of hospital doctors to diagnose dementia (or delirium)[a disoriented condition with

clouded consciousness], finding that the diagnosis was missed in between 16 and 77% of cases.

Such research findings are rather worrying. Not only can a diagnosis of dementia be missed, it can also be incorrectly attributed – which will be even more damaging to the individual concerned and his or her family. Byrne *et al.* (1991) conclude that the failure of the diagnostic process appertains to the complexity of the dementia syndrome, and that knowledge, clinical skills and the attitudes of the examining doctor all play a part. As they suggest 'the foundation of knowledge on which clinical skills rest and from which attitudes (in part) may arise is not as secure as could be wished' (p. 205). But such knowledge is increasing in substance, as Huppert's (1991b) review of the neuropsychological assessment of dementia attests. She notes, however:

> The presence of cognitive decline in the normal elderly population, together with the individual differences referred to above, results in a large degree of overlap in the scores of normal and demented subjects on cognitive tests . . . whatever cut-[off] point is selected for dementia, a proportion both of demented and normal subjects will be wrongly classified.
>
> (Huppert 1991b: 161)

This is even more likely to be the case when attempting to diagnose 'early' dementia, while differentiating Alzheimer's from multi-infarct dementia, Lewy Body dementia or any other of the 'new' dementias (some of which we consider in more detail below) remains equally problematic. There is always the possibility that differences in 'types' of dementia may be attributed to what are, in fact, random variations in the appearance of the disorder.

In essence, in dementia the more complex cognitive processes are the first to become impaired, while the simplest tend to remain intact until dementia is quite advanced. This might imply that tests of complex processes should be used to detect early dementia. But tests, especially those for screening, have above all to be practical and acceptable. Naming the objects in six pictures and thereby affording the opportunity for incidental memorization (to be tested later), as well as making an effort to memorize a name for later recall, may suffice for screening purposes. Someone with dementia may be able to read aloud correctly a word such as 'psalm' which cannot be predicted from its spelling, but not know the meaning of it, or may be able to correct the grammar of a sentence they no longer understand. This preserved ability forms the rationale for using acceptable short forms of the National Adult Reading Test (NART) as a measure of pre-morbid (verbal) intelligence (Beardsall and Brayne 1990). Comparing community norms for both verbal and more fluid aspects of cognitive performance may begin to suggest the range where measurable decline is possibly morbid.

The ageing brain

The structural and chemical changes that appear to typify the ageing brain in the absence of known disease are heterogeneous. The brain consists largely of the neurons which convey signals, the glial cells which support and repair neurons, and the blood vessels which supply energy and nutrition to – and carry away waste products from – the cells. Not surprisingly, certain subsets of cells and areas of the brain seem more prone to age-associated change than others, and a single underlying mechanism for their production seems unlikely. According to Selkoe (1992), although the overall number of brain neurons decreases, the pattern is far from uniform, for example, few seem to disappear from the areas of the hypothalamus which regulate the secretion of hormones by the pituitary gland. But many more nerve cells do disappear from specialized areas in the brainstem like the substantia nigra and locus coeruleus. Older people who exhibit symptoms rather like mild Parkinson's disease – decreased flexibility, slowness of movement and a stooped shuffling gait – may have lost up to 30 per cent of the original complement of such cells.

Some areas of the hippocampus,[1]* which as part of the limbic system influences emotional and motivational behaviour and hence aspects of learning, as well as the formation of long-term memories, may lose up to 20 per cent of cells, with other areas showing little decline. Even when neurons themselves survive, their cells bodies and extensions – the single axon that relays signals to another neuron, and the dendrites[2] which are found in large branching arbors and generally receive messages from other neurons – may waste away or atrophy. Some net growth in dendrites in some areas of the hippocampus and cortex, which occurs between middle and old age, is thought to be due to viable neurons coping with the age-associated loss of their neighbours. This suggests a capacity for dynamic remodelling, which as yet does not appear to extend to late old age, where dendrite regression is again in evidence.

Neurons may also undergo changes in their internal architecture. For example, the protoplasm of the cell outside its nucleus can begin to fill with protein filaments, helically wound as screw-shaped spirals, known as neurofibrillary tangles. This change in cellular scaffolding might lead to inefficient signalling and, when present in sufficient numbers of cells vital to memory and learning, may contribute to Alzheimer's disease. Another internal alteration that can occur in cells in many parts of the brain involves the accumulation of granules containing the pigment lipofuscin. Whether this is just a marker of longevity (like grey hair) or is actively disruptive for cells is a matter of debate. There is also an increase in the size and number of certain glial cells capable of releasing factors that promote neuronal and neuritic growth. Again it has been suggested that this might be part of a compensatory mechanism for decrements in the number and structure of neurons.

The extracellular spaces also undergo change, accumulating moderate numbers of spherical deposits called senile plaques, which are primarily aggregates of a small molecule known as beta-amyloid protein. This protein also gradually accumulates in scattered blood vessels and in the connective tissue that envelops the brain, the meninges. The production and consequences of this accumulation of beta-amyloid protein are under intense

---

* Superscript numerals refer to numbered notes at the end of the chapter.

investigation because of its relative abundance in the brains of individuals diagnosed as having Alzheimer's disease.

The biological processes hypothesized to contribute to ageing in general may also have their effect within the brain. For example, several enzymes that synthesize neurotransmitters or their receptors seem to become less active as an individual ages, perhaps influenced by oxidation via free radical activity.[3] But does free radical activity cause DNA damage, or does DNA damage produce free radical activity? Probably both. Among other changes, the vesicles (i.e. small fluid-containing sacs) involved in the storage and release of neurotransmitters may function less efficiently, and the composition of the white fatty substance, myelin, that sheaths and insulates axons (rather like the plastic covering for domestic electricity wires),[4] can subtly change with age, thus affecting the efficiency of electrical impulse distribution. Once many such processes start, there is the likelihood of a cascade effect (Selkoe 1992).

The exact nature of the links between all the diverse observed changes in the ageing brain and their behavioural or mental consequences or counterparts remains obscure. Even if neurochemical changes might constitute a 30 per cent deficit by the time an individual is in his or her eighties and nineties, their effect on thinking seems relatively slight. Positron emission tomographic imaging,[5] for example, indicates that the brains of healthy people in their eighties are almost as active as those of people in their twenties. The brain seems to have a great deal of physiological reserve and to be able to tolerate small losses of neuronal function.

The 'new' dementias and beta-amyloid protein in Alzheimer's disease

Holden-Cosgrove (1992), in considering the new dementias, suggests that 'senile dementia' is a non-existent disease, and that, like Alzheimer's, it is an umbrella term for a variety of processes affecting the brain. She divides such encephalopathies into four main groups: those that affect the cortex, the outer layer of the brain; those that affect areas of the brain below the outer layer; those that affect both; and those that she describes as multi-focused. Within the cortical group are sub-groups largely defined by where in the brain pathology appears most evident. A variety of sub-cortical conditions are listed which, though frequently found, are little understood. Lewy Body disease, for example, can affect both the cortex and sub-cortex. Lewy Bodies, bodies which readily stain with the dye eosin and form in the protoplasm of cells outside the nucleus, particularly in pigmented neurons, have been thought to be associated with Parkinson's disease for many years. It is possible that a significant percentage of what have hitherto been labelled 'Alzheimer's cases' are in fact people with Lewy Body disease, of which there are thought to be several types.

In some rare instances of inherited forms of Alzheimer's, it is now clear that mutations in the gene that gives rise to beta-amyloid precursor protein somehow leads to accelerated extracellular and vascular deposits of the beta-amyloid segment. Perhaps some mutations lead to more or faster deposition than others, which could explain in part why certain individuals show some symptoms earlier than others (Selkoe 1992). Individuals with Down's syndrome, who are born with three copies of chromosome 21, where the gene that gives rise to the beta-amyloid precursor protein is located, also develop an excess of senile plaques and neurofibrillary tangles, usually in their forties and fifties. While the deposition of amyloid protein is now demonstrably associated with certain forms of Alzheimer's disease, and some would argue with a variety of the symptoms we might have labelled as being due to 'ageing', it remains to be discovered how the initially inert protein influences (over a long time) the extensive structural and biochemical changes in axons, dendrites, neuronal cell bodies and glial cells that characterize the brains of individuals with Alzheimer's disease. The consequence, however, would seem to be the effective progressive disconnection of neuronal circuitry that underpins memory and produces some of the changes in memory described previously. The assorted initial symptoms witnessed in Alzheimer's perhaps reflects the varied nature, extent and locus of such 'disconnecting'; it may be visible in impaired memory or judgement or reasoning, or in language problems or in personality change, or in capacity for abstract thought. Clearly, several central questions need to be answered: What speeds up amyloid deposition? Why does it seem to occur predominantly in the brain? Why do some areas of the brain seem more susceptible than others? Which cells actually secrete it?

Given the complexity of the issue it is not surprising that Byrne *et al.* (1991) found different accounts for defining the microscopic structure (i.e. the histological characteristics) of Alzheimer's disease. Some suggest the numbers and locations of senile plaques are the key, and correlate closely with the degree of dementia as observed. Others suggest that neurofibrillary tangles (NFTs) in the neo-cortex (i.e. the frontal, parietal, temporal and occipital lobes of the brain) are the defining characteristics, along with senile plaques and other changes, and that the numbers of NFTs in the cerebral cortex correlate more closely with the degree of dementia observed than does the presence of senile plaques. And others suggest that it is changes in the hippocampus alone that serve to distinguish Alzheimer's from normal ageing, since senile plaques and NFTs are almost always found to a greater or lesser extent in the brains of individuals not thought to have had dementia.

It is, of course, possible that dementia does not become observable until a certain threshold of brain change occurs, be it due to Lewy Bodies, 'ageing', Alzheimer's, or other cerebral infarctions where small parts of the brain might die due to lack of blood. Indeed, 'multi-infarct dementia', as its name suggests, is a form of dementia comprising a multitude of disparate small areas of the brain which are dying, and its progress is correspondingly patchy with deterioration being focal rather than global. Sometimes, of course, such infarcts are large, as in a stroke.

Strokes

The death of brain cells may occur when the blood supply fails because a blood vessel bursts, or because it becomes blocked or so narrowed as to make the supply of blood inadequate. Stroke accounts for 10–12 per cent of all deaths in industrialized countries and for more deaths among females than among males, but rates vary from country to country and have been dropping dramatically in the last few decades, in particular in Japan. The incidence of stroke rises exponentially with age, from about 3 per 10,000 population in their thirties and forties to almost 300 in the eighth and ninth decades. The cumulative risk of recurrence over five years is high, ranging from about one-third to one-half of people who have a stroke, and on average some 24 per cent of individuals will die within one month of an acute first stroke. In a population of one million, 1250 will experience their first stroke in any one year, and an additional 350 may have a recurrent episode. Of these 1600 individuals, only 880 will survive six months. Of the 640 (of the 1600) who will be living at home, about two-thirds will regard themselves as back to their pre-stroke functional status after six months; the remainder, representing about 15 per cent of all acute events in a one-year period, will have residual difficulties of varying degree in caring for themselves.

Because national variations and the general decline in mortality from stroke are not fully understood, achieving government targets in stroke reduction (40 per cent for people aged 65–74 in England, in the next decade) may be a difficult task. Nevertheless, strokes are to some extent preventable. Reducing high blood pressure, serum cholesterol levels, overweight, smoking, and sodium and alcohol intake have all been suggested as preventive measures. A daily dose of aspirin is thought to reduce by some 25 per cent the likelihood of having a subsequent stroke in individuals who have had transient losses of oxygen supply to the brain cells (transient ischaemic attacks). Lowering the average blood pressure of a population would probably be the most effective in reducing the number of deaths from stroke attributable to high blood pressure, and perhaps reducing the daily salt intake is the clearest way of achieving this. Marmot and Poulter (1992) suggest there are no grounds for assuming that the rise in blood pressure with age observed in western societies is 'normal' and being 'normal' therefore requires less attention in older people. Hachinski (1992) not only considers that strokes are preventable, but so also is the form of dementia known as multi-infarct dementia, a form of vascular dementia singularly responsible for some 20 per cent of dementias among older people.

Depending on the nature, severity and location of the stroke, individuals may be left with a variety of impairments – of speech, muscular control and coordination – which can benefit from the help of physiotherapists and speech-therapists, as well as occupational therapists. Physical recovery has become the most important outcome measure of stroke rehabilitation, dictating, for example, the timing of discharge from hospital, the provision of community services and the need for respite care. This has arguably led to the relative neglect of the emotional, personal and social consequences of having a stroke. As with Alzheimer's disease, as we shall suggest later, the *person* can be lost behind attention to a condition. Helping an individual adapt as best as possible to the difference between his or her desired and achieved role may be a goal for rehabilitation, but one can question how well this objective is being achieved. Many people who make a good physical recovery may nevertheless become socially inactive, even to the extent of becoming 'house-bound', despite their ability to walk indoors and climb stairs. More attention needs to be paid to loss of the power of speech, since aphasia is often mistakenly taken to indicate diminished or vanished mental powers, with an accompanying reduction in civil rights.

Some individuals who have had a stroke may well be depressed, both as a reaction to their changed circumstances and as a direct physiological effect of the stroke. Compared with age-matched controls, depressive symptoms are about twice as common in individuals who have had a stroke. Clearly, physical impairments may perpetuate depression, and depression may also inhibit functional recovery. Both individuals who have strokes and their carers require longer-term support, more support at the time of discharge from hospital, access to counselling, and more information about services for disabled people – rather than more physical rehabilitation. Translating gains in physical ability to improvements in well-being and access to a richer social world seems to remain, however, fairly resistant to conventional attempts at rehabilitation.

Another common sequela of a stroke, about which more information can prove beneficial, concerns emotionalism. Emotionalism may affect as many as one in five individuals, often manifesting itself as a heightened tendency to cry, but sometimes to laugh. Emotionalism is considered to be more than a feature of a depressive condition, or a response to frustration, or even a way of communicating. Some three-quarters of individuals showing emotionalism seem to be induced to cry by the social context; for example, by being asked about symptoms, or by having thoughts about changed family life provoked by the presence of family members. Allman (1991) suggests that simple education and advice is the best 'treatment' and that most individuals exhibiting emotionalism benefit from knowing that the symptom is common and that it tends to improve with time. He also suggests that 'consoling' behaviour by those around the elderly person should not be automatic lest it inadvertently promotes the crying episodes. In responding automatically, we react to the distress of the person perhaps, rather than to what their condition requires. In responding to the symptoms of the dementias, we may tend to do the obverse – that is, respond to the condition, not to the person. With dementia we have to rise to the challenge of helping to maintain personhood rather than thoughtlessly contributing to its deconstruction.

The prevalence, nature and experience of the dementias

The image we are given of dementia is, as Sweeting (1991: 6) suggests, one of a slow living death, of a relentless disease with nightmare results, and our attention is usually focused on the end result: being unable to exist independently; unable to communicate meaningfully; unable to recognize once familiar persons. She provides some illustrative academic article titles and newspaper headlines:

- 'Death of a mind: A study of disintegration'
- 'A never-ending funeral: One family's struggle'
- 'Living with dementia: The ongoing funeral'
- 'Slow, steady and heartbreaking'
- 'Alzheimer's: Slow death in Dickensian squalor'
- 'My husband: The stranger'

And a quote from Jonathan Miller in conversation in *The Independent on Sunday* (15 April 1990):

> . . . I'm president of the Alzheimer's Disease Society, and when I talk to public meetings about it, I talk about an uncollected corpse; there is this terrible thing which is walking around which the undertaker has forgotten to collect.

Given this imagery, it is not surprising, then, that the disclosure of a diagnosis of dementia is not without its problems. Perhaps, as with HIV, counselling should be available *before* an informed decision is reached as to whether to go ahead with testing, whether for psychological indicators or for biological markers. Cheston and Marshall (1994: 5) point out that systems of coordinated assessments and feedback available in the few existing 'memory clinics' tend to be the exception rather than the rule, and 'It may be thought that it is not in the patient's best interest to disclose fully the results of the assessment, but more often than not such decisions are taken to protect the professionals or the carers than to protect the patient. Breaking bad news in the dementia field is an uncharted area'. Perhaps President Regan's announcement that he has Alzheimer's disease will prove a turning point.

Given that the earlier a diagnosis of dementia is attempted, the less it may be reliable and valid, the justification for early diagnosis must be based on its pros outweighing its cons; if little positive response is made as a consequence of reaching the diagnosis, is it worth having? Such is the stigma of the label 'dementia' that many researchers studying the carers of older people with dementia avoid using the term. And even the 'low-level' help such carers request – with heavy jobs in the house or garden, or just 'having some company' – may not be readily available from Dementia Community Resource Teams comprising social workers, psychiatrists, nurses and therapists. Pollitt and Anderson (1991: 32), talking of early diagnosis, write:

> To intervene early in such cases – other than to offer the kind of low level help which is actually asked for – involves changing perceptions: making people aware of potential problems. How justified are we in telling people that their relatives have dementia – when it may not get worse or they may die of something else before it does? We need to think carefully about the implications – both for families and services – of bringing forward from

normal to abnormal the reclassification of elderly people in the early stages of a dementing illness.

The prevalence of dementia depends on the instrument or set of procedures used to detect it, what sort of dementia one is attempting to detect, and whether one is looking for 'early' dementia or established dementia. Reviewing such issues and the relevant data, Black *et al.* (1990: 88) conclude that despite apparent variations in prevalence rates in different countries:

> Nevertheless, the rate of dementia changes with age in a strikingly consistent manner. According to a theoretical model derived from 22 studies, the age-specific prevalence rate approximately doubles every five years, from an average rate of 5.6 % at 75–79, to 10.5 % at 80–84 and 39 per cent in the 10th decade. The corresponding rates in Melton Mowbray were much lower, 2.1%, 3.7 % and 13%, respectively. However, the Melton Mowbray study was not included as a data source in this analysis, and the fit of the model beyond age 85/90 is conjectural because actual observations are scanty. It is of course possible that dementia is in fact uncommon in Melton Mowbray.

It would perhaps be unwise to plan to retire to Melton Mowbray as a way of reducing your 'risk factor' for dementia on the strength of such prevalence figures! Prevalence rates do not appear to have changed much in recent years, and men and women do not differ in their age-adjusted rates, although forms of Alzheimer's may affect women more than men and multi-infarct types of dementia affect men more than women (Kay 1991). Dementia among minority ethnic groups within the UK is a hidden problem, and consequently we have little relevant and reliable information about prevalence. But within the human lifespan, prevalence never reaches 100 per cent in any population group. Of all forms of dementia among older people, roughly 50 per cent are thought to be due to forms of Alzheimer's alone, 20 per cent due to multi-infarct dementia alone, 20 per cent due to both existing together, and some 10 per cent from other causes. But misdiagnosis rates for Alzheimer's, for example, may be as high as 20 per cent. Dementia is probably second only to joint disease as a cause of disability in later life. It is, therefore, not surprising that various studies report a prevalence of dementia among residents of homes for old people of between 33 and 50 per cent.

Assessing cognitive ability: The outer presentation of inner changes

The 1987 revised edition of the American Psychiatric Association's *Diagnostic and Statistical Manual of Mental Disorders* (DSM-III-R) stresses that the difference between dementia and normal ageing is that in the former cognitive deficits have to be sufficient to interfere with 'social function'. Clinical descriptive definitions of the dementia syndrome usually cover changes in cognitive and intellectual skills, and changes in personality and behaviour. We will look at some aspects of these in a little more detail, since they illustrate the range of changes that may be observable in dementia and which receive attention in assessment protocols like CAMDEX.

Orientation may be examined through a variety of questions, such as 'What season are we in now?' or 'What county are we in?' Language difficulties can be assessed through motor responses to directions, for example by asking someone to follow verbal instructions to nod their head or to look at the ceiling and then the floor, or through verbal responses to questions such as 'Is this place a hotel?' Sometimes naming is difficult; for example, someone may not be able, when shown a pencil, to say what it is. Sometimes definitions are difficult, as in 'What is a bridge?'; sometimes a person may not be able to repeat an expression like 'No ifs, ands or buts', or describe spontaneously what is happening in a picture he or she is shown. Memory recall can be assessed by asking individuals if they can remember what objects were present in pictures they were shown earlier, and recognition by presenting some of these pictures again, together with others, and asking which of them were seen earlier. Remote memory might be assessed by a variety of questions concerning the past such as 'Who was the leader of the Germans in the Second World War?', and more recent memory by asking for the name of the current prime minister. Registration might be assessed by naming a few objects like an apple and a penny and asking for the names to be repeated and to be remembered for recall later on.

Attention and concentration are often assessed by asking individuals to count backwards from 20, or to subtract 7 continuously starting from 100. Reading comprehension might be examined by showing individuals a card with an instruction on it like 'Close your eyes', which they then have to follow. Being able to do things – *praxis* – is often a problem for people with dementia and it is sometimes assessed through an individual's ability to copy designs, or put the hands and numbers on a clock face, or follow an instruction to fold a piece of paper in half and put it somewhere, or to wave good-bye. Writing ability, whether it is to dictation or spontaneous, is usually examined, as is tactile recognition. For example, recognizing a coin just through touch may be a problem. An ability to calculate is usually assessed using coins, and abstract thinking can be assessed through questions such as 'In what way are a shirt and a dress alike?' Visual perception can be assessed through recognition of famous people in photographs, such as the Queen, and through recognition of everyday objects, such as a cup and saucer photographed from unusual angles. The ability to judge the passage of time may be assessed, for example, by asking the individual how long he or she has been with the interviewer doing the testing.

Such assessment of cognitive and intellectual status is not, however, without its problems. It may tell you little about what a person *can* do, even if the individual is achieving very low scores. Because they are designed to show failure, cognitive appraisals can be stressful, and the person being appraised may not be motivated to perform well on material that may appear fairly irrelevant to 'real life'. For this reason, other measures of incapacity – behavioural assessment scales – have been developed, in particular for individuals who are considered to be 'severely demented' (Ritchie and Ledesert 1991).

Changes in memory, behaviour and personality

Changes in personality and behaviour are usually documented through interviews with the relative of a person being assessed or with some other informant who knows the individual well. Questions concerning changes in personality may concern such things as exaggeration of normal character, change in concern for others, or being more or less stubborn or awkward. Interviews with informants usually cover changes in ability to undertake everyday activities, such as eating and drinking, mobility, dressing and undressing, bathing, use of toilets, levels of emotional control, and alterations in sleep patterns – such as being restless or wakeful during the night. When collected together into a research instrument such as CAMDEX, cognitive tests, interviewer's observations and informants' answers to detailed questions, along with biochemical and physiological assays and various forms of brain imaging, can provide a procedure for attempting a differential diagnosis of mental disorders or dementias such as Alzheimer's, as well as other conditions such as depression. Since the latter can sometimes mimic the former, it is crucial that depression *is* diagnosed for what it is, and treated appropriately. Given the higher than chance co-morbidity of depression and dementia in later life, the question of whether having dementia predisposes to having depression, or vice versa, needs to be answered.

Quotes from a National Health Service (1993) brochure illustrate some of the ways in which dementia becomes visible to others:

She'll have her breakfast and then she will say 'When are we having breakfast?'

Suddenly odd things began to happen. She would lose things, forget her keys, go for her pension on the wrong day and very often not answer the phone when I used to ring every day. I took her on holiday with my two girls and when I was with her all the while, she used to answer questions very strangely, and that was the time my worries started.

Often, though, the changes in dementia, particularly of the Alzheimer's type, are insidious rather than sudden, and only recognized later for what they are, after a diagnosis has been made. Gilleard (1984: 11) describes one example:

I didn't really notice, until much later, but looking back, now, I can find things that happened . . . she used to be a good card player, you see, especially at solo whist, she belonged to a club, went every week, twice a week, and several times she was forgetting the numbers of the cards . . . then she gravitated to bingo, but even that was getting too much for her – but we didn't think no more of that either, for some reason, but eventually it just gradually came, she would just stand in the kitchen, and wonder why she was there . . .

Sometimes the changes noticed are less to do with memory and more to do with personality or behaviour. Gilleard (1984: 12) continues:

Well, he started on the motorists, what business had they parking in front of the door, and telling them to take their cars away or he would get the police. He would use very bad language . . . if the children came near the garden, he would tell them to clear out and things like that, and threaten them . . .

Experiencing dementia

The most common linguistic problem first noticed by relatives concerns difficulties the individual with dementia has in writing a meaningful letter to someone. Following this, word-finding difficulties and a difficulty with naming objects are often noted (Bayles and Tomoeda 1991). However, awareness of such difficulties by the person with dementia may not be particularly acute.

Individuals with dementia are thought to under-report their symptoms, perhaps in part in self-defence and perhaps in part out of a lack of a real awareness of their circumstances. In particular, depressive symptoms and paranoid features seem under-reported in comparison with accounts by close friends or relatives (Ballard *et al.* 1991), and a lack of self-awareness for memory deficit may be more acute in individuals who maintain their verbal fluency. Given that individuals with dementia may rate their degree of deficit as significantly less severe than do 'normal' individuals acting as 'controls', it is not surprising that the experience of a global diffuse dementia like Alzheimer's is problematic to communicate: one has to use one's imagination.

You wake up in the middle of the night in your own home and you don't know where you are. You think you had better get dressed, go downstairs and find someone who can tell you what is going on. But you can't remember where all your clothes are. Your wife or your husband finds you downstairs in the dark, with one shoe on, wondering who they might be.
(Ignatieff 1991: 21)

Given that we all may experience the condition in others or indeed in ourselves as we age, reflection on the experience of dementia is important in order to consider what we would wish to do for ourselves or others should the necessity arise. How, for example, would you react if the person who stands in front of you saying she is your daughter clearly isn't? When such misidentifications of persons occurs, is it surprising that the perceiver behaves in a way we might label 'paranoid'? What would you suspect? Presumably something untoward – in such an appearance of a 'double'. Trying to understand the situation from the point of view of the person with dementia might well give us insight into at least some of the behaviour labelled as a 'management problem'.

Wilkie (1992: 17) quotes from individuals with a known familial genetic form of Alzheimer's disease, which may become evident in mid-life rather than in old age. Such individuals can now be genetically tested for the condition, as indeed in the future many more of us may be.

'There are a lot worse ways to die than Alzheimer's', says Carol Jennings.

'I'm not so frightened by the disease, although I would like to put it off a bit and get in my three score years and ten'. In 1982, Mrs Jennings' father was diagnosed as having Alzheimer's disease. He was 58 years old. Mrs Jennings, 37, has a 50 per cent chance of developing the disease . . .

Andrea Paddison is 32, and her father showed the first signs of the disease when he was 40 . . .

Both women condemn the stigma that is still attached to Alzheimer's. 'A physical illness seems more acceptable than something that affects your brain', says Ms Paddison.

'One of my jobs is to get this understood as a disease and to stop the taboo. People are still very frightened of it, and there's no need to be'. A Methodist lay preacher, Mrs Jennings recounts how she was shaking hands with the congregation after a service when one woman said her husband was ill. 'He gave me a little smile. I thought he had Alzheimer's and once I'd have been frightened. But it's just someone who's ill'.

Responding to dementia

Whether Alzheimer's is just an illness or a more pronounced form of what have hitherto been accepted as 'normal' age-associated processes, our response to it of late has been primarily medical. It has been formulated as a medical problem and the search is on for medical solutions (Robbert 1990), and it has become an integral part of what Robertson (1990: 430) refers to as the biomedicalization and gerontologization of old age:

> The view that the 'problem' of aging is primarily one of physiological decline medicalizes old age; that is, the phenomenon and experience of aging are brought within the medical paradigm as individual pathology to be treated and cured . . . Accompanying the biomedicalization of old age is the 'gerontologization' of the experience of aging itself. With their search for scientific laws and theories about aging, their emphasis on the physical and psychological aspects of aging, and their adherence to scientific methodology in investigating aging, the disciplines of gerontology and geriatrics constitute old age as observed phenomenon rather than lived experience, and old people as objects of study.

Such perspectives tend to ignore the contribution of, for example, poverty, isolation, loss of role and status to the experience of later life and thus effectively depoliticize the 'problems of ageing'. With Alzheimer's and other dementias, it also has the consequence of turning the person into a patient. Stockton (1991: 19) goes further and suggests that, in the Unites States at least: 'The result of all the recent publicity surrounding Alzheimer's disease is to generate anxiety in everyone over the age of 50 who has ever forgotten a name, and to send others to medical specialists seeking diagnostic testing for reassurance. Memory testing institutes have been set up to cater for the "worried well"'. Stockton considers that the present emphasis on early detection of cognitive decline serves only to transform people who feel healthy into patients anxious for a verdict, and to divert even more resources into the acute health care sector.

Since loss of 'personhood' or 'self' is often deemed to be an end-product of the dementias, the challenge is how to maintain personhood. Clearly, becoming defined as a patient, which lends itself to giving others the opportunity to think the most important thing to know about you is that you have this 'dementing disease', contributes to the deconstruction rather than the construction of personhood. With regard to the 'self', Sabat and Harré (1992: 459–10) note that:

> In the cases we have described the threatened disappearance of any self is not directly linked to the process of the disease. Rather, it is related to the behaviour of those who are regularly involved in the social life of the sufferer, though to react positively to such fragile clues requires persistence and dedication.
>
> If such behaviour is founded on story lines that paint the sufferer as inadequate, confused, helpless [one might add 'suffering'] etc., then that person will be so positioned and will have his or her behaviour so interpreted by others in such a way as to confirm the initial story line and positioning. The ultimate result of such a situation is the fencing off of the sufferer so that no adequate self can be constructed. Perhaps it is not stretching the point too far to refer to such a situation as a species of self-fulfilling prophecy. Thus, if there is a loss of the capacity to present an appropriate self, in many cases the fundamental cause is to be found not in the neurofibrillary tangles and senile plaques in the brains of the sufferers, but in the character of the social interactions and the interpretations that follow in the wake of the symptoms.

The challenge, then, is to react positively and with persistence and dedication to the fragile clues concerning the existence and maintenance of the self. The theme of maintaining personhood by relating to individuals with dementia in an appropriate social rather than medico/technical frame of reference is emphasized by Kitwood (1993: 104), who also suggests how the social context itself can, with the unwitting collusion of professionals, family and friends, facilitate the dementing process:

> A few years ago, I spent a good deal of time looking at what might be called the 'malignant social psychology' surrounding the dementing process. The method involved collecting vignettes from everyday life, and putting these into 10 categories, as follows:
>
> • *Treachery*: the use of dishonest representation or deception in order to obtain compliance.

- *Disempowerment*: doing for a dementia sufferer what he or she can in fact do, albeit clumsily or slowly.
- *Infantilisation*: implying that a dementia sufferer has the mentality or capability of a baby or young child.
- *Condemnation*: blaming; the attribution of malicious or seditious motives, especially when the dementia sufferer is distressed.
- *Intimidation*: the use of threats, commands or physical assault; the abuse of power.
- *Stigmatisation*: turning a dementia sufferer into an alien, a diseased object, an outcast, especially through verbal labels.
- *Outpacing*: the delivery of information or instruction at a rate far beyond that which can be processed.
- *Invalidation*: the ignoring or discounting of a dementia sufferer's subjective states – especially feelings of distress or bewilderment.
- *Banishment*: the removal of a dementia sufferer from the human milieu, either physically or psychologically.
- *Objectification*: treating a person like a lump of dead matter; to be measured, pushed around, drained, filled, polished, dumped, etc.

Thus Kitwood (1993) suggests that a destabilized and diminished sense of self can arise from the interaction between neurological impairment and interpersonal processes. It must indeed be challenging to recognize such interpersonal processes, and to have the time, energy and inclination to change our behaviour accordingly. 'Dementia care mapping', devised by Kitwood, provides a useful technique for helping carers, particularly professional ones, to become sensitized and mindful to the effects of what they do, and to the 'personhood' of the individual with dementia. By getting carers to 'map' in detail what goes on in care settings, and to give evaluative appraisals of what they describe, carers should be in a better position to help people with dementia to keep some sense of agency, of personal worth, to have more social confidence, and to have hope. Carers need to be more sensitive to clues about underlying feelings as well as making an effort to see what sense can be made out of 'surface behaviour'.

Perhaps a 'There but for the grace of God go I' perspective can also help. Over time, relating appropriately to someone who has Alzheimer's is likely to become increasingly effortful, and such efforts are bound to be undermined for carers when the necessary energy is drained away through lack of sleep, for example, or deflected on to other necessary but more mundane activities such as the twice-daily washing of soiled bed-linen, or showing someone how to eat or to clean his or her teeth. Having to pay continuous attention means that for many carers time is a resource that can never be taken for granted. But as Orona (1990: 1255) notes, carers hang on to the caregiving experience long after 'identity' has diminished, to the point that the person was felt to have 'gone':

However the loss of the person 'as once known' did not occur without a struggle. These struggles took place in the arena of everyday living.

Moreover caregiving relatives fought to maintain vestiges of the person as known, even when it was not clear if the Alzheimer's person 'knew' what was happening . . .

Gilleard (1992) widens the social context in which we respond to brain changes in individuals – from their immediate carers to wider society. What we think of our fellow dementing citizens, he suggests, is a part of and a place in our collective consciousness, and that place itself is a function of the institutions and practices we create in response to our various perceptions of the problem. He suggests a dialectic between losing one's mind and losing one's place in society, and that by maintenance of the latter, particularly by keeping people with dementia as autonomous, engaged and identifiable as possible, society can grasp its responsibility for maintaining the personhood, citizenship and individuality of all adults irrespective of their individual competency. The challenge that faced those who reclaimed personhood for individuals with developmental learning disabilities now appears before us as we face the learning difficulties and degenerative brain changes that later life can bring. *We create the stigma surrounding such changes and therefore some of the problems attached to them. Could not dementia be seen as part of *la condition humaine*? Should we not be detecting residual abilities and finding ways to support them?*

Explicitly therapeutic as opposed to broadly social responses to Alzheimer's disease can be divided into two camps: the search for drugs to influence brain functioning, and more focused and considered ways of responding to 'symptom' or 'problem' behaviour. The latter we return to in the next chapter. As to the former, Koenig (1991: 3) suggests that the search for drugs is developing apace. To drug companies, Alzheimer's presents a vast untapped market and 'the person who discovers a cure for Alzheimer's will have discovered the equivalent of penicillin'. So far, a variety of drugs – including those like desferrioxamine, which mop up molecules of iron and aluminium – have been tested on a small scale with some positive results, although the underlying mechanisms are not well understood. More common are headlines of the variety 'Hopes overdose on the "wonder drug"', although reports on tacrine suggest that one in ten individuals with mild Alzheimer's disease might get a six-month 'stay of execution', as the newspaper coverage put it. Although after taking the drug 'people who have been unable to dress have been able to dress', the assistant director of the UK Alzheimer's Disease Society was reported as saying that false hopes must not be raised. Tacrine can cause such side-effects as liver damage, nausea and vomiting, and three-quarters of those given it cannot tolerate the high doses necessary. If prescribed freely, many individuals would suffer the side-effects but not the benefits.

According to Spagnoli (1991: 266), a researcher at a geriatric neuropsychiatry institute, where the effects of drugs on Alzheimer's have been investigated:

No drug with firm evidence of efficacy is available and Alzheimer's disease is a medical disorder where there is a serious tension between the rapid development of the biological understanding of the disorder and the depressing lack of effective drugs, despite the enormous efforts of pharmacological research.

Spagnoli appears far from sanguine about a 'drugs breakthrough'. Reporting on a study he conducted in which individuals given a drug showed a statistically significant slower decline on behavioural and cognitive measures compared with controls not given the drug, he concluded that, in clinical terms:

> . . . the treatment gave neither an actual real improvement nor stopped the course of the disease. Patients taking the drug at the end of the trial were worse than at the beginning. 'Are you sure' someone asked me 'you would not have obtained the same results by regularly taking those patients for a walk?' No, I am not sure. For a number of reasons at present no-one would conduct such an imaginative trial. Who would fund a large and expensive trial testing a drug against a rational caring system?
>
> (Spagnoli 1991: 266)

For the vast majority of older people with or without dementia (i.e. those who live in the community), the 'caring systems' that exist are, of course, provided by families and friends; only for a small minority are they provided by workers within special residential or institutional settings. Such 'systems', whether supportive or therapeutic, comprise patterns of relationships between individuals, which at best can nourish a sense of place and of belonging, of purpose and autonomy, as well as fostering self-esteem and providing for a need to help and be helped. It is to some of these issues that we now turn.

Notes

1 The hippocampus is an area of the brain below the outer cortex, a principal function of which appears to be in transferring information from short- to long-term memory. When damaged, individuals have pronounced problems in remembering new information.
2 Dendrites are the 'ends' of neurons where impulses from other neurons are first received.
3 This free radical is a volatile form of oxygen with an extra electron. It can damage cell molecules in several ways.
4 Axons are the nerve fibre projections from a cell body through which impulses pass on their way out to make connections with the dendrites of other neurons.
5 Positron emission tomography is an electronic scanning procedure which detects how a section of the body derives energy from a dose of mildly radiocative glucose.

6

Belonging – supportive relationships

For most people, a sense of belonging develops first within a domestic context, second within a community and educational setting, and third through engagement in occupational and leisure activities. In this chapter, I look at the importance of family and friends to the lives of older people, and in the next I look at home and place, at work and 'play'. In all these contexts, it is mainly within the relationships which are formed that our self-esteem and sense of personhood and place are nourished and sustained.

Friends and friendship

What are friends for? After having lived and worked in the USA, the Australian actress Judy Davis remarked of the way some Americans use therapists:

> It's like, if you want the maximum amount of friends, you don't talk about your troubles with them, and you're always in a really good mood. So in order to achieve that difficult challenge, you've got to pay somebody to sort all that out so you can be happy when you meet your friends. It's very logical and it makes a lot of sense.
>
> (Cooney, 1994: 61)

Such notions might seem very foreign to current generations of older British individuals who have clear but very different expectations about with whom it is appropriate to share one's troubles, for example. In a study of the meaning and measurement of friendships for 94 older adults, Rainey *et al.* (1992) remark how older people may be able to express certain personality character-istics and social patterns differently with friends than with family and other associates. This may be because the functions that such relationships serve are different. They suggest that among various functions are:

- *Guidance*: having knowledge, advice and expertise to hand.
- *Social integration*: providing a sense of belonging to a group.
- *Opportunity for nurturance*: being responsible for the care of others.
- *Attachment*: developing feelings of intimacy and peace.
- *Reassurance of worth*: having a sense of competence and esteem.
- *Reliable alliance*: receiving assistance.

Perhaps the key values expressed in having friends in later life can be expressed as the three As: aid, affect and affirmation. The older women in the study by Rainey *et al.* indicated that they received greater advice and assistance from their friends than did the older men and that there was less conflict in their friendships. Interestingly, the older men perceived themselves as having a greater opportunity for nurturance than did the older women, perhaps because older women see their nurturing role as lessening once their children are married and move away from home, whereas men (rightly or wrongly) still perceive their wives as relying on them.

The vast majority of women in Rainey and co-workers' (1992) study described their friends as being of the same sex and living close by, but relatively few men had friends of the same sex. On average, males in the sample said they had five friends and the females three, but this may have been due in part to the men being more inclined to include ex-work colleagues as friends, whom the women may have regarded as acquaintances. Arber and Ginn (1991) suggest that usually older women have more friends than do older men. Women reported having much more frequent 'phone contact with their friends than did men, and women were more likely to name someone who was not a relative or family member as 'best friend', whereas men were more likely to name their spouse as their only best friend.

When asked, 'Who would you confide in if you had any personal problems?', the large majority of older women included their best friend in those to whom personal details could be told, but relatively few men felt able to talk about confidences outside the family, many saying they could only confide in their spouse; something relatively few women reported. Many women suggested that it depended on the problem when one chose in whom to confide; some problems were best kept within the family, and some were best kept away from the family.

But having someone to confide in over a problem is not the same as having someone 'to turn to for help in times of trouble'. First and foremost, both older men and women reported that in times of trouble their spouse or a family member or relative would be the person to whom they would turn; but fewer women than men said they always tried to work troubles out by themselves. Perhaps the older men in Rainey and co-workers' (1992) study had been in part socialized to be more independent and less emotionally oriented than the women. The importance for mental health of having a *confidant* in later life (Wenger 1984), to which we will return, suggests that a challenge in later life, for older men in particular, may be to develop more confiding relationships with one or two of their peers, rather than investing all their emotional energy in their wives. They may well need to start doing this in middle age.

Friends and family

Over time, people probably sift through acquaintances and friends and retain those who are most valued; therefore, by late adulthood, as Ishii-Kuntz (1990) notes, many members of the older person's social network have become part of what she calls a person's 'social convoy':

> This partly explains a surprising finding: older people's satisfaction with life has little relationship with the quantity or quality of their contact with the younger members of their own family, but shows a strong correlation to the quantity and quality of their interaction with friends.
>
> (Ishii-Kuntz 1990: 19)

She goes on to suggest that many older people are concerned not to be a burden on anyone, and to help others just as others help them. Such mutual reciprocity may be easier to achieve in friendship relations that in familial relations. Although older people may support their children financially when they are able to, and can provide child-care support in a grandparenting role, their concern not to be or become a burden to their children, or that they are not as fully reciprocal in their relationships with them as they would wish to be, can 'become a psychological burden for the elderly' themselves (Ishii-Kuntz 1990: 19).

According to Ishii-Kuntz (1990), the primary providers of emotional support for older people 'are their close friends whose relationship is based upon more "equal" status'. Friends may also provide complementary support for older people who have suffered the loss of family members, in particular their spouses. Since friendship may rest on mutual choice and need, and includes an exchange of sociability among individuals who are more or less equals, friendship may sustain a person's sense of usefulness and self-esteem more successfully than do many kin relationships with children. Kin relationships often have a perceived obligatory aspect, and generational differences in interests, expectations and experiences may induce strain, resulting in relationships that are relatively symbolic or ritualistic.

Ischii-Kuntz's (1990) analysis of data from 3692 respondents age 18 and over interviewed in the Quality of American Life survey shows that the *qualitative* dimension of social interaction with family and friends, not the *frequency* of social interaction, is an important predictor of psychological well-being, with the impact on well-being of family relationships tending to decrease with age, whereas that of relationships with friends increases. Perhaps in the future, among the relatively well-off in Los Angeles if not among anyone else, we will also see research being undertaken on the changing significance with age of relationships with one's therapist!

Jerrome (1990), in her study of frailty and friendship, considers that the importance of equity in friendships, as noted above, has been exaggerated.

Gerontologists, she suggests, have traditionally considered that friendship and long term ill-health, for example, are incompatible. Her own systematic observations of friendships among older people in the south of England also suggests how new friends may be made later in life, where 'equity' in the relationship is far from obvious to the outsider.

> Edna (81) describes Jenny (76) as her best friend and vice versa. They met seven years ago at the death of Edna's younger sister, who had been Jenny's best friend. Now Jenny is Edna's most frequent visitor. She has taken over the departed younger sister's role, performing a range of practical tasks, providing companionship and emotional intimacy. Seeing them together, the age gap seems much greater than five years. Edna adopts the role of passive dependent old woman while Jenny takes on the reciprocal role of cheerful, youthful helper, a link with the outside world. The relationship is mutually rewarding, though different items are involved in the exchange.
>
> (Jerrome 1990: 61)

A mutual satisfaction of emotional needs can give a sense of equity to a relationship even if the relationship appears unequal in terms of such things as reciprocal aid. And when a person is dying and cannot reciprocate, for example, friendships may often be bestowed as a gift. Jerrome suggests that in our culture, 'elderly friends measure a caring attitude by the ability to receive care without the need to reciprocate immediately'.

There is perhaps more potential within family relationships for a friendship-type of influence on self-esteem to be developed, than Ishii-Kuntz's (1990) review of the literature would have us believe. But as Jerrome (1990) herself notes, although friendship may sometimes have a protective quality that brings it close to kinship in the practical response to ill-health and disability, the affection between friends which underpins a caring attitude has the distinctive quality of a basis in choice rather than obligation. Perhaps the very existence of friends is beneficial, promoting self-esteem and a sense of worth.

One challenge for policy-makers in the future, therefore, is to acknowledge the importance of friendships as well as familial relationships in later life and to enable individuals to maintain and develop their friendships as well as find new ones. If friendships are more easily formed among age peers, for example, perhaps one should think more than twice before labelling age-homogeneous retirement complexes, and other residential schemes, as 'geriatric ghettos' which should be 'integrated' into mixed-age communities.

For men who outlive their wives, the problem of friendship formation may be particularly acute, as indeed it may be for men whose friendships hinged on occupational contact which is no longer available. With the greater partici-pation of middle-aged women in the labour force, it is likely that the importance of occupational contact as a basis for friendship will increase for women too. Whether they will be more able than men to sustain such relationships across retirement remains to be seen.

The notion that older men may be emotionally and psychologically relatively less well equipped than women to cope with the transitions and vicissitudes of later life is considered by Giesen and Datan (1980). They suggest that the myth that ageing is swifter and harsher for women than it is for men is, in reality, a double-edged sword. The women in their sample seemed to have acquired a wider range of occupational skills than their husbands and had encountered and resolved a greater range of emotional and material problems, and they had not had to leave their occupational world behind them as they aged. 'If prior skill, experience, and a sense of usefulness are determinants of successful aging, then the competent older woman, whom we have failed to recognize, is advantaged over men in the transition to old age' (p. 71). Perhaps this is one factor to be taken into account in explaining the consistently higher suicide rates of men in later life.

Living alone

We noted above that frequency of social interactions is a poor predictor of psychological well-being. Nevertheless, a relative absence of social interactions, as indexed by living alone, has often been suggested as making older people 'at risk'. Iliffe *et al.* (1992) suggest that while this notion historically may have had a basis in fact, their own study of 239 people aged 75 and over, identified from the age–sex registers of general practitioners, suggested it was no longer the case. As they point out, being alone may be mistaken for being isolated or be associated with being lonely, 'even though there is ample evidence that isolation and loneliness can occur within families and that elderly people living alone can have extensive social networks' (p. 1004).

It would be appropriate to acknowledge that many older people are enmeshed in complicated systems of mutually *inter*dependent relationships, as the discussion of carers and caregiving, which follows later, will suggest. Although living alone may not lead directly to clinical morbidity, as Wenger (1984) notes in her study of older people living in eight rural communities in north Wales, individuals living alone *are* more likely to feel lonely and to be isolated. Some 33 per cent of the older people in her study who lived alone were childless; put another way, half of those without children lived alone. Wenger suggests that, with increasing age, brothers and sisters may become more important, in part because they too share one's childhood and adolescence. They are among the few who have clear memories of one's parents, early home and growing up, and sometimes siblings who have never been particularly close may seek a closer relationship in old age if any threat of loneliness increases. In her sample, Wenger (1984: 80) found that contact with siblings increased after 75, with as many people in the over-85 category having at least a weekly contact with a brother or sister as those in the youngest (65–69) age range. Contact with siblings also increased after widowhood. Almost half of Wenger's sample saw a relative every day of their lives, as did over a third of those without children. For those with children, however, children were the relatives with whom most frequent contact was maintained.

Friends and neighbours

Arber and Ginn (1991) note that among people under the age of 75 living alone in more urban settings, women are more likely than men to be visited and to visit others in their neighbourhood, despite being, on average, less physically fit and more housebound. After age 85, women are less likely to make visits than men, due to their greater disability. Among her rural sample, Wenger found the numbers of those who never made a visit to relatives' or friends' houses increasing with age, with age 75 marking a steep decrease in visiting. Under the age of 80, some 25 per cent made a visit at least once a week. On Christmas Day, however, nine out of ten of the people in her sample visited family or friends.

Arber and Ginn (1991) suggest that the 'good neighbour' element of friendship may be more evident among older women than men, partly because it extends the caring role into which many women have been socialized. It also gives a sense of 'being useful', which many older women – in particular, those who live alone and who also have surplus time and income – express as a need. Despite living in rural settlements, 85 per cent of both men and women in Wenger's (1984) study felt they had 'real' friends living nearby. By the age of 90, however, this had fallen to 58 per cent. Wenger remarks how friendship and providing instrumental help were allied in the minds of many in her sample: a friend is someone you help or someone who helps you. But: 'Company and emotional support do not appear to be valued as highly by the giver as the performance of tasks, although the receiver may feel quite the other way!' (p. 97).

Confidants and clubs

While families may provide the linchpin of instrumental relationships, for women in particular, emotional sustenance may be also derived in the main from friendships. But having a confidant appears equally important for men and women – having someone to whom you can talk about life's joys, sorrows and uncertainties and with whom you can freely discuss personal problems. Having a confidant may even help ward off depression.

Wenger (1984) found 95 per cent of her sample had someone who fulfilled this role (while noting that some studies of older people in urban communities have found upwards of 15 per cent to be without a confidant). For those who were married, the majority confided with their spouse; for the never married, most confided in a brother or sister. Half of the widowed confided in a child and with advancing years children became more significant as confidants. Some 43 per cent of Wenger's sample had known their confidant for more than 50 years, some 75 per cent for 30 years or more. As Wenger (1984: 98) notes:

> The implications of this for communication in the context of shared knowledge and understanding those things which do not have to be said are obvious . . . What is reassuring is the apparent ability of the elderly to

adjust to the emotional shock of the loss of spouse or other confidant and to establish new confiding relationships.

Jerrome's (1993b) discussion of intimate relations in later life would suggest, however, that establishing new confiding relationships may be more of a challenge to older men than it is to older women. The clubs that older people – women in particular – may belong to can provide a setting for the development of friendships, confidants and forms of mutual support. But they may not be quite the place in which older men blossom, because as Jerrome (1993a: 96) notes, 'There, the assertiveness which develops over the course of a woman's life . . . can be seen in full flower. The members and leaders alike organize their affairs with vigour and a general disregard for the few men present, who are socially invisible'. In the conclusion to her study of settings for, and in the main run by, older people (many being 'pensioners' clubs'), Jerrome (1992: 189) remarks that:

> It is difficult to convey the vitality and intensity of life in the setting of old people's organisations. The richness of the experience for participants and its importance in their lives is summed up in the fervent remark, 'It's a life-line!'

Using participant observation as a research method to get to know some 170 members, Jerrome points out that people who voluntarily make a positive decision to join peers in the formal settings of old people's clubs and Christian fellowships are likely to differ from non-joiners in several respects: they are more likely to have already established social relationships, have high morale, and 'they share a model of ageing which stresses struggle and resistance'. Already likely to be better off also in terms of income and health, club members can reap the additional rewards of a practical, social and psychological nature. Companionships and a recognition of one's worth, as well as confirmation of one's identity, may be achieved with others familiar with the local culture and its history. Indeed, joining an organization may itself be proof to members of their ability to cope with ill-health and mobility problems and lead an independent and active life.

Nevertheless, Jerrome (1992) suggests such clubs are in decline, in part because the solidarity of members rested on an experience of hardship – the Depression and the Second World War – and in part because club members endorse 'a model of ageing which stresses activity and involvement and produces a reluctance in leaders to relinquish their control to the younger, fitter members' (p. 191). Jerrome (1992: 191) continues:

> Clubs and fellowships – the individuals in them, the groups they represent, the buildings and equipment, the ideas they express – are objects of attachment. Attachment in the psychological sense of strong feelings (both positive and negative) and emotional intensity characterises members' relationships with each other, with the group and the physical environment. It is sometimes assumed by younger people that with the loss of significant relationships the potential for attachment diminished [sic]

through the life-span. But though the objects of attachment may change, people go on being attached – to people, to groups and organisations, to beliefs and values, to places and possessions, and to the self.

Most older people, Jerrome suggests, are engaged in a search for social integrity, and other people are required for its attainment. In the process of attaining it in groups, they are likely to achieve companionship, interest and 'good company' – the title of her book. Should we, then, be striving to find ways to encourage and support group organizations for and run by older people, or indeed other voluntary initiatives run by older people for the benefit of others? Age+Resource (1992) is an organization set up to do specifically that. It seeks to foster the potential capacity of many older people to be actively involved with, and to find personal satisfaction in, a variety of activities which are both economically and socially viable, including self-help schemes in the community in which older people organize mutual support for leisure, health and social activities.

We shall return in the next chapter to the notion that such 'doing' can give rise to a sense of belonging. But here it is worth asking if the development of such groups, and others like the University of the Third Age, or the National Federation of Retirement Pensioners' Associations, is a defensive response, a consequence of the age-segregation found elsewhere in society and of the relative marginalization of older people? Or are age-segregated patterns of association initiated by some older people simply because they have a preference to associate with their peers, because peers can provide resources of various kinds that non-peers cannot? Jerrome suggests that members of the older peer group both support one another and preserve for one another the tragic sense of life; they allow growth with an acceptance of the finiteness of existence.

Grandparenting

An overtly positive conventional image of later life concerns grandparent–grandchild relations. It can be seen in advertisements for life insurance or pension schemes, where grandpa watches while little Sarah has a swing in the playground. Not everyone becomes a grandparent as we have noted, but the majority of us do. For example, it has been estimated that three-quarters of Americans and some 60 per cent of British people over the age of 65 are grandparents (Jerrome 1993b), and the number of people without descendants is likely to decline rapidly. Indeed, for the first time in history perhaps, some women may simultaneously be grandmothers and granddaughters.

The strongest feature of modern grandparenting is its diversity. Married or remarried grandparents may be very different from those who are single, divorced or widowed, and those in employment may be different from those who are retired, just as those who are 30 will be different from those who are 100. The myth that all that grey-haired grandmothers and pipe-smoking wheelchair-rocking grandfathers do is 'grandparent' needs laying to rest.

Troll (1985) suggests that grandparenting is generally a secondary activity in the lives of most grandparents unless they have reason to believe that their values are not being handed down, or unless trouble in the lives of their children leads them to pitch in and help. She continues:

> It is, therefore, not surprising that research has found that those older people who are most involved with their families have the lowest morale. It is true that grandparents are not necessarily old but one suspects that at any age, finding your children and grandchildren in trouble does not make for happiness. Besides, it is much more fun to do your own, new thing and be with your own friends than to repeat earlier behaviors, no matter how enjoyable they were the first time around.
>
> (Troll 1985: 149)

Clearly, longer life along with better health and early retirement (now taken by some two-thirds of men and half of women) may be redefining role possibilities within the family. Hanna (1993: 10) suggests that 'granddada taking a toddler on a slow trail through the park can give more time to childcare than when his own children were small; and grandmothers are promoting an economic role for their daughters that they themselves may have been denied'. Perhaps if men do become less assertive and less instrumentally oriented with age, they might also develop more potential and personal resources to sustain better relationships, which they can put into effect with their grandchildren, and become more 'generative', in the sense proposed by Erikson (1963), which we consider further in a later chapter.

Part of the diversity in grandparenting opportunities is influenced by the increase in the divorce rate. Paternal grandparents are more likely to have problems with access to their grandchildren than maternal grandparents, since divorced mothers still are more likely to bring up their children than fathers. Furthermore, paternal grandmothers are probably more likely to retain contact than paternal grandfathers. As Jerrome (1993b: 237) points out, the frustration of grandparents denied access 'has led to the formation of pressure and support groups such as The Grandparents' Federation'. Their legal position is more secure after the 1989 Children Act, which gives any relative or person important to the child the right to apply to the court as a suitable caretaker in a case of divorce. In previous years, when youthful illegitimacy was less tolerated, many grandparents brought up their grandchildren. It is reported, for example, that after the death of his mother, the actor Jack Nicholson discovered his 'sister' was in fact his mother and his 'mother' was in fact his grandmother.

In Wenger's (1984) study, it was noted that the photographs of grandchildren in many an older person's living room attested to the pleasure that grandchildren brought. While Wenger found that contact with children increased with the age of the subjects in her rural samples, contact with grandchildren did not. More than half of those with grandchildren saw at least one grandchild every week, and three-quarters said they were satisfied with the amount of contact they had. Wenger suggests this level of satisfaction is raised by rationalizations like 'They come as often as they can', or 'They've got their own lives to lead'.

The belief that grandparents fulfil an important need within family life is strong enough, suggest Thompson *et al.* (1991), to make both older and younger generations seek out substitutes. Perhaps this is where schemes linking schoolchildren to older people perform a useful function, because 'to be deprived of a grandparent can be almost as grievous for a child as to be deprived of a parent' (Lord Young of Dartington, quoted in O'Connor 1993: vi). It may also explain in part the success of some 'adult' fostering or placement schemes.

The fact that the grandparents' role *qua* grandparents embodies relatively few, clear rights or responsibilities, suggests a freedom of choice which might be somewhat challenging to exercise. When grandparenting is a major activity, it is usually because of problems being faced by the younger generations. When grandparenting loses its 'voluntary' nature, it can become a burden.

Although parents may exercise control over grandparents' access to grandchildren, the variety of relationships possible with grandchildren can be determined to some extent by the personal preferences of the grandparents and the extent to which they also choose to control the relationship. The lack of strictly defined role behaviours for grandparents legitimates both the question, 'What part do I want relationships with grandchildren to play in my life', as well as attempts to negotiate with one's children-as-parents to achieve mutually acceptable outcomes or compromises. Perhaps in the future, opting out of the grandparent role in the pursuit of self-development might increasingly have an appeal to older people who are affluent, active and healthy (the 'me' generation in old age?). But, the longer-term consequences of doing so might well be to weaken their inter-generational relationships, as well as their own sense of 'generativity': their feeling of contributing to the future.

Some of the grandparents in Thompson and co-workers' (1991) study felt that grandparenthood had given them a feeling of biological renewal, or a renewed sense of purpose in their life, but even those who spent a lot of time with their grandchildren were not explicitly involved in child-rearing: intervening here usually being resented and labelled as 'interfering'. Because of their traditional childcaring role, grandmothers appeared to be more easily 'brought into the family' than were grandfathers. It remains to be seen if the pressures on younger generations of males to become 'new men', to be more involved in childcare and more traditional 'housewifely and motherly' activities, translates in the future into their easier embrace into the bosom of three-generational families.

While just 'being there' and 'being taken for granted' might characterize a not unimportant, an almost symbolic, facet of grandparent–grandchild relationships, it appears to be men who are more likely to become socially invisible and lose sustaining relationships. Perhaps this is another factor contributing to the higher suicide rates of men in later life mentioned earlier.

Caring

In some societies, among Navajo Indians for example, the mutual caring obligations of women across generations, both upwards and downwards, remain. In modern western societies, responsibility upwards for one's parents in their old age is becoming less clear-cut. Although in Britain it is normatively accepted that adult children should do something to support their parents if the need arises, there is less broad agreement as to exactly what children might be expected to undertake. However, fiscal pressures and political decisions may lead governments to make some form of responsibility a legal requirement.

In Germany, for example, the European Commission subsidiarity principle is interpreted as meaning that first the individual in need of assistance is responsible for changing his or her situation, second his or her immediate family is responsible, third social security organizations, and finally social assistance organizations. 'Thus the notion of family responsibility is stated explicitly and dominates attitudes and feelings in such a way that help from outside the family is not taken for granted' (Jamieson 1990: 14). Conversely, in Denmark, state help is automatically expected, and adult children continue in a social relationship with their parents without feeling obliged to embark, in addition, into an instrumentally supportive one. In Germany, families with sufficient financial wherewithal can be made to pay for the domiciliary and residential care parents receive.

Grandparents who had no option but to care for their own frail parents may well not want to be a 'burden' to their own children, nor may they be keen to use all their savings or realize the capital value of their house in order to pay for care in their own old age. Many have intended such monies to be passed on to their children in their will. They may have assumed that, as members of a civilized society, they had been making lifelong contributions to the state so that state help would be forthcoming when needed. Enforced individual responsibility, of (older) people for themselves in the future, or of children for their parents, may produce more relationship problems than it appears to solve fiscal ones for the state. Already there are instances of children having to sell their family home, which they bought with some financial help from a parent, so that that parent could come and live with them, in order now to pay for the parent's institutional care. As Twigg and Atkin (1994: 9–10) point out:

> . . . caring takes place in a relationship. As important as the carer is the cared-for person. They, after all, are the reason why the caring exists, and it is the presence of their difficulties that transforms a family or social relationship into a caring one . . .
>
> Caring is embedded in relationships of obligation such as marriage, parenthood, kinship, in which people feel responsible for spouses, children or parents, and obliged to give care. These are not voluntary relationships, and these feelings of obligation have consequences for their lives – often, as we shall see, severe consequences . . .
>
> Public agencies cannot treat carers as they might more distant members of the informal network such as neighbours, where there is an assumption

that they will withdraw if the involvement becomes too burdensome. Carers pose moral problems to welfare agencies precisely because they cannot be assumed to pursue their own interests in a straightforward way.

Just as grandmothers seem to play a more significant role in the care of grandchildren, it is daughters who, by and large, play the largest role in the support of 'nan' or grandpa when spouses are no longer available to do so. Thompson *et al.* (1991) point out how heavy a burden this can and may continue to be, despite the availability of services such as home helps and meals on wheels, the impact of which they suggest has been exaggerated. Without appropriate support, the desire many people have to give care may be thwarted and the sense of belonging that receiving care can engender may become transformed into rejection or abuse. No-one plans to be the active or passive agent behind newspaper headlines like 'Why granny is down in the dumps' (Weale 1993), but the fact that the phenomenon of 'granny dumping' exists demonstrates how desperate and destructive relationships can become. Weale (1993: 13), for example, notes that:

> Preliminary results from a study of elder abandonment (doctors and carers' organisations reject the emotive tag 'granny dumping') revealed that at least once a year one hospital in three in England and Wales sees a case of 'complete abandonment' when an elderly person is found in the hospital confines and relatives are difficult or impossible to trace. One hospital claimed more than 20 such cases in a year.

In the same newspaper report, the clinical director of medicine for the elderly at St. Bartholomew's Hospital in London was reported as saying he saw a case of abandonment of the less dramatic kind once every three months: 'What we usually see is people presenting late, with exhausted carers who have limited help because they've not known how to go about getting it', and 'Even if they have, it's often not the help they need'. What impressed him was how the large number of relatives 'box on against the odds'. Under the headline '80-hour week for carers of dementia patients', Brindle (1993: 6) notes:

> Half the people caring for a relative or friend with dementia are having to do so for more than 80 hours a week and more than a quarter are spending at least £100 a month according to a survey by the Alzheimer's Disease Society . . . Twenty-per cent of those surveyed had been forced to take early retirement to concentrate on caring, one in four losing full pension rights, and 41 per cent had met costs by drawing on savings, taking out a loan, or selling property or other assets.

How might one resolve this state of affairs more acceptably in the future? *Answers for adult children of aging parents* is the title of an American magazine which encourages rational forethought and inter-generational discussion of the caring issues that will continue to confront us as we get older. There must be discussion of what care we are prepared to give, or to receive, and at what cost to whom. Should long-term caring be assumed to be a duty one takes up as 'a natural part of family life' with little or no support? Perhaps tailoring services to individual needs – often relief care at night, and easily accessible and more frequent respite care – should be one aspect of policy priority, if your answer is 'No'.

Twigg and Atkin (1994) remark that some older carers see the restrictions imposed by caring as little different from the other limitations of old age, and as a result make little attempt to seek help. Other older carers, like younger carers, may well want a chance to go out and enjoy themselves. 'As one young assistant social worker put it, carers in their fifties accept that "their days are gone". In such cases he would give support "as required . . . [but] would be careful not to overstep the mark"' (p. 136). It seems unlikely that, in the future, many people in their fifties will accept that 'their days are gone'! But understanding what community care services are, or should be available to support caring relationships, and knowing how to go about obtaining them, is something we should all feel confident about, although middle-class individuals as yet have the relative advantage in this respect. Should, for example, employers be encouraged to give employees paid or unpaid leave of absence for caring, or facilitate flexible or shorter working hours to enable carers to continue caring *and* working?

Dementia care

Although there are problems in generalizing about the community care of dementia sufferers, services to support carers do appear to be insufficient, patchy and uncertain. As Twigg *et al.* (1990: 76) point out:

> Simply obtaining help can be a major problem; one compounded by lack of knowledge and by some of the other forms of indirect rationing operating with the system . . . Few carers have received or been offered a variety of support packages sufficient to enable them to express a view as to their relative acceptability or effectiveness. One of the difficulties of asking carers about the effectiveness of support is that so many carers have little or no experience of services to discuss.

Carers are likely to continue to provide the majority of care, and caring relationships should be adequately supported so that they are mutually enhancing rather than destructive. But it is readily acknowledged that caring for someone with a dementing illness can pose particularly acute problems. For example, there may be a problem in the sexual aspects of marital relationships for the spouse carer, or in the fact that the person with dementia doesn't seem to be the same person he or she used to be.

> Spouse carers often want to get away from the other person's company, yet the person they most want to go out with is their spouse. Carers often experience guilt about enjoying themselves when the person they love cannot . . . Building up a separate social relationship may seem to

undermine the relationship, yet, at the same time, constantly being in each other's company creates enormous strains.

(Atkin 1992: 31)

Ways of intervening therapeutically when individuals with dementia become tagged with the unfortunate label of being a 'management problem' are considered in some detail by Jones and Miesen (1992). Sometimes, however, the greatest improvement in the mental health of carers of older people with a mental infirmity only comes with either the institutionalization or death of the person being looked after. The outlook, though, is not always so bleak. Farran *et al.* (1991), in their study of 94 family caregivers of individuals with dementia, suggest that even in difficult circumstances people can 'grow and find meaning through their caregiving experiences'. Caregiving, then, can be a source of satisfaction for some informal carers. Grant and Nolan (1993: 147) suggest that studies of informal carers 'have concentrated largely on the difficulties and problems of carers to the virtual exclusion of the gratifications and rewards that can be experienced'; 'caring can be a source of personal satisfaction for many individuals and . . . such satisfaction can co-exist with high levels of stress'.

It would appear, however, that it is factors in the social context of care, rather than the personal or dependency characteristics of the cared-for person, that are important concomitants of whether satisfaction is experienced. Grant and Nolan (1993) suggest that sometimes carrying on with caring is seen as the least worst option and hence as an achievement in itself, but that 'for families who wish to continue to care, the realization of rewards and satisfactions *from* caring is as justifiable a goal, and as meaningful to them, as the alleviation of stress' (p.156). They go on to suggest that the provision of information, counselling, educative approaches and respite services among others, all have something to offer, coupled with the adoption of empowerment models designed to assist family support, based as it often is on love and attachment. Even in – perhaps, especially in – dementia care, by supporting meaningful relationships with family and friends, and neighbours even, feelings of belonging and being wanted can be strengthened, and feelings of losing one's place, perhaps even fears of losing one's mind, may be lessened.

7

Belonging – place and purpose

People can be very attached to, and in a sense love, their home, neighbourhood and town. You can feel you belong to a place and that the place belongs to you. 'Charles wants me to go, he's had a room built for me. Our Norman has had a room built for me. But I'm not giving my little home up, and that's what upsets them. They think I shouldn't be on my own now. But I'm not giving up my home for nobody' (Thompson *et al.* 1991: 210). And as well as being attached to people and places, both pets and personal possessions come to have significant meanings for people, as Csikszentmihalyi and Rochberg-Halton (1981:101–102) note in their book *The Meaning of Things*:

> . . . the possibility that older persons may see their furniture as extensions of themselves or as a personal record of their memories and experiences is often ignored. Advice issued from government agencies stresses the importance of simple, hygienic, uncluttered rooms with the bare minimum of objects and furniture . . . From this viewpoint furniture is seen only in terms of its physical function, not a culturally defined 'frame' for structuring the experiential living space, thereby missing its importance as a means of establishing a sense of personal continuity and meaning in an otherwise impersonal environment. Yet if, as we have argued, the self of mature adults tends to be structured around networks of past and present relationships, which are often embodied in concrete objects, then depriving an older person of such objects might involve the destruction of his or her self.

Settings

McCready's (1985: 58) study of grandparents in white ethnic groups in America came to what might seem at first a surprising conclusion concerning their sources of satisfaction:

Although some of the findings concerning relative differences in the salience of the family are like those findings we see in the ethnographic literature, the more important fact may be the importance that so many of the older people attach to the place where they live, their home, or perhaps their neighbourhood . . . The role of the neighbourhood should take a much more prominent place in the research literature on the elderly – both as a social context for their lives and perhaps as an important source of satisfaction and support.

While living in a succession of different hotels in different countries may suit some film stars, many people feel their roots are in one location. Migrating after retirement to the north coast of Wales or the south coast of England, for example, or more recently to the 'Costas' of Spain, has always been a minority activity. It remains to be seen whether migration to warmer climes will increase in the future. Denmark began sending patients to Spain for rehabilitation and recovery some 20 years ago. Others also seek the sun for health reasons – as a form of 'balneotherapy' – as well as financial ones. Living abroad, for whatever motive, will be facilitated when getting access to one's retirement pension anywhere in the European Community becomes as easy as going to the local post office at home, and when the 'Europass' gives older people EC-wide access to travel concessions. Perhaps for some of the more affluent, taking to a life on the open road in campervans will be a retirement choice, as it has been for many Americans. However, headlines like 'Shadow over a new life in the sun' or 'A sour taste of paradise' suggest that the gleam of Eldorado may become somewhat tarnished if you become physically or mentally frail in a foreign land, where you may indeed begin to feel far from *home*.

Home and 'Home'

'Care and Repair' and 'Staying Put' schemes represent one practical way of helping some older people remain where most usually want to be – namely, in their own homes. Only a minority move to purpose-built retirement housing or apartments, sheltered accommodation, or into group homes like those provided by Abbeyfield. 'Life care communities', to which affluent persons might retire, and where as part of a package deal they would pay to be cared for, as and when necessary for the rest of their life, have been part of American retirement options for some time, but are only in the developmental stage in Britain.

In terms of such options, Sixsmith (1990: 173) asks: 'do we really know what the elderly want or do we as a society provide what we think they want, or ought to want?' Do we know what we would want for ourselves, and how can we help make it possible? For most people, the meaning of *home* has to do with family life, comfort, a place where you can do what you want. For older people, in particular, it is also likely to have something to do with having good neighbours and friendly people around, with memories, and a sense of ownership. For some their home is their refuge and for many it is a source of their sense of independence and personal control; it may literally and metaphorically be *terra firma*, as opposed to the 'sea of change' of the outside world (Sixsmith 1990: 178). Such 'external' changes may contribute to feelings of ambivalence about, for example, the neighbourhood, but feelings about *home* tend to be uniformly positive for most older people. It is little wonder, then, that a move from *home* to a 'home' can provoke feelings of loss akin to those of grief reactions to attachments severed by death.

Only for a very small minority of individuals does entry into a residential or nursing establishment become the 'positive choice' that, ideally, it should be. For many, the decision is effectively made for them by a relative or professional when a lack of other appropriate support services leads to some sort of crisis. Until 'homes' can genuinely foster residents' sense of independence, power and control, and self-worth, moves into them, understandably, will be resisted by and unwelcome to many.

The frailer older people are, the more likely it is that relocation may have deleterious health effects, sometimes making an earlier death more likely, although the evidence is less than clear-cut and positive outcomes have been reported (Danermark and Ekström 1990). But when addressing members of the Royal Society of Medicine on the topic of the interaction of physical and mental symptoms in older people, Grimley Evans (1991), a professor of geriatric medicine at Oxford University, noted that:

> Many elderly people adapt to deterioration in their intellect and memory by the progressive restriction of lifestyle and life-scope so that they no longer venture outside a familiar and repetitive environment . . . In settings such as these the victim's dementia gives rise to no functional problems since it is compensated by behavioural, environmental and social factors. Any disruption of the social or physical environment may precipitate acute decompensation as the patient cannot assimilate or adapt to new elements in his or her surroundings . . . Housing authorities should not move old people out of their homes for upgrading without appropriate consultation.

One moral of the story might be that individuals should give rational consideration to moving house and setting up a final home before 'old' old age is reached. But doing what you would *like* to do may become increasingly constrained by the consideration of how much of the cost of your future care you are going to have to pay for. Individuals might well postpone such decision-making if they are worried they might lose out financially.

Community care policies – which must include appropriate housing policies – should enable us to remain at home or to move, from choice, to more suitable settings which can become *home*. They should help us maximize the control we have over our lives, even when we are physically or mentally frail. Such 'care' is likely to enhance our quality of life, and indeed may prolong it. That people should feel they have to 'pay for their old age' by selling their homes in order to release capital to cover care and other service costs (while at the same time denying their offspring the inheritance they might have hoped to leave them), hardly seems a characteristic of a caring or civilized society, or of a welfare state to which they have made lifelong contributions.

Work and leisure

We have noted that a sense of belonging is engendered in relationships, both with individuals and with places. Along with a sense of purpose, it can arise also from activities undertaken in the company of others. For a significant number of individuals, a sense of belonging and purpose will have been derived from aspects of their working life as well as from their family. But working life eventually comes to an end, and to the extent that it fulfilled psychological functions – providing a routine, a sense of purpose, social contacts perhaps – its disappearance may represent for some individuals another significant loss.

Patterns of retirement have been changing, with fewer and fewer individuals continuing to work full-time after retirement, and more and more people – men in particular – retiring early (i.e. before the statutory retirement age of 65). However, whether this pattern will change remains to be seen. Early retirement gives the state an opportunity to control rising unemployment and provides employers with a means of rapidly shedding employees without involving industrial confrontation. But the social security implications of fewer individuals in the workforce contributing to the financial welfare of increasing numbers outside it have led to suggestions that early retirement should be discouraged and the statutory retirement age be increased. Furthermore, the financial implications for the individual volunteering for early retirement require close and expert scrutiny. Summarizing a Coutts Career Consultants Report 'Retire now – Pay Later', Smith (1991) notes how early retirement may look like a dream come true, until it transpires that the pension you get if you retire at 60 is double that which you might get at 60 if you actually retire at 50.

In the UK, the retirement age for females has been changed from 60 to 65 to bring it into line with that of men, as required by EC equal opportunity legislation. Had the official age of retirement been revised upwards in line with increasing life expectancy, it might currently stand at 70 and perhaps be nearly 75 by 2025 (Young and Schuller 1991: 10).

That age tells you relatively little about the performance at work of any particular individual is now well accepted and was one reason behind the adoption in Finland of a flexible policy towards retirement. If older people are to have equal employment opportunities, then employers' traditional prejudices about older workers will need tackling, perhaps through the encouragement of appropriate re-training schemes. Within the EC, some states have anti-age discrimination in employment legislation in place, while others have voluntary codes – as yet the UK has neither.

Retirement has become less of an 'all or nothing' affair – in work full-time one day, out of work full-time the next – even if this still happens to the majority of people. The route into detachment from the workforce has become more varied. People might be forced into early retirement or take it voluntarily; they may be made redundant; be among the group who have experienced one or more spells of long- or short-term unemployment and who have not been able to find work; they may become disabled or have long-term ill-health that precludes them from working; they may become unpaid carers; or they may indeed follow the 'traditional' path of working full-time until they reach the state retirement age of 65. Such routes, together with variations in access to occupational pensions and in health status, will markedly influence the patterns of life we can create for ourselves in what is increasingly, but perhaps unfortunately, called 'The Third Age'. Unfortunately, because much that is stereotypical and ageist about ageing might get uncritically lumped into a 'Fourth Age', one which you only enter at your peril.

The Third Age?

'Dear Mr. Slater', started the computer-personalized letter from the Association of Retired Persons (ARP), and continued:

The best years of your life

Why shouldn't the years after 50 be your happiest and most productive years? We believe that retirement and pre-retirement years are there to enjoy. But are you making the most of them?

ARP Over 50 can help you make new friends, lead a more active life and save money. At the same time you can join the other over 50s who are standing up for their rights on issues that affect you such as pensions and age discrimination in employment and the National Health Service. With a growing membership of 125,000 the Association is constantly campaigning on behalf of all the over 50s within the UK.

The leisure and self-development retirement lifestyle hinted at by the ARP, and developed almost into a philosophy for the future by Young and Schuller (1991: 20) in their book *Life After Work*, seems almost like a dream come true:

'An era of personal fulfilment' sounds very hopeful, and it would be wholly unrealistic to suggest that this is what necessarily happens in the third age . . . So when we refer to the third age in this way, what we are emphasising is its potentiality rather than its actuality. We are thinking of older people as having a certain kind of freedom – a negative freedom from coercion – which they may or may not convert into another kind of freedom, the positive kind. 'Freedom from' is contrasted with 'freedom for'.

This invites speculation as to when and how one wants to free oneself from work (assuming one is *in* work) and for what kind of life in retirement. Clearly, the more arbitrary and uniform retirement and pensions policies are, the less they will suit the preferences of individuals. Should there be a mandatory retirement age or could it become more a matter of individual negotiation?

Perhaps you want to work full- or part-time after the normal retirement age, or part-time for a few years before it. Such individual flexibility might be bureaucratically inconvenient, but the variety of options currently available within EC member states suggests it is not an impossible political goal, and it is certainly a desirable social and psychological one.

Given reasonable health and financial resources, just what potential is there for fulfilment in later life? For some, 'freedom for' may be a somewhat daunting and unmanageable prospect, which, along with other pressures, results in the leading of more passive home-centred leisure lives. Among Young and Schuller's sample of people between 50 and retirement age (who, for whatever reason, had left full-time employment within the past two years), one in three had what was termed a 'positive' approach to their life. The most striking fact was that:

> ... the positive people were engaged in activities which, in a way, resembled what they had done before. Many of them were engaged in 'work', although not paid work . . . a 'portfolio' of different bits of work – was for many the most satisfactory arrangement . . . Some of their portfolios included personal hobbies as well as a voluntary job in a church or some other organisation. This variety may itself go a long way to explain why many of them found the unpaid more satisfying than the single paid job they had had before. Perhaps it would have been better still if they had a paid part-time job as well.
>
> (Young and Schuller 1991: 150).

In the next century, perhaps, new kinds of people will emerge in large numbers who are less ready to put up with repetition in their lives than has been customary so far – people who are more 'leisure literate'. With one eye on the idealized image of retirement to the 'Costas' and life as one long round of golf, sea, sun, surf and gin and tonics, Young and Schuller (1991: 154) warn, however, that:

> The ever-present and growing danger is of increasing polarisation between those already better-off, with fine pensions, choice about when to retire, a range of opportunities for paid and unpaid work and an easy acceptance of their past and present status in a solidly male gerontocracy on the one hand, and on the other the marginalised people who are impoverished and insecure, without access to paid work, striving if they can to earn a few pounds in the black economy.

Education for life and leisure

Young and Schuller (1991) suggest that older people should be entitled to education vouchers to enable them, if they so want, to spend one year full-time, or its part-time equivalent, at an institution of higher education. Certainly, the idea of older people being actively involved in education in later life appears less novel, as public discussion about making education a lifelong experience gets noted under newspaper headlines such as 'Cradle-to grave-learning goals', which reported the proposals of the independent National Commission on Education. Furthermore, with the publication of books such as Peterson and co-workers' (1986) *Education and Aging*, the study of the topic has gained academic legitimacy. In the foreword to their book, Birren remarks (p. xiii):

Earlier in this century, no one would have expected that one of the tasks of education was going to be the fostering of personal growth in middle-aged and older adults . . . Our ideal is the self-constructing individual, the person who can transcend the bruises and limitations of the environment and exercises creativity in finding a pathway that is both productive and satisfying. Environmental opportunity is often limited and many persons do not transcend their environments; instead, with age, they become victims of the environment. It is at this point that education must intervene. Older adults have a need to develop strategies for good health, management of personal resources, finding durable interpersonal relationships in the face of family changes, and maintaining self-esteem in the face of change and stress.

At an annual conference of the Association for Educational Gerontology held in Keele, the focus was on the European dimension of education and training for an ageing society. There, Tom Schuller, as Director of Continuing Education at the University of Edinburgh, raised the fundamental question of whether education and training for older persons should be viewed as a right or a privilege, and put forward several arguments as elements of what was termed an 'advocacy gerontology':

Society cannot afford the waste in human capital from older persons' expulsion from the labor force at arbitrary ages nor the lost opportunity for postponing dependency.

Is it not likely that the 'use it or lose it' approach widely recognised in the medical field is also applicable to other areas of human activity, including human learning?

Intergenerational justice requires that special educational measures be directed to the cohort now entering the 'third age' because it is the last group *not* to have benefited from the post-war expansion of educational opportunities.

The traditional splitting of the life course into distinct periods of education, work and leisure is a model that is becoming increasingly inapplicable.

(Anon 1990: 48)

However, the opening speaker, Tom Mcghay – a member of the European Parliament – pointed out that much remained to be done to make the voice of older persons and their educational needs better known to decision-makers in the EC. Other participants pointed out that pre-retirement education should be more than a retirement ritual and company conscience saver. Rather, pre-retirement courses should provide the opportunity for participants to reflect on their situations and the degree to which they can influence the direction of change.

Older people as students are, however, making their presence increasingly visible in Universities of the Third Age, at local authority evening classes, or as students of the Open University. Yet a report by Tuckett (1994) shows that only 3 per cent of people over 65 are currently studying, compared with 10 per cent of the population aged 17 or over. One in five of the public also seemed to have swallowed the myth that they are too old to learn anything new, but as Glendenning (1991: 344) notes 'Old dogs can learn new tricks so why should they be denied the possibility of self-growth, self-knowledge, self-fulfilment and genuine enjoyment and satisfaction?' The challenge is to dispel the myth and make learning in later life more appealing to others than those who are middle-class and already relatively well educated. In an ageing society, strategies to equip people for continuing active citizenship, and for delaying morbidity, are vital.

Role models are needed who can't be dismissed as the exceptions that prove the rule; ones perhaps like those described by McGill (1994), who are neither film nor TV stars. Of Doris Van Hooydonk, he writes:

> When she retired at the age of 72, she signed up for all three courses available in her local school – swimming, German and old-time dancing . . . Now, aged 80, she is working for A-level German and GCSE Italian . . . 'When I fell last year and damaged my arm I could no longer drive, so the class formed a rota to take me to classes'. 'Just going to classes has opened up a whole new world for me. I have a wonderful circle of young friends, which helps to keep me young', she said.
>
> (McGill 1994: 3)

One response to the withdrawal or higher costs of courses, especially day-time courses, has been the do-it-yourself movement represented by the University of the Third Age. Founded in the early 1980s, UK membership stands at around the 38,000 mark, spread through some 246 local branches. According to Geoff Peacock of the Thamesdown U3A:

> 'It is the blurring of the distinction between "teacher" and "taught", this acceptance of responsibility for our own learning and helping others too, that makes a U3A group distinctive and innovative'. It is also possible to offer more courses more flexibly if people use their own resources.
>
> (McGill 1994: 3)

U3A also produces a newspaper, *The Third Age*, and it is noted in one of its publicity flyers that 'travel is also very popular and many U3As organise their own visits at home and abroad'. There is also a national programme of study holidays and residential activities where members of U3A mix together. At the Cardiff branch, talks given at a general meeting ranged from 'Living in Hong Kong' to 'Living with technology', and from 'Care and housing in the community' to 'Topical tips for gardeners'. For good measure there have been visits to 'Techniquest', the Wales Science and Technology Centre.

While some older people find a self-generated 'university' to their satisfaction, others want the 'real thing'. The Open University has some 75,000 undergraduate students of whom more than 3000 are aged 60 or over, and it is those in the 60–64 age range who are most successful academically of any age group. In a report by the Older Students' Research Group (1993: 3), it was noted that the very competent group of Open University students who were studied were not exceptional, 'but were indeed representative of older learners as a whole'. Like other older students in Europe, they too are predominantly middle-class and relatively well educated. Given that the generations of older people currently studying are relatively less well educated than those following, there is reason to be optimistic that learning in later life might become more broadly based than it is. It is certainly crossing national boundaries. The 'European Federation of Older Students at University' already produces a journal, *News*, containing information for older people about relevant welfare issues and matters concerning 'senior study'.

Maintaining and developing relationships, having a confidant, feeling you are 'at home', belong and have a place, as well as keeping up interests and contacts through engaging in volunteering, joining the bowls or walking club, being a regular at the day centre, or becoming a student, may all help – as the dog food advert used to run – to 'prolong active life'. They are certainly unlikely to hinder it. But many people may also find fulfilment in later life through what, for them, are forms of 'positive disengagement', perhaps in contemplation and solitude. Nevertheless, both for those who keep physically, socially or psychologically engaged, and for those who disengage either from choice or out of necessity, morbidity of one form or another leads to something we all have to face eventually – death: that of others and that of ourselves. Facing up to dying and death, accepting it and giving it meaning, looking forward to it even, are some of the topics we consider in the following chapters.

8

Looking back

A good look at the conditions of old age in our stage of history makes it obvious that we are all facing the prospect of a steadily increasing longevity in an unpredictable technological future – a future in which, in fact, it must first be proven that mankind as a whole can survive its own reckless inventiveness. From here on, old age must be *planned*, which means that mature (and, one hopes, well informed) middle-aged adults must become and remain aware of the long life stages that lie ahead. The future of these long-lived generations will depend on the vital involvement made possible throughout life, if old people are somehow to crown the whole sequence of experience in the preceding life stages. In other words, a life-historical continuity must be guaranteed to the whole human life cycle, so that middle life can promise a vivid generational interplay and old age can offer what we will describe as existential integrity – the only immortality that can be promised.

(Erikson *et al.* 1986: 14)

Restrospections

It may seem odd to suggest that looking back can help us look forward – that it is something we might plan to do even. Looking back in a particular way – as a process of reminiscence – is something many older people engage in. Judging by the enthusiasm by which it has been embraced by residential care workers, reminiscence as reinterpreted by Butler (1963) as part of the life-review, appears to have become seen as a necessary, if not quite obligatory, activity for older people to undertake in order to come to better terms with their own ageing and eventual death (Woodward 1988).

The concept has taken on physical form in 'reminiscence centres' like the one in Rochford Hospital, benefiting from the help of the *Challenge Anneka* TV programme. Here Southend Health Authority were helped to transform an old Nightingale ward into a 1930s-style tea-room and conservatory, plus an old-fashioned kitchen and fully stocked corner shop. In the tea-room, 'olde tyme' music hall acts take place most afternoons, and patients and visitors are able to buy coffee and biscuits.

'Reminiscence rooms' are a visible expression of 'something being done' for older people who hitherto may have simply languished in the day-rooms of psycho-geriatric wards. At Raikeswood Hospital in Skipton, North Yorkshire, 'the idea was to create a thirties-style sitting room to rekindle memories in patients aged typically between 85 and 90 . . . it echoes to the melodies of traditional music hall songs . . . and a wealth of photographs from the Bradford Recall and Recognition group, which was set up to promote reminiscence therapy' (Illman 1991: 33). And, in line with the importance of the meaning of 'things', the term 'reminiscentia' has been coined for cherished objects that serve as memorabilia in late life reminiscence (Sherman 1991). In Sherman's study of some 100 older people, a total lack of cherished objects was associated with significantly lower scores on a measure of positive mood.

Aids to reminiscence have evolved to live theatre. The Age Exchange Reminiscence Project has a theatre company which performs plays and musicals based on the writings of older people. The only project of its kind in Europe, from its inception in 1983 it has developed training programmes, workshops, books, tapes and videos, all aimed at facilitating reminiscence. 'The project has two main aims: to stimulate residents' memories in a creative and therapeutic way, and to pass reminiscence skills on to care staff' (Francis 1992: 16). But, if not undertaken with care, group reminiscing has the potential for producing a stereotypical view of life past – the 'good old war years', for example. Similarly, reminiscence performances without appropriate follow-up may become entertainment (no bad thing in itself), masquerading as therapy.

Age Concern organizes some thirty reminiscence courses a year, and as one of their training coordinators put it:

> I think people are bloody sick of just wiping bums in care. People don't just go in to it to do basic care, they want to have a real attachment to the people. Long-term residential care can be a time of loss. Reminiscence training tries to minimise that loss and introduces new areas to work on.
>
> (Francis 1992: 17)

Expressing a genuine interest in someone's past of necessity is a form of taking interest in that person as an individual, and helps him or her feel interesting – something positive in its own right. Reminiscence work helps residential staff get to know the people they work for better, and clearly fosters forms of interaction that are more meaningful and personal than those seen on many occasions (i.e. those which may be limited to functional requirements about eating, dressing, toileting and such like).

Even for individuals who are severely 'confused', reminiscence can be an effective activity, with 'engagement' being higher in reminiscence groups than even at very busy times on a ward, with verbal interaction being stimulated in particular. A person who is 'confused' may not know what they had for breakfast, but they may well be able to recall the coronation of King George in 1936. And they may be able to respond more to things with personal meaning that they can hold and touch than to slides and photographs; things such as ration books or skipping ropes, for example.

Of course, reminiscence may be one of the few, perhaps the only stimulating experiences on offer. Some might argue that a visit to a local museum with a section on the everyday life of the rich and the poor in the early part of this century, is more in line with the tenets of reality orientation. How orientating is a trip to another 'ward' in a hospital – a ward which has mysteriously become, transmogrified, as by a time machine, into a 1930s tea-room? As Hopkins and Harris (1990: 7, 9) note:

> . . . the predominance of this approach with semi captive audiences of working-class people emphasises the homogeneity of their experiences . . . reminiscence groups which stress the commonality of people's war-time experiences, and the solidarity in evidence at that time, may ignore other important features of the period such as continued class antagonisms, industrial strife and conflictual gender relations.

Continuing their critique of some of the organized reminiscence groups which are to be found in residential or continuing care settings, Hopkins and Harris note that too often the selection, deployment and evaluation of materials is very much in the hands of the service providers. They suggest that a more reflexive and open approach may lead to different ideas about which past experiences older people regard as important and about the sense they make of them. Reminiscence groups run the danger of implicitly reinforcing ageist attitudes to older people, by confirming a narrow view of them as conservatively preoccupied with personal memories and collective expressions of nostalgia.

But reminiscence groups are not completely confined to institutional settings. Reporting on community-resident older people's discussion groups of everyday life history, Sprinkart (1988: 51) enthusiastically asks:

> What is it that turns afternoons like this into educational events, into places of lively learning. What is it that changes worry-laden, one-dimensional thinking into a mode of thought which doesn't allow itself through powerlessness to be made speechless, even in the face of death, a mode of thought which in spite of the inevitability of death, generates hope, a joy of living and a healthy perspective on life?

Perhaps one function of a reminiscence group might be to enable anger at past injustices to be expressed, and illuminate for care staff and others how ideological forces have shaped the past with a view to understanding ways for change in the future. Sprinkart (1988: 61) considers that:

. . . social-historical work with life history can become a form of learning in which personal formative processes and political awareness coincide. The objectified reinterpretation of individual biographical experience can then form the basis of social as well as personal identity.

Life history *can* be conceived as oral history with a political agenda, wherein older people are cast as the actors who should help shape the future.

Haight's (1991) review of ninety-seven published articles on reminiscence revealed only seven where negative outcomes were reported, the remainder being positive or non-evaluative, and she concludes that clinicians should use reminiscing in their practice, and researchers should continue to define the variables that lead to successful reminiscing. This is a conclusion also drawn by Bornat and Adams (1991), who note that while reminiscing may be a meaningful, adaptive and enjoyable activity for many in later life, its long-term potential as a 'therapeutic' enterprise is more questionable. It can degenerate into 'diversion as therapy' or become simply another form of distraction. Moody (1988) somewhat sceptically suggests that, according to the therapeutic point of view, the working assumption is that life history activities help older people attain psychological integration:

. . . the psychological integration promised by the Romantic myth extending from Wordsworth to Proust and beyond. But now, we are told, instead of merely an aesthetic image of wholeness, therapeutic life history methods hold out a scientifically validated technique for accomplishing the goal of fulfilment in old age.

(Moody 1988: 13)

But whose goal *is* 'fulfilment' in old age? Does it assuage our guilt over the conditions of life for many people in old age to think that we can help 'them' become fulfilled through some process of psychic reorientation of a tranquillizing kind, which anaesthetizes them (and de-sensitizes us) to their painful realities?

Reminiscence and life review

By no means all older people reminisce or want to, and one wonders just to what extent 'informed consent' is obtained from individuals in residential care, some of whom might find 'reminiscence' an intrusion that is thrust upon them. In his study of reminiscence, Coleman (1986) interviewed and collected standardized data from twenty-seven men and twenty-three women, with an average age of 80, all of whom were residents of sheltered housing schemes. Over a two-year period, he met these individuals several times, getting to know them well on a personal basis. Of the fifty people studied, twenty-one indicated that reminiscence 'played a significant and positive part in their lives' (p. 40). But eight individuals who also reminisced dwelt on the past in ways which gave them few satisfactions, their retrospective views of themselves being in some way unacceptable. Some fifteen people did not reminisce and saw no point or purpose in it. What they shared in common was a belief that, for them, there were other, better ways of coping with life in old age.

In the euphoria of psychologizing reminiscence into a form of therapy, of being able to give older people nearing the end of their lives 'some really useful psychological work to undertake', there has been a tendency to consider those who find reminiscence irrelevant as part of the 'awkward squad', like those who don't want to do other activities laid on in residential care settings. Coleman, however, suggests that the fifteen people whom he studied who had a dismissive attitude to reminiscence seemed as equally adjusted to the stresses of later life as those who had a positive, valuing attitude to personal memories. However, another six of the older people studied actively disliked reminiscing and expressed a distinct uneasiness about thinking of the past. This was the group described in a chapter titled 'Loss and depression', a group of individuals who perhaps might have benefited from help with resolving past problems which were still of psychological concern.

Coleman (1986) suggests that the four orientations to reminiscence should be viewed as dynamic characteristics whose presence was felt at times more strongly and at other times negligibly in individuals' thoughts. Even in those whom Coleman identified as nearest to the state of 'integrity' – the end-state which Erikson (1963) suggested must dominate over despair, if 'wisdom' is to be achieved – attitudes of serenity and hope fluctuated: 'even the most cheerful person knows at times what despair is'.

Although 'creative reminiscing' needs distinguishing from brooding on the past, there are those who are more sceptical about the value of reminiscing at all, largely because it involves looking backward rather than living in the present. Coleman (1986: 160), too, notes that:

> For some the past is genuinely over. Experiences, positive and negative have been fully assimilated. A state of serenity and inner peace has been reached, living in the present and just 'being' are now the goals. Others will be more oriented to the present because their current life situation invites them to be so involved. For others it will be a natural preference.

But how many older people find themselves 'invited' to look backwards because little in their current situation invites them to look forward – because there is nothing better to do? Woodward (1988) notes how reminiscence has to some extent sentimentalized 'the elderly', making us feel anything they recall is worthy of reverence or that any insight they express must have the glow of wisdom about it, rather than banality. It is natural to want a satisfactory old age for ourselves, but do we need to take action towards it rather than cognitively reconstructing our view of it? We run the risk of wishing away dark and tragic portraits of old age, which is perhaps one reason why Simone de Beauvoir's book on old age, *La Viellesse*, met with a wave of censure in the USA in particular, where it was published under the euphemistically 'positive' title, *The Coming of Age*.

Butler's (1963) view that we need to resolve guilt over past action or inaction, and to come to terms with loss and depression in order to accept our ageing and death, seems somewhat at odds with the advice of (the young) Dylan Thomas, who, like the rock singer Neil Young, seemed to consider that 'It's better to burn than to fade away'. Going out with a bang rather than a whimper seems to reflect juvenile romanticism, perhaps?

> Do not go gentle into that good night,
> Old age should burn and rave at close of day:
> Rage, rage against the dying of the light.

Woodward (1988) notes that both Butler and de Beauvoir agree that at the root of an older person's interest in her past is her evaluation of life in the present (which implies a question about satisfaction), and the imminence of death. But whereas Butler sees reminiscence as positive, for de Beauvoir the past is only a weight or burden and reminiscence is an ignoble means of escape. De Beauvoir sometimes seems like the group of Coleman's subjects who don't reminisce because it is emotionally threatening, and sometimes like those who feel it serves no purpose. For de Beauvoir, only 'projects', which give one something purposeful and meaningful to do and which lead on into the future, are positive. Of course, with death somewhere around the corner, the nature of the 'projects' need tailoring to circumstances; perhaps *in extremis* tending to a window box, for example.

One of the predominant metaphorical elements in Butler's presentation of the life review is the figure of reconciliation, of the ends of a life being knitted together, of the satisfactions of resolution. For de Beauvoir, identity is not 'solidified' in the old age of frailty, but rather 'evacuated' (or emptied, as has been suggested happens in a more obvious way in the dementias). But Woodward suggests that denying selfhood to the frail, as de Beauvoir seems to do, dispossesses them of themselves, of their selves which have now changed. De Beauvoir appears to project her own inability to accept – and her distaste for – old age into her description of it, which in turn seems to reflect the particular texture of her own mind. Butler is for acceptance, de Beauvoir is for struggle. Butler challenges psychic repression, whereas de Beauvoir challenges social repression. As Woodward (1988: 36–7) notes:

> . . . their two views represent opposing cultural and personal choices regarding aging in Western society . . . it is certain that many people working and writing in the field of aging studies project their hopes and fears – or reproduce aspects of their own temperament – onto the inchoate period to which we affix the label 'old age'. Important as it is, Beauvoir's own work is a case in point.

But so too may be Butler's, and there is little doubt that such projections exist in this book. For example, I personally feel that since death is inevitable, one should accept it and try and 'leave' the way one chooses to. But why should Butler's and de Beauvoir's views be seen as opposing? Perhaps they can be complementary and mutually useful? Surely there are both psychic *and* social forms of repression to be tackled? But if, as Woodward suggests, contemporary western societies deny late old age through a form of psychic cultural repression, of which, paradoxically almost, de Beauvoir's writing might be an example, we should perhaps reflect on the extent to which we too are complicit in it.

9

Finding meaning

Writing of his work as a pastoral counsellor with twenty-six chronically ill older people living in a hospital in Helsinki, Gothóni (1990: 70) notes that:

> . . . to ask questions and to find answers regarding the meaning of life is a matter everyone has to do in her or his own way . . . an elderly patient usually has plenty of time to reflect upon his or her life, discover its meaning and accept the course life has taken with all its failures and successes, changes and limitations, as unique and good after all. This means rebuilding one's self-identity despite the changes in the body and cultivating one's personality despite changes in the culture and the social networks.

Has life a purpose?

Discussing meaning, particularly the meaning of life, like the discussion of wisdom, tends to raise smiles. Was 'the meaning of life' a Monty Python episode? Perhaps it can in part be approached through a series of questions: 'What would it mean to you if . . . : you won the pools; you couldn't play golf anymore; your teenage son died in a car crash; you learned a new language; you lost a cherished possession; you got an OU degree; you were told you had terminal cancer and ten months to live?' Dittmann-Kohli (1990) investigated the topic by getting a sample of older and younger people to complete sentence stems like: 'When I think about myself . . .'; 'Perhaps I can . . .'; 'I am afraid that I . . .'; 'In the next few years . . .'. In reporting her findings, she asks:

> How is it possible that the elderly, on the one hand, are aware of many adverse facts of old age and anticipate threatening events but, on the other hand, do not express negative feelings about themselves and their lives.

Why does the younger group, whose members seem to be in the best period of life course, demonstrate more negative and ambivalent attitudes to self and life?

(Dittmann-Kohli 1990: 288)

The answer she gives is that older people change their frames of reference and standards of self- and life-evaluation. For example, 'they stop wanting things no longer available.' But 'such strategies as downward comparison or devaluation of reference standards' seem to echo the resident of the old people's home who said, 'You get used to anything over time, don't you; if you have to?' Which elements do we 'have to', and which can actually be changed? Turning to the present and generating positive meanings about the current situation and self is understandable when there seems to be 'little future'. But how much do we ourselves contribute to the circumscription of what future there is?

'Meaning' is hard to quantify, as Reker's (1991) cross-sectional study of 'provisional' and 'ultimate' sources of meaning across the life-span shows. Like others, Reker suggests that individuals discover meaning from the givens of life (ultimate meaning) and create (provisional) meaning through exercising choice, taking action and entering relationships. Provisional meaning might come from leisure activities, personal relationships, or tradition and culture, for example. He adopts Frankl's (1979) conviction that the full meaning of life can only be achieved by transcending self-interest, and suggests that provisional meanings exist at different levels of comprehensiveness. At a low level there are those derived from hedonistic pleasure and comfort (self-preoccupation); then there are those concerning the development of one's potential (individualism); at the third level are those derived from service given to others or to societal or political causes (collectivism); and at the highest level 'the individual entertains values that transcend individuals and encompass ultimate purpose' (self-transcendence) (Reker 1991: 4). Using romantic metaphorical imagery, Reker describes life as a tapestry, woven from meanings derived from different sources and levels of comprehensiveness, resulting in (for some) 'a beautifully integrated and pleasing mosaic'. And for others, no doubt, something more like the chaotic splodges of a Jackson Pollock.

Reker's (1991) brave, though some might think misguided, attempt at quantification in this conceptual minefield led him to construct a measure of the 'purposive' and 'coherence' aspects of 'ultimate meaning'. Purpose referred to having life goals — a sense of direction; coherence referred to 'having a logically integrated and consistent intuitive understanding of self, others, and life in general' (p. 12). The measure comprised a 12-item, 7-point Likert scale of such statements as: 'I have discovered a satisfying life purpose' and 'The meaning of life is evident in the world around us'. After offering caveats about cohort effect and cause–effect issues, Reker concludes that his data support the notion that individuals who create meaning by transcending self-interest are those who experience a greater degree of 'ultimate' meaning in life, and that a greater diversity of sources of meaning contribute to higher levels of psychological well-being. He also found evidence of a shift to sources of provisional meaning that transcend self-interest among the older people in his sample, and that females derive greater meaning from sources reflecting self-transcendence than do males. Is this further evidence that older men tend to have more difficulty than older women in extracting a satisfactory meaning for their lives?

Kimble (1990), in a paper entitled 'Aging and the search for meaning' asks the question 'Is growing old worth one's whole life to attain?' This book's answer to that question is that we have to work at it to make it so, for ourselves and for others. Now that the struggle for human survival for many in the west has subsided, the question has emerged – survival for what? Kimble cites Frankl as suggesting that ever more people today have the means to live, but no meaning to live for – except to consume, perhaps. Some will sympathize with Kimble's belief that there is a widespread spiritual malaise and confusion over the meaning and purpose of life, particularly in old age. Little wonder, perhaps, when the advertising hoarding asks 'What is the most used word in the world after OK?', and the answer you get is 'Coca Cola'. What happened to God?

Kimble espouses a 'hermeneutical phenomenology' which he sees as a revolt against the attempt to replace the world of everyday experience by a system of meanings organized by science, which inevitably suggest determination, whether social or psychological, leading individuals to feel they have little control or responsibility for themselves. According to Kimble (1990: 118):

> The awareness of possibilities and the understanding that an individual is a deciding being conveys hope. Hope must be seen in relation to freedom. To be free is to stand before possibilities. It is to transcend the present situation and see one's capacity to alter the *status quo*, even if limited to one's own attitude toward unavoidable suffering.

Do we choose to change what is within, or what is without? For Kimble (1990: 124) as for Frankl, 'the spiritual core of a person is recognized as capable of taking a stand not only toward negative and painful external circumstances but also toward its own psychological structure'. The future remains to be shaped; it is to some extent at the disposal of our responsibility. According to Kimble (1990: 126), it is religion that 'has the inescapable challenge in this technocratic age to try to bring wholeness to older persons plagued with the brooding sense of emptiness which characterises . . . the sickness of our time'.

We shall return to the part that religion plays in people's lives later. Here we briefly turn our attention to another suggested 'goal' for older people as they move towards the end of their life – the achievement of wisdom.

Wisdom, and successful ageing

Erikson *et al.* (1986) consider that towards the end of one's life two pervasive senses are in tension. One they label 'integrity', the struggle to integrate the strength and purpose necessary to maintain a sense of wholeness despite disintegrating physical capacities; the other they label 'despair'. Clearly, later life brings many quite realistic reasons for experiencing despair. We may wish many aspects of the past had been different; we may be in unremitting pain; the uncertainties of the future may be frightening. They suggest that the sense of integrity needs to be dominant if 'the final strength' (p. 37) of later life – wisdom – is to emerge. Their definition of wisdom is 'detached concern with life itself, in the face of death itself'. We shall meet others.

The most inescapable thing in life is death, that one aspect of the future which Erikson *et al.* suggest is both wholly certain and wholly knowable. They also suggest that, throughout life, the individual has on some level or other anticipated the finality of old age, experiencing an existential dread of 'not-being'. At a point in the life-cycle where far more life has been lived than remains, the challenge is, they consider, for the person to consolidate a sense of wisdom with which to live out the future, and to place him or herself in perspective among those generations living, and to accept his or her place in an infinite historical progression. In the effort to do this, the individual will have to admit legitimate feelings of cynicism and hopelessness in a dynamic balance with feelings of human wholeness. Wisdom devoid of elements of despair could become presumptuous. Erikson *et al.* (1986: 288) note that:

> To have experienced this world and our human inadequacy to deal with one another and our mutual problems in living and growing is consistently to know defeat. To balance this pull of despair, which may well increase with waning strength, we need to muster all the ingredients of the wisdom we have been garnering throughout the life stages.

And what are these ingredients of wisdom? Erikson *et al.* suggest in part it is a realization that prejudice is maladaptive and impertinent, since 'with age one is forced to concede how little one knows'; and it embraces an understanding that situations are complex and many factors have to be distinguished. These facets are echoed in Birren and Fisher's (1990) overview and integration of the elements of wisdom as presented by the authors of chapters in Sternberg's (1990) edited volume, *Wisdom: Its Nature, Origins and Development*. In that book, some authors are cited (p. 325) as suggesting that 'wisdom is an intellectual ability to be aware of the limitations of knowledge and how it impacts [*sic*] solving ill-defined problems and making judgements'; 'knowing that one does not know everything'; 'an awareness of the fallibility of knowing – a striving for balance between knowing and doubting'. Others suggest that wisdom 'involves recovering age-old types of knowledge that have been forgotten'. For some, integration holds a key: 'a multidimensional balance of cognition with affect, affiliation and social concerns'; 'a dialectical integration of all aspects of the personality, including affect, will, cognition, and life experiences'; 'the organismic integration of relativistic dialectical modes of thinking, affect, and reflection – *a perspective on reality* developed within interrelationships'. For others, wisdom is 'closely associated with problem-finding ability – a fundamental process of reflection and judgement'.

Putting an overall perspective on this variety of propositions made about wisdom, Birren and Fisher (1990: 326) suggest that:

Wisdom is the integration of the affective, connative, and cognitive aspects of human abilities in response to life's tasks and problems. Wisdom is a balance between the opposing valences of intense emotion and detachment, action and inaction, and knowledge and doubts. It tends to increase with experience and therefore age but is not exclusively found in old age.

As the old expression goes – 'some people never learn'; so perhaps Tennyson was wrong on at least one count when he wrote:

A young man will be wiser by and by;
An old man's wit may wander ere he die.

Birren and Fisher present wisdom as a dialectic – a form of resolution of contradictions – in particular concerning the rejection of limitations on the one hand and their acceptance on the other. Wisdom is tested, they suggest, by situations in which we have to decide what is changeable and what is not.

Joan Erikson (1988) is more specific in her characterization of the attributes of wise people, listing ten 'character strengths' associated with wisdom:

- a capacity for appropriate dependence;
- an acceptance of the life-cycle from integration to disintegration;
- resilience, essential to recover from the adversities which can beset us in old age;
- empathy for the experiences of others;
- humour, which enables one to turn things around and upside down;
- humility, a prerequisite for learning throughout life;
- a sense of the complexity of living;
- recognition of the complexity of sustained relationships;
- caring for and about people and the world; and
- an existential identity which transcends the self and attends to intergenerational links.

Baltes *et al.* (1992) take a more pragmatic approach to the topic, perhaps because this is to some extent necessary in an attempt to examine wisdom empirically, through the analysis of data collected by social scientific means. Rather like Reker (1991), in his study of ultimate and provisional meaning, they 'boldly go where no man has gone before'. For Baltes *et al.* a main component of wisdom is 'expertise in the domain of fundamental life pragmatics', such as in life planning or review. It requires rich factual knowledge about life matters, rich procedural knowledge of life problems – about likely causes and effects – and an understanding of the influence of contexts, values and priorities, as well as an understanding of the unpredictability of life.

While the Eriksons suggest that wisdom is a desirable outcome of the tension between integrity and despair, Baltes *et al.* place it firmly in the context of 'successful ageing'. Clearly, all have in mind an 'end-state' they see as desirable, but which many of us are going to find it hard to achieve without the appropriate cultural support. Judged in reference to these frameworks, many of us are going to be found wanting. Rather than sensing we are 'good enough' in our ageing, we may – paradoxically – by being made to feel that someone could be giving us 'marks out of ten' for the way we are ageing, be reinforced as 'ageing under-achievers', or feel we are 'ageing failures'. When, as Baltes *et al.* (1992: 138) put it, 'older adults can be among the top performers' on tests of wisdom-related knowledge, we may fear trying in case we don't quite come up to scratch.

Earlier, reference was made to Woodward's (1988) comment that people working in the field of ageing may project their own temperament onto their subject matter. How, then, do we interpret Baltes and co-workers' finding that clinical psychologists perform better than controls on tests of wisdom-related material? There may be some temptation to sketch the wise person in one's own image. Workshops on 'Growing older and growing wiser', or movements like 'Ageing to Sageing', which invite one to harvest the experience of a lifetime and promote 'spiritual eldering' may, not surprisingly, have an appeal to like minds. But some of us will not feel competent to join the club and have yet another reason for feeling inadequate. As Thomas (1991) notes, definitions in this area are often based, implicitly or explicitly, on value judgements, but conceptions of desirable end-states, personalities or lifestyles vary from culture to culture, as well as over historical time.

Religion and spirituality

To make his point, Thomas recounts dialogues with three 'religious renun-ciates' – older men of the Hindu faith living in India who had renounced secular life. He writes:

> If we are to come to an understanding of maturity, or wisdom, or whatever term is used for optimal personality development, it is clear that we cannot limit our investigation to Western societies, let alone elderly adults residing in 20th century North America. Indeed, there is reason to believe that our society militates against elderly adults attaining either maturity or wisdom, which would make it even more suspect as a sole source of one's definition.
>
> (Thomas 1991: 212)

Hindu beliefs outline four *ashramas* or stages of life: the student, the householder, the religious seeker and the religious renunciate. Though few reach the final stage, the ideal provides agreed-upon guidelines to aid individuals in their later years. Thomas suggests that a significant contribution of the *ashrama* model is the sanction it gives the older person for engagement in contemplation. The ethos of western society, in popular culture and often in advice from gerontologists and other professionals in the ageing field, tends to extol the virtues of active modes of ageing. Older people in India, however, have cultural support to engage in reflection. They are relatively free, suggests

Thomas, from pressures to live the second half of the life-cycle by the agendas of the first.

Thomas: Are you afraid of death?

Baba Ramshiva: One should not be afraid of death [speaking emphatically]. There is no need to fear death. It is definite the moment a person is born. To have birth is to have death. Both religious and non-religious will die. But the soul never dies, only the body changes. Like the pants and shirt you are wearing, when the body is old you will cast it off.

What happens, though, if you don't believe in a soul or have no religious or spiritual convictions, when you have to search for your own private meaning, and when an absence of norms and values makes looking forward something of a daunting do-it-yourself project? Does a sense of fulfilment in later life require a larger supportive cultural context and framework of meanings of the kind that religion has provided, or are secular solutions possible?

Honour thy father and thy mother: that thy days may be long upon the land which the LORD thy God giveth thee.

(Exodus 20, v. 12)

The only one of the ten commandments to offer a reward offers longevity, and it may seem a little ironic that older people appear to have least respect in those cultures where Christianity predominates. Do the children of a more secular age – 'the first generation without God', as the bookshop poster I passed today put it – understand the needs of some of their elders, their metaphorical fathers and mothers, for religious and spiritual engagement?

In a paper titled 'Inner beliefs', Froggart (1991: 15) writes:

Those people who are elderly now mostly grew up in an environment which included religious practice. The development of a sense of the spiritual involves a recognition of the presence of God within life. Where this has been built up, it is something which cannot be denied or ignored by the individual without real damage to the sense of self. The rituals of religion give a rhythm and purpose to life. For those becoming older, habits of spiritual expression are a comfort and support. Many elderly people can sustain their spiritual life for much longer than they can deal competently with a shopping list.

But there are problems here. As Koenig (1990: 24) points out, considerable interest has focused on whether religious behaviours and cognitions 'are indeed healthy coping responses, or, rather, reflect underlying pathology in an unstable and insecure individual'. Jung saw religious conviction as healthy, Freud considered it neurotic. For Freud religion was something created by man to help him deal with his insecurities and helplessness in the face of the powerful uncontrollable forces of nature – such as ageing and dying. Jung, however, noted that people have always and everywhere spontaneously developed religious forms of expression and that from time immemorial human experience has been shot through with religious feelings and ideas.

Jung considered those who cannot see this aspect of the human psyche to be 'blind', and whoever chose to explain it away, or 'enlighten' it away, to have no sense of reality. Our own convictions in this area will obviously inform (or constrain) our understanding of the place religion and spirituality has, or could have, in our own life and in the lives of others.

The positivism of science is often blamed for undermining religious and spiritual forms of understanding, but many scientists need religion to derive meaning and achieve it by locating God outside the universe defined by science. For others, perhaps, science has become the new religion, one which in an increasingly secular society supplies the root metaphors for meaning, one which has removed the positive metaphors that the church and theology have traditionally proposed to give meaning to growing old, death and dying. Spirituality may not require religion, as a succession of humanists have demonstrated, but many would consider that it helps.

James E. Birren, some of whose publications we have already referred to, is an eminent scholarly researcher and academic psychologist in the positivist tradition. In later life, he has become the 'grand old man' of psycho-gerontology. It is interesting to note how he has turned his attention to the topics of wisdom and spiritual maturity. Indeed, he has devised courses in 'psychological development through autobiography'. This suggests a not insignificant development in research and teaching orientation, one might think. Birren himself suggests that in the later years many people shift in the direction of introversion, and this increased internal focus lends itself to a more spiritual outlook. Here, let us examine some empirical studies of personality, before we turn in the next chapter to a more theoretical discussion of other forms of adaptation in later life.

Personality

Personality has often been described in terms of 'types' or 'traits'. Types suggests discontinuity, in that you get labelled as one type of person rather than another. It suggests that there are a certain number of individuals of a similar sort who, by their similarity, are sufficiently different from other sorts, to be worthy of a label. Traits are more suggestive of finer degrees of differenti-ation. With regard to types, for example, in a study of adult development, Shanan (1991) interprets his data as suggesting that some individuals in later life can be characterized as 'active integrated copers'; they are people who are hard working (but not at the expense of family life) and concerned with the welfare of the community; they are dependable and honest. As with most typologies for older people, the conception of 'personality' blurs somewhat into a consideration of 'patterns of adjustment' as evidenced in a much-quoted but seldom replicated study by Reichard *et al.* (1962). This introduced, for example, types of people who were 'mature', 'rocking-chair men' or 'arm-ored'. Shanan suggests that active integrated copers are, on the whole, socially well integrated and adjusted. He identifies other types: the 'failing over-coper', the 'tired hero' and the 'disenchanted moralist'. In order to escape the danger of providing a spuriously scientific basis for stereotyping older people – as in 'Dad's turning into a grumpy type' – others have talked of 'styles' or 'forms' of ageing, or even 'fate-determined trajectories'.

McCrae and Costa (1989), after an examination of what is perhaps the most popular 'type' indicator – the Myers-Briggs – concluded that the sixteen 'types' did not appear to be qualitatively distinct, and that 'personality dimensions do not appear to interact to form distinct types of persons' (p. 34). According to Costa and McCrae (1992), personality is best described on five factors or dimensions: neuroticism, extroversion, openness to experience, agreeableness and conscientiousness. Each dimension has several sub-facets. For example, agreeableness comprises elements of trust, straightforwardness, altruism, compliance, modesty and tender-mindedness. This trait approach is purely empirical and descriptive; it provides no explanation for the origins of personality, nor for the mechanisms that account for individual differences in profiles.

After reviewing the literature and presenting much of their own evidence, Costa and Macrae conclude that individuals have pervasive and enduring characteristics which influence their thoughts, feelings and behaviour. In short, they propose that whereas 'personality' might change in the early years up to young adulthood, thereafter it is remarkable for its continuity. Although there may be age-related changes in specific behaviours, by and large they do not amount to changes in personality. Even the 'changes in personality' associated with dementia are usually much less in evidence than the intellectual changes. For the personality as a whole, Costa and Macrae conclude that the total picture is one of remarkable consistency across time.

There may, however, be some changes over time in individuals' scores on sub-facets of the trait dimensions. They suggest, for example, that increasing age may be associated with lower 'impulsiveness', 'excitement seeking', 'openness to fantasy', and 'openness to values' scores, and with higher 'straightforwardness' and 'modesty' scores. Lower scores on openness to values, they suggest, may be one example of the influence of generational differences as opposed to age changes. Interestingly, the few men who changed seemed, if anything, to exhibit a decline in activity and openness to feelings and ideas scores, but an increase in openness to fantasy scores.

Field and Millsap (1991) in a separate longitudinal study of personality 'in advanced old age' (forty-seven respondents were aged 74–84 years and twenty-seven were aged 85–93 years), found that 'agreeableness' increased slightly over time for more than one-third of responents. Agreeableness was considered to be a dimension influenced by socialization (while 'extroversion', for example, was considered to be more biologically based). Extroversion seemed to decline somewhat, while other traits remained stable.

What are we to make of these interesting results? Does one become more open to fantasy and less open to feeling when reality becomes harder to bear? Socialization implies the influence of external factors, as does the notion of generational differences. Do we socialize older people into becoming more agreeable because they realize that being disagreeable will not get them anywhere (although it might get those with more power somewhere). Who wants to be labelled with the stereotype of 'disagreeable and cantakerous old sod'? Who wants to fill the stereotype of the miserable moaner, going on perhaps about their aches and pains and the injustices inherent in poverty?

According to Field and Millsap (1991), 'agreeableness' describes a person who is open-minded, cheerful and accepting. As far as the latter two elements are concerned, might it not be the psychologically defensive response of individuals who have little alternative, those 'who get used to anything, over time, if they have to'. Better to cover stoicism with a socially acceptable veneer? And how much of a decline in extroversion is due to a change in the underlying energy level which outgoing activities may require, and how much due to expectations of what is 'appropriate at your age' and lack of opportunity to actually do what you want to do? Perhaps more of us need the courage and support to 'grow old disgracefully' and to be more demanding and disagreeable.

How much of personality change in later life, where it exists, is due directly or indirectly to the social and economic circumstances in which older people find themselves? As several writers point out, the notion that older people become more 'grumpy' is an incorrect stereotype. But maybe they should be. There is, after all, enough to be grumpy about. Are we to be expected to become so 'agreeable' that we agree to being dispensed with? As Woollacott (1994: 16) notes under the headline 'When people in the margins are pushed off the edge':

> At the other end of life, there is a clear possibility that the new animus against the aged evident in all industrial societies could produce, by a combination of cuts in medical care and pensions and morale factors arising from a sense of being unwanted, an increase in the death rate in this sector of the population. The change in attitudes toward the old has to be, in part, a result of the changing economic situation. If employers have little need for lifetime labour, they have less reason to support the state's system of care in old age . . . people are seen as a liability not an asset . . . people are becoming surplus to requirements.

10

Reconstruing reality

Birren (1990: 43–4) suggests that many individuals move from logical analytical orientations to more interior, emotional, affective ones:

> . . . spirituality in the later years is less focused on the external formalism of religion and more on the interpretation of life and its feelings . . . I have the impression that mature and elderly adults seek a wholeness, a meaning in life, that is more integrative of actions and emotions, and less analytical in thought.

Changing perspectives

For those who prize the more youthful powers of analytic thought, this may constitute another loss, but for others the blending of mental boundaries might lead to different sorts of insight. Birren (1990) considers that finding meaning in later life is more of a challenge for men 'displaced by technology . . . in our evolving post-industrial information society', and hints that females are also biologically the stronger sex. He suggests that if people are to be helped in their spiritual quests in later life, they have to understand, and be understood, in their own terms and not in the terms of youth.

A similar theme is highlighted by Tornstam (1989), who suggests that in throwing out 'disengagement' as a viable option in later life we, in the west, have thrown the baby out with the bath water. He suggests that the element of disengagement theory which posits that there is an intrinsic tendency to disengage and withdraw in the later stages of life, ran counter to the personal values of the gerontologists who criticized it and to their wishes of what reality ought to be like. 'The defeat of disengagement theory was insured by an almost "religious" conviction of its incorrectness' (p. 56).

What appears as isolation and loneliness for one may be peaceful solitude to another. Tornstam suggests that what is lacking is an understanding of the meaning the individual imparts to engagement or disengagement, not the meaning which the gerontologist attributes. For Tornstam, disengagement may be a positive step towards what he calls 'gero-transcendence', in which there is a radical reconstruing of reality. But this reconstruing is one which is not simply a cognitive defence mechanism to make the unbearable bearable. In essence, the individual's meta-perspective shifts from a materialistic and rational vision to a more cosmic and transcendent one.

'Social' withdrawal occurs not because gero-transcendence necessitates it, but because in our society no roles conforming to this state are provided. Rather, we collude to make older people feel guilty over their disengagement, or the way they may now see things. Urging 'activity' can thus be a form of tyranny. Throwing positivism to the wind (though a researcher in the positivist tradition himself), Tornstam suggests that introspection is probably one of the most important ways to test the hypothesis that there *is* a process ultimately leading to gero-transcendence: to, among other things, the diminishment of self-centredness as a more cosmic sense of self develops; and to a sense of affinity with past, present and future generations.

One might expect that religious contact would facilitate gero-transcendence, so there is a slight irony about Moberg's (1990a: 18) suggestion that: 'Far too many religious groups serving the aging pay so much attention to empirically observable needs related to health, transportation, food, home services, and social relationships that they fail to minister to spiritual needs in any but the most perfunctory modes'. Nevertheless, as Moberg (1990b) notes, religious affiliation, behaviour and belief are associated to varying degrees with what one might broadly term 'positive psychological health', even when one partials out intervening variables and difficulties of interpreting cause and effect.

Older individuals are more involved in religious matters than are the young, and this appears to have been the case for long enough for us to suppose it is not simply a generational effect. Moberg interprets the evidence on religious participation, thought and behaviour as indicating that the ageing process itself contributes to a deepening of religious concern in the later years, particularly at the private, non-organizational level. This may in part be attributable to closeness to death – 'preparing for their finals' as Moberg (1990b: 224) puts it – and to the fact that the pressures of life in youth and middle age do not foster the time and stillness required for reflection and contemplation.

Another partial explanation may be that some people experiencing ill-health may turn to private religious activity as a form of support; frequency of prayer is reported to increase with age, especially among those who are in ill-health. But, by and large, positive self-assessed health and positive religious engagement are the best predictors of morale (Moberg 1990b) and many individuals, women in particular, report that religion has helped them cope at times of great stress. As Koenig (1990) notes, even among those at higher risk for mental ill-health, those who use religion to help cope may exhibit higher levels of adjustment than those known to be less at risk. Given the methodological problems inherent in 'religion and mental health' as an area of research, he nevertheless concludes that no data at this time support a negative association between religious cognitions and mental health in later life. Even when functional status and health are controlled, a positive relationship tends to exist between religious activity and well-being. Professionals without faith may find it somewhat difficult to comprehend such relationships, let alone facilitate them. As Koenig (1990: 39) suggests:

> For some older persons, especially those disabled with chronic illness, religion may be the only way to cope with the trials and struggles of life. With little control over their situation and few social or economic resources from which to draw, that person may find solace in their personal beliefs alone. For those particular patients, it is our observation that religion acts as the underlying force that enables them to function, provides their life with meaning and motivates their will to live.

Others, cited by Moberg, have suggested that religious belief, in particular a belief in life after death, enables people to fear death itself less, although in the west at least, the 'process' of dying is of concern to the religious and non-religious alike. Few can shrug off pain, for example, as a useful 'shock mechanism to awaken people from the mirage of this-worldly existence' (Tilak 1989: 159).

> I would prefer to die than to suffer going to a doctor. I should bear the pain, because I should dissociate myself from the pain. Detach yourself from the physical body, from the mind, from the intellect. That way you become yourself. So I should practice when the body is decaying, at that time is the best opportunity to detach. I should not miss that opportunity by going to somebody else.
>
> (Thomas 1991: 215)

Dying and death

> The living man [and woman] has both a future and a past; the dying man has no future in the usual sense, but only a past; the dead, however, 'is' his past. He has no life, he 'is' his life . . . he does not become a reality at his birth but rather at his death; he is 'creating' himself at the moment of his death. His self is not something that 'is' but something that is becoming, and therefore becomes itself fully only when life has been completed by death.
>
> (Frankl 1979: 112–13)

For most modern westerners, the idea that we can somehow 'develop' through the processes of growing older, dying and death, is an unfamiliar and perhaps uncomfortable notion. We feel more 'at home', paradoxically, with death when it is taken off our hands and occurs, as it nowadays most commonly does, in a hospital. A 'hands on' approach to death and dying, physically and psychologically, literally and metaphorically, is something to which we are no longer accustomed.

How do you want it to be for yourself? Most of us have some notion of 'a good death', and attitudes to death and dying are clearly influenced by our culture, religious beliefs and contact with medicine. Perhaps peacefully passing away in one's sleep at a ripe old age would be a stereotypic example of a good death for many. But even a sudden unexpected death in mid-life can be construed as 'good' by those bereaved. If we are to get a terminal cancer, some of us might like hospice care at home, with family and friends all around and involved in the caring and nursing, while others might prefer to die with hospice care but in a hospital, so that the direct involvement of family is somewhat lessened. Some might even prefer the anonymity and lack of self-involvement – the 'not knowing' – that was common in the first half of this century. But what if you get Alzheimer's disease? Or what if you get to a point where life seems unbearable and little can be done – and you want out? And on a more pragmatic level, what if, like my father, you think burning a coffin is a waste of money, and you want to be cremated in a plastic bag?

Getting what you want, whether dementia is in store or not, is more likely to happen if you express your wishes to family, friends and GP, and perhaps if you write a 'living will'. Under circumstances when you can no longer give instructions yourself, you may want an 'enduring power of attorney' to come into play. As Farrand (1989: 645) notes:

> It follows that the principal's [i.e. your] wishes as to the decisions which should be taken in the future on the occasion of a range of hypothetical circumstances might be written into the power. Whether this could effectively extend to the giving or withholding of consents to medical treatment is obviously problematical.

Several safeguards obviously need to be built in so that older mentally infirm individuals, for example, are not exploited by those to whom they have given enduring powers. The same safeguards also need building in to the laws concerning guardianship, the invocation of which should be seen as the least restrictive alternative. Such laws are often used to facilitate transfer of an unwilling individual into residential care. How can others be expected to act in your best interests if you yourself have never expressed what you consider your best interests, your wishes for the future, to be? Related to the issue of who will control your life in the future should certain circumstances arrive, are 'advanced directives' about medical treatment:

> The case is the first in which the High Court has been asked to rule on the validity of an advance directive expressing a patient's wishes about future medical treatment. It gives court sanction for the first time to US-style 'living wills' refusing, for example, life prolonging treatment in the event of a catastrophic brain injury or serious mental deterioration.
>
> (Dyer 1993: 3)

What if your present wishes are that if you get Alzheimer's disease you would like your life to be terminated at a certain point in its progression – when you are unable to recognize your husband, perhaps, or when your husband thinks it is best for you because 'you' are not there any more? What if when you reach a 'persistent vegetative state', you would prefer a fast-acting injection (active euthanasia) to being 'allowed' to die over several days by the withdrawal of food and water (passive euthanasia)? If the Law doesn't allow what you want, what then?

The Natural Death Centre in London, according to Schwarz (1991:6), writing under a headline 'New centre aims to lift gloom and put ecstasy into dying', offers 'midwives for the dying, death exercises, recyclable coffins and a DIY guide to getting bodies to graveyards'. My father would have loved the practical bits. The centre 'aims to give people the right to their own death without being taken over by the state', an allusion to the fact that older people in particular are more likely to die in hospital or other institutions, women in particular. For many of us, though, it is difficult to genuinely reconstrue funerals as celebrations for the life lived, or to put 'ecstasy' into dying other than by massive shots of euphoria-inducing drugs. We have no equivalent to the Mexican 'Day of the dead', when death is celebrated. We probably find it bizarre that in Hong Kong celebratory meals are taken to the graveyard. Clifford (1992:11) points out that death and bereavement are no longer thoroughly integrated into our daily routine as they were, for example, in Post-Reformation England:

> . . . there is now no sense in which society 'prepares' its members for death. Nor in modern Britain do we have a general metaphysic of death, or a set process of mourning . . . secular death as a social 'event' exists really as an absence, something to be avoided . . . death has ceased to be socially 'real' – existing only as a kind of metaphorical ending which entails nothing in particular.

And Clifford reminds us that, having news flashed the shooting of President Kennedy, the BBC went ahead with its next show, the Harry Worth TV comedy programme.

But it is the process of dying that concerns older people more than death itself, and while hospice care – whether at home or in hospital – can certainly ease the process for those individuals who can get access to it, the best palliative care is often not available to patients dying of acute or chronic illnesses, or of 'old age'. But shouldn't it be? The philosophy of the Cardiff-based George Thomas Trust and Centre for Hospice Care, published in its annual report, is not untypical of the 'hospice movement':

> Central to the philosophy . . . is a belief in the dignity and value of all persons. This belief is enacted in the care of those approaching death, and those close to them. The care offered unites this belief with one that does not separate death and dying from life and living. Death is seen as part of life's journey. Difficulties in this passage can, we believe, be eased with skilled, respectful and continuing care in whatever environment is most

appropriate. Such care enables life to be lived, even in the knowledge of approaching death.

Only about 7 per cent of people receive some form of hospice care in the year before their death, and only 3–4 per cent actually die in a hospice (Seale 1995a). Very few people dying of 'old age' die in a hospice. But hospices have brought some visibility to dying. The dying, and people with such diseases as cancer, are no longer social lepers, and the sharing of their thoughts, by those dying in the public gaze, may help more ordinary mortals to talk about what is happening to them. In 1994, for example, the playwright Dennis Potter gave an interview, part of which considered his knowledge of his imminent death. Derek Jarman's film *Blue* reflected on AIDS and his approaching death, as did several articles by the American novelist Harold Brodkey. The well-known journalist Jill Tweedie talked about her terminal motor-neurone disease. The stiff upper lip is going; fears can be aired:

> Brodkey worries that he might become incontinent and have to wear diapers; Tweedie talked of the panic attacks, the 'ferrets nibbling at my brain'; Guilbert filmed himself slowly and painfully washing his genitals and anus.
>
> (Bunting 1994: 22)

The movement of dying and death back towards the public domain – the revival of death awareness from a period of relative denial – has revealed that there are many different ways in which individuals face death. For example, Tweedie's response was blind fury and fear, while Potter appeared tranquil and serene, though the morphine he sipped may have helped. Even humour can enter. The comedienne Marti Caine, when asked if her bouts of cancer were making her live more intensely, replied: 'You do initially . . . You start by watching the daffodils and end up watching *Neighbours*'. But the colonization of dying, death and grieving by expertise tends to provide a framework by which, again, we can be judged to have failed. Are we dying well? Did we have a good death? Have we resolved our grief properly? Should we *still* be in stage 3?

With respect to dying, we are said to have to work through five stages:

- *Denial*: 'No, not me, it can't be true'.
- *Anger*: 'Why me?'
- *Bargaining*: 'Please let me be here to see the new baby'.
- *Depression*: 'I'm losing everything'.
- *Acceptance*: 'It's happening'.

(Seale 1995a)

But for individuals reaching 'a ripe old age', this pattern, as witnessed in studies of younger cancer patients, may not hold true. Dying may be what it is that you have been expecting to do next; you may feel enough is enough. And so too may the people looking after you.

With grieving we are said to have to work through four stages (Seale 1995b).

We have to accept the reality of the loss, experience the pain of grief, adjust to the environment from which the deceased is missing, and withdraw emotional energy from the deceased in order to invest it in other relationships. And many of us will be grateful to such self-help organizations as CRUSE for the aid and comfort their members give to those grieving. But what if, to you, the exhortation to withdraw emotional energy sounds like an invitation to forget about the woman you have loved for the last fifty or so years? What if you want to keep her room just the way it was? Was the actor Peter Cushing, star of many Hammer Horror Films, who died in the summer of 1994, 'wrong' to have spent the last twenty years of his life after his wife's death 'waiting to join her'?

Peter Cushing clearly didn't die forthwith of a broken heart. Even the notion that ill-health and earlier mortality are widespread concomitants of the loss inherent in, say, the death of a spouse, has been questioned by Fasey (1990) In his review of studies of grief in old age. It would seem that if there is an effect, it is that some older widowers suffer increased mortality from vascular disease in the immediate post-bereavement period. Again, men are more 'at risk'. More evident is the fact that bereavement can precipitate depression, which may have a poor prognosis.

Our understanding of the processes of dying and grieving becomes tinged with prescriptions for 'normality' that are inevitably culture-bound as well as tied up with our religious, spiritual or secular understandings. While in an increasingly secular society completing *your* life in the manner *you* would like seems a laudable goal, what feels right for us should not be forced on others. It is not too difficult to imagine that 'in contemplation of the desirability of an easy, self-controlled death, we have moved inexorably into the field of voluntary euthanasia as a universal rite of passage' (Vincent 1994). If we choose not to afford 'ourselves in the future', we must be prepared to be expected to loosen our hold on life perhaps sooner than we might have wished. In that brave new world perhaps, 'the elderly' who 'relinquish' their hospital beds to worthier patients will at last regain status – as national heroes.

Gaining control

> 'In Revolutionary activity', Marx and Engels write, 'the changing of oneself coincides with the changing of circumstances' . . . If we conceive of revolutionary activity as a process often taking place over long periods of time involving individuals in collective action, we can see that such activity helps the individual to be rid of the psychological 'muck' (guilt, lack of self-confidence, low self-esteem), which subordinacy to the social order often entails.
>
> (Leonard 1984: 206–7)

Subordinacy of older people to the social order seems evident in the way they are treated as a commodity to be processed by the 'ageing enterprises', which, in one way or another, have earned their living by regarding older people as different, to be stigmatized, examined, studied and isolated from the rest of society. Empowerment implies questioning what we take for granted. In their introduction to a collection of papers on community development in an ageing world, Derricourt and Miller (1992: 117) suggest that:

> . . . there is clearly a need for greater emphasis to be placed on the process through which elderly people can speak for themselves, identify their own needs, assert their rights, contribute their skills and knowledge, and work alongside those who are interested in ensuring that elders receive an appropriate level of material resources, which in turn means continuing to struggle against inequalities that have been experienced throughout their lives.

Clearly, what one considers to be an 'appropriate level of material resources', and how it is best raised and delivered, are political issues. Laing (1991), for example, in a book entitled *Empowering the Elderly: Direct Consumer Funding of Care Services*, advocates that a consumer-led market for care services should extend to the National Health Service (NHS). He argues that the NHS should be obliged to charge patients the full costs of long-stay beds, as well as for their community care services such as district nurse visits. Older people would be given vouchers (but not cash) which they could use to buy the services of their choice. He suggests that direct payments to consumers would stimulate care service innovation by private for-profit service suppliers.

Laing's argument is set in a context of not risking 'expenditure getting out of control' and 'tight public expenditure control'. Older people are expected to have to sell their homes, as and when necessary, in order to pay themselves for care costs. While there seems some truth in the notion that 'he who pays the piper calls the tune', just how much real 'empowerment' such a voucher scheme would give a person must depend on how much cash he or she has to spend in the market. Less cash usually means less choice and less power. Laing seems to assume rather than question inequity in wealth distribution. Nevertheless, the idea of giving the residents of an old people's home, say, the voucher equivalent of the real costs of their care to spend – perhaps with the advice of specialist brokers – on setting up a more tailor-made care package for themselves, is not without its merits.

Such ideas of empowerment are behind the thrust to community care. But the rhetoric of empowerment may become suspect, and the initiative wrecked, if it is under-resourced. Empowerment is a complex issue and requires change in far more than just the behaviour of front-line workers with older people. Empowerment through access to cash is only one, albeit very important form.

Empowerment may require power sharing in the context of trusting relationships. This is highlighted, for example, by Thorsheim and Roberts (1990) in their study of storytelling. They found that storytelling led to empowerment through reciprocal social support among older people and, interestingly, men's stories often seemed to be focused on 'mastery' – I am what I have done – whereas women's stories seemed to be filled with considerations of 'relationships' – I am the relationships which I have established.

Most of our significant relationships are with people, and it is by knowing people as individuals – not as objects to be serviced – and by hearing their life histories and by listening to what they have got to say, that we also help empower them. This is because in so doing we become willing to let others exert influence over us. We tend to consider later life a particularly precarious time for older women, associated as it can be with chronic illness and relative impoverishment. But, as has been suggested at various points in this book, later life may be a psychologically more precarious time for men, in part because relationships have less salience for them than power. Perhaps before power sharing has to come a power struggle and women, who make up the majority of older people, may need more encouragement to reclaim their power.

Another form of empowerment can involve the giving of information and the provision of help in the development of skills which promote autonomy and independence. Brown and Furstenberg (1992: 81) provide a good example of this in the context of home health teams empowering older patients, who had had hip fractures, and their families: 'Successful recovery and the rehabilitation of the older patient is contingent upon restoring the patients' perception of control over their recovery'. They continue:

> Empowerment activities have two aspects: content, that is specific actions, skills and information that the professionals can do, teach or impart, that increase control; and a process by which professionals help patients and families see themselves as 'causal forces' . . . capable of, and responsible for, control.
>
> (Brown and Furstenberg 1992: 89)

To produce change we have to exercise our capacity for psychological reconstruing; not to reinforce the *status quo* by accepting the constructions of others, but by questioning. Why should we take as legitimate, for example, the acceptance by women of lower wages and benefits throughout life, and their resultant impoverishment in old age, as the norm? What *should* people feel entitled to in return for a lifetime of paying taxes and national insurance contributions?

Perhaps one answer to that question is 'a future with a caring face', which may be more likely to come about if older people can achieve some coherent political clout. Is it not possible to develop moral, philosophical and political leadership to which people could give their full and informed consent because the policies to which it would give rise were in their own best long-term interests? Jack Jones, as president of the National Pensioner's Convention (with a membership of some one million), puts the issue starkly: 'It's a matter of human understanding. Either we look after our old people . . . or you might as well bloody well shoot them'. But looking for coherent political clout for older people seems almost to fall into an ageist trap. Age may be less important than such other influential factors as class, race and gender; 'older people' are not a homogeneous coherent group, and nor, of course, are women or black people. Nevertheless, in America, the Gray Panther Movement (some 80,000 members) and the Association of Retired Persons (some three million members) have been effective in getting 'grey issues' onto the political agenda.

It does not have to be denigrating to past generations to suggest that we must find the psychological strength to transform ourselves into – as Maggie Kuhn, the founder of the Gray Panthers put it – a new breed of older people 'who look to the future'. We have a better opportunity to do so.

References

Abrams, M. (1988) Use of time by the elderly in Great Britain. In K. Altergott (ed.), *Daily Life in Later Life*, pp. 23–41. London: Sage.

Age Concern England (1992) *Dependence: The Ultimate Fear*. London: Age Concern England.

Age+Resource (1992) Information Pack, from Age+Resource, 1268 London Road London, SW16 4EJ, UK.

Aldwin, C.M. (1991) Does age affect the stress and coping process? Implications of age differences in perceived control. *Journal of Gerontology (Psychological Sciences)*, 46(4): 174–80.

Allman, P. (1991) Depressive disorders and emotionalism following a stroke. *International Journal of Geriatric Psychiatry*, 6(6): 337–83.

Anon (1990) European dimensions on education and training for an ageing society. *Ageing International*, 17(2): 48 9.

Anon (1992) The agony of trial by your peers. *The Guardian*, 5 October, p. 10.

Anon (1993) Everest record. *The Guardian*, 12 October, p. 10.

Arber, S. and Ginn, J. (1991) *Gender and Later Life: A Sociological Analysis of Resources and Constraints*. London: Sage.

Atkin, K. (1992) Similarities and differences between informal carers. In J. Twigg (ed.), *Carers: Research and Practice*, pp. 30–58. London: HMSO.

Balarajan, R. (1991) Ethnic differences in mortality from ischaemic heart disease and cerebrovascular disease in England and Wales. *British Medical Journal*, 302(6776): 560–4.

Ball, K. and Owsley, C. (1991) Identifying correlates of accident involvement for the older driver. *Human Factors*, 33(5): 583–95.

Ballard, C.G., Chithiramohan, R.N., Handy, S., Bannister, C., Davis, R. and Todd, N.B. (1991) Information reliability in dementia sufferers. *International Journal of Geriatric Psychiatry*, 6: 313–16.

Baltes, P.B. and Baltes, M.M. (eds) (1990). *Successful Aging*. Cambridge: Cambridge University Press.

Baltes, P.B., Smith, J. and Staudinger, U.M. (1992) Wisdom and successful aging.

Current Theory and Research in Motivation, 39: 123–67. Nebraska Symposium on Motivation, 1991. Lincoln, NB: University of Nebraska Press.

Bayles, K.A. and Tomoeda, C.K. (1991) Caregiver report on prevalence and appearance order of linguistic symptoms in Alzheimer's patients. *The Gerontologist*, 31(2): 210–16.

Beardsall, L. and Brayne, C. (1990) Estimation of verbal intelligence in an elderly community: A prediction analysis using a shortened NART. *British Journal of Clinical Psychology*, 29: 83–90.

Benbow, S.M. (1991) Guardianship orders: Underused and undervalued. *Care of the Elderly*, 3(8): 351–2.

Bennet, K.C. and Thompson, N.L. (1991) Accelerated ageing and male homosexuality: Australian evidence in a continuing debate. *Journal of Homosexuality*, 20(3/4): 65–75.

Birren, J.E. (1990) Spiritual maturity in psychological development. *Journal of Religious Gerontology*, 7(1/2): 41–53.

Birren, J.E. and Fisher, L.M. (1990) The elements of wisdom: overview and integration. In R.J. Sternberg (ed.), *Wisdom: Its Nature, Origin and Development*, pp. 317–32. Cambridge: Cambridge University Press.

Birren, J.E. and Fisher, L.M. (1992) Aging and slowing of behavior: consequences for cognition and survival. *Current Theory and Research in Motivation*, 39: 1–37. Nebraska Symposium on Motivation, 1991. Lincoln, NB: University of Nebraska Press.

Black, S.E., Blessed, G., Edwardson, J.A. and Kay, D.W.K. (1990) Prevalence rates of dementia in an aging population: Are low rates due to the use of insensitive instruments? *Age and Ageing*, 19: 84–90.

Blessed, G., Black, S.E., Butler, T. and Kay, D.W.K. (1991) The diagnosis of dementia in the elderly: A comparison of CAMCOG, the AGECAT program, DSM-III, the Mini-Mental State examination and some short rating scales. *British Journal of Psychiatry*, 159: 193–8.

Bornat, J. and Adams, J. (1991) Models of biography and reminiscence in the nursing care of frail elderly people. Extended version of a paper presented at SYSTED '91, Barcelona, 10–14 June.

Brayne, C. and Calloway, P. (1988) Normal ageing, impaired cognitive function, and senile dementia of the Alzheimer's type: A continuum? *The Lancet*, 1(8597): 1265–6.

Brewer, M.B., Dull, V. and Lui, L. (1981) Perceptions of the elderly: Stereotypes as prototypes, *Journal of Personality and Social Psychology*, 41(4): 656–70.

Brindle, D. (1991) Public health doctors urge contact for elderly among health targets. *The Guardian*, 18 June, p. 2.

Brindle, D. (1993) 80-hour week for carers of dementia patients. *The Guardian*, 5 July, p. 6.

British Gas (1991) *The British Gas Report on Attitudes to Ageing 1991*. London: British Gas.

Bromley, D.B. (1988) The idea of ageing: An historical and psychological analysis. *Comprehensive Gerontology Series C*, 2: 30–41.

Brown, J.S.T. and Furstenberg, A.-L. (1992) Restoring control: Empowering older patients and their familes during health crisis. *Social Work in Health Care*, 17(4): 81–101.

Brown, R. (1986) *Social Psychology*, 2nd edn. London: Free Press.

Bunting, M. (1994) Bowing out in front of the final curtain. *The Guardian*, 7 April, p. 22.

Bury, M. and Holme, A. (1991) *Life After Ninety*. London: Routledge.

Butler, R.N. (1963) The life review: An interpretation of reminiscence in the aged. *Psychiatry*, 26: 65–76.

Byrne, E.J., Smith, C.W. and Arie, T.T. (1991) The diagnosis of dementia. 1. Clinical and pathological criteria: A review of the literature. *International Journal of Geriatric Psychiatry*, 6(4): 199–208.

Bytheway, B. (1990) Age. In S.M. Peace (ed.), *Researching Social Gerontology*. London: Sage.

Cheston, R. and Marshall, A. (1994) Consent to treatment: Issues with older adults. *PSIGE Newsletter*, 49: 4–6.

Claxton, G. (1991) Psychosophy: Are we ready for a science of self-knowledge? *The Psychologist*, 4(6): 249–52.

Clifford, A. (1992) A dying art. *The Guardian (Weekend)*, 4–5 January, pp. 10–11.

Coleman, P. (1986) *Ageing and Reminiscence Processes*. Chichester: John Wiley.

Cooney, J. (1994) Judy Davis: Antipodean actress. *Empire*, 61: 61–2.

Costa, P.T. and McCrae, R.R. (1992) Trait psychology comes of age. *Current Theory and Research in Motivation*, 39: 169–204. Nebraska Symposium on Motivation, 1991. Lincoln, NB: University of Nebraska Press.

Crook, T.H., Larrabee, G.J. and Youngjohn, J.R. (1990) Diagnosis and assessment of age-associated memory impairment. *Clinical Neuropharmacology*, 13 (suppl. 3): S81–91.

Csikszentmihalyi, M. and Rochberg-Halton, E. (1981) *The Meaning of Things: Domestic Symbols and the Self*. Cambridge: Cambridge University Press.

Danermark, B. and Ekström, M. (1990) Relocation and health effects on the elderly: a commented research review. *Journal of Sociology and Social Welfare*, 17(1): 25–49.

Derricourt, N. and Miller, C. (1992) Community develpment in an ageing world. *Community Development Journal*, 27(2): 117–21.

Dittmann-Kohli, F. (1990) The construction of meaning in old age: Possibilities and constraints. *Ageing and Society*, 10(3): 279–94.

Dixon, R.A. (1989) Questionnaire research on metamemory and aging: Issues of structure and function. In L. Poon, D.C. Rubin and B.A. Wilson (eds), *Everyday Cognition in Adulthood and Late Life*. Cambridge: Cambridge University Press.

Donaldson, L. (1993) An age-old question of discrimination. *The Independent*, 18 March p. 22.

Dyer, C. (1993) Patient wins bar on future treatment. *The Guardian*, 15 October, p. 3.

Eisenhandler, S.A. (1990) The asphalt identiket: Old age and the driver's licence. *International Journal of Aging and Human Development*, 30(1): 1–14.

Erber, J.T. and Rothberg, S.T. (1991) Here's looking at you: The relative effect of age and attractiveness on judgments about memory failure. *Journal of Gerontology (Psychological Sciences)*, 46(3): 116–23.

Erikson, E.H. (1963) *Childhood and Society*. New York: W.W. Norton.

Erikson, E.H., Erikson, J.M. and Kivnick, H.Q. (1986). *Vital Involvement in Old Age*. London: W.W. Norton.

Erikson, J.M. (1988) *Wisdom and the Senses: The Way of Creativity*. London: W.W. Norton.

EurolinkAge (1990) *Age and Disability: A Challenge for Europe*. London: EurolinkAge.

Evans, J.G. (1991) Paper presented at the meeting on *The interaction of physical and mental symptoms in older people*, held at the Royal Society of Medicine, London, 25 June.

Farran, C.J., Keene-Hagerty, E., Salloway, S., Kupserer, S. and Wilken, C.S. (1991) Finding meaning: An alternative paradigm for Alzheimer's disease family caregivers. *The Gerontologist*, 31(4): 483–9.

Farrand, J.T. (1989) Enduring powers of attorney. In J.M. Eekelaar and D. Pearl (eds), *An Aging World: Dilemmas and Challenges for Law and Social Policy*, pp. 637–52. Oxford: Clarendon Press.

Fasey, C.N. (1990) Grief in old age: A review of the literature. *International Journal of Geriatric Psychiatry*, 5(2): 67–75.

Fenton, S. (1987) *Ageing Minorities: black people as they grow old in Britain*. London: Commision for Racial Equality.

Field, D. and Millsap, R.E. (1991) Personality in advanced old age: continuity or change? *Journal of Gerontology (Psychological Sciences)*, 46(6): 299–308.

Fisk, A.D. and Fisher, D.L. (1994) Brinley plots and theories of aging: The explicit, muddled, and implicit debates. *Journal of Gerontology (Psychological Sciences)*, 49(2): 81–9.

Folstein, M.F., Folstein, S.E. and McHugh, P.R. (1975) 'Mini-mental state': A practical method for grading the cognitive state of patients for the clinician. *Journal of Psychiatric Research*, 12: 189–98.

Ford, J. and Sinclair, R. (1987) *Sixty Years On: Women Talk About Old Age*. London: Women's Press.

Foy, S.S. and Mitchell, M.S. (1991) Factors contributing to learned helplessness in the institutionalised aged: A literature review. *Physical and Occupational Therapy in Geriatrics*, 9(2): 1–23.

Francis, J. (1992) Remembrance days. *Community Care*, 938: 16–17.

Frankl, V. (1979) *The Unheard Cry for Meaning: Psychotherapy and Humanism*. London: Hodder and Stoughton.

Froggart, A. (1991) Inner beliefs. *Community Care*, 876: 15–16.

Gadow, S. and Berg, G. (1978) Towards more human meanings of aging: Ideals and images from philosophy and art. In S.F. Spicker *et al.* (eds), *Aging and the Elderly: Humanistic Perspectives in Gerontology*, pp. 89–92. Atlantic Islands, NJ: Humanities Press.

Gee, E.M. and Kimball, M.M. (1987) *Women and Aging*. Toronto: Butterworth.

Gibson, H.B. (1992) *The Emotional and Sexual Lives of Older People: A Manual for Professionals*. London: Chapman and Hall.

Giesen, C.B. and Datan, N. (1980) The competent older woman. In N. Datan and N. Lohmann (eds), *Transitions of Aging*, pp. 57–72. New York: Academic Press.

Giles, H. (1991) 'Gosh, you don't look it': A sociolinguistic construction of ageing. *The Psychologist*, 14(3): 99–106.

Gilleard, C.J. (1984) *Living with Dementia: Community Care of the Elderly Mentally Infirm*. London: Croom Helm.

Gilleard, C.J. (1992) Losing one's mind and losing one's place: a psychosocial model of dementia. In K. Morgan (ed.), *Gerontology: Responding to an Ageing Society*. London: Jessica Kingsley.

Glendenning, F. (1991) Old dogs and new tricks: Education for older adults. *Care of the Elderly*, 3(7): 344.

Gothóni, R. (1990) From chaos to cosmos: The telling of a life story reconsidered. *Journal of Cross-Cultural Gerontology*, 5: 65–76.

Grant, G. and Nolan, M. (1993) Informal carers: Sources and concomitants of satisfaction. *Health and Social Care*, 1(3): 147–59.

Greer, G. (1991) Body to soul. *The Independent on Sunday*, 13 October, pp. 9–10.

Grover, D.R. and Herzog, C. (1991) Relationships between intellectual control beliefs and psychometric intelligence in adulthood. *Journal of Gerontology (Psychological Sciences)*, 46(3): 109–15.

Gubrium, J.F. (1986) *Oldtimers and Alzheimer's: The Descriptive Organization of Senility*. London: JAI Press.

Gupta, M.A., Gupta, A.K., Schork, N.J., Ellis, C.N. and Voorhees, J.N. (1990) The aging face: A psychocutaneous perspective. *Journal of Dermatologic Surgery and Oncology*, 16(10): 902–4.

Gurland, B. (1992) The impact of depression on quality of life of the elderly. *Clinics in Geriatric Medicine*, 8(2): 377–86.

Gutmann, D. (1987). *Reclaimed Powers: Towards a New Psychology of Men and Women*. London: Hutchinson.

Hachinski, V. (1992) Preventable senility: A call for action against the vascular dementias. *The Lancet*, 340(8820): 645–8.

Haight, B.K. (1991) Reminiscing: The state of the art as a basis for practice. *International Journal of Aging and Human Development*, 33(1): 1–32.

Haldeman, V.A. (1990) The identification of resources for effective stress management in later life. Paper presented at the *2nd International Conference on the Future of Adult Life*, Leeuwenhorst, The Netherlands, 4–8 July.

Hamilton, D.L. and Trolier, T.K. (1986) Stereotypes and stereotyping: an overview to the cognitive approach. In J.F. Dovidio and S.L. Gaertner (eds), *Prejudice, Discrimination and Racism*, pp. 127–63. London: Academic Press.

Hanna, L. (1993) A big job for Rosie's granny. *The Guardian (Society)*, 13 January, pp. 10–11.

Hazan, H. (1990) Victim into sacrifice: The construction of the old as a symbolic type. *Journal of Cross-Cultural Gerontology*, 5: 77–84.

Heim, A. (1990) *Where Did I Put my Spectacles?* Cambridge: Allborough Press.

Henwood, K.L. (1990) Stereotyping and self-disclosure: A discourse approach to ageing. Paper presented at the *2nd International Conference on the Future of Adult Life*, Leeuwenhorst, The Netherlands, 4–8 July.

Holden-Cosgrove, U. (1992) The 'new' dementias. *PSIGE Newsletter*, 44: 15–18.

Holland, C.A. and Rabbitt, P.M.A. (1990) Autobiographical and text recall in the elderly: An investigation of a processing resource deficit. *Quarterly Journal of Experimental Psychology*, 42A(3): 441–70.

Holland, C.A. and Rabbitt, P.M.A. (1991a) The course and causes of cognitive change with advancing age. *Reviews in Clinical Gerontology*, 1: 81–96.

Holland, C.A. and Rabbitt, P.M.A. (1991b) Ageing memory: Use versus impairment. *British Journal of Psychology*, 82: 29–38.

Holland, C.A. and Rabbitt, P.M.A. (1992a) People's awareness of their age-related sensory and cognitive deficits and their implications for road safety. *Applied Cognitive Psychology*, 6(3): 217–31.

Holland, C.A. and Rabbitt, P.M.A. (1992b) Effects of age-related reduction in processing resources on text recall. *Journal of Gerontology (Psychological Sciences)*, 47(3): 129–37.

Hopkins, T. and Harris, J. (1990) Back to the future: Reminiscing in the '90s. Paper presented at the *British Society of Gerontology Annual Conference*, Durham, September.

Huppert, F.A. (1991a) Age-related changes in memory: learning and remembering new information. In F. Boller and J. Grafman (eds), *Handbook of Neuropsychology*, Vol. 5, pp. 123–47. Amsterdam: Elsevier.

Huppert, F.A. (1991b) Neuropsychological assessment of dementia. *Reviews in Clinical Gerontology*, 1: 159–69.

Huppert, F.A. and Garcia, A.W. (1991) Qualitative differences in psychiatric symptoms between high risk groups assessed on a screening test (GHQ–30). *Social Psychiatry and Psychiatric Epidemiology*, 26(6): 252–8.

Huppert, F.A. and Kopelman, M.D. (1989) Rates of forgetting in normal ageing: A comparison with dementia. *Neuropsychologia*, 27(6): 849–60.

Ignatieff, M. (1991) A taste of ice-cream is all you know. *The Observer*, 7 July, p. 21.

Iliffe, S., Tai, S.T., Haines, A., Gallivan, S., Goldenberg, E., Booroff, A. and Morgan, P. (1992) Are elderly people living alone at risk? *British Medical Journal*, 305(6860): 1001–4.

Illman, J. (1991) Untitled article on a reminiscence room. *The Guardian*, 11 January, p. 33.

Ince, M. (1993) Strains of too long a life. *The Times Higher*, 19 February, p. 9.

Ishii-Kuntz, M. (1990) Social interaction and psychological well-being: Comparison across stages of adulthood. *International Journal of Aging and Human Development*, 30(1): 15–36.

Jamieson, A. (1990) Informal care in Europe. In A. Jamieson and R. Illsley (eds), *Contrasting European Policies for the Care of Older People*, pp. 3–21. Aldershot: Avebury.

Jerrome, D. (1990) Frailty and friendship. *Journal of Cross-Cultural Gerontology*, 5: 51–64.

Jerrome, D. (1992) *Good Company*. Edinburgh: Edinburgh University Press.

Jerrome, D. (1993a) Intimate relationships. In J. Bond, P. Coleman and S. Peace (eds), *Ageing in Society: An Introduction to Social Gerontology*, (2nd edn), pp. 226–54. London: Sage.

Jerrome, D. (1993b) Intimacy and sexuality amongst older women. In M. Bernard and K. Meade (eds), *Women Come of Age*, pp. 85–105. London: Edward Arnold.

Johnson, J. and Bytheway, B. (1993) Ageism: Concept and definition. In J. Johnson and R. Slater (eds), *Ageing and Later Life*, pp. 200–6. London: Sage

Jones, G. and Miesen, B. (1992) *Care-giving in Dementia: Research and Applications.* London: Routledge.

Jones, K.J, Albert, M.S., Duffy, F.H., Hyde, M.R., Naeser, M. and Aldwin, C. (1991) Modeling age using cognitive, psychosocial and physiological variables: The Boston normative aging study. *Experimental Aging Research*, 17(4): 227–42.

Jones, S.J. and Rabbitt, P.M.A. (1994) *Familiarity Versus Recollection: Effects of Age on Recognition of Proper Names.* Manchester: University of Manchester Age and Cognitive Performance Research Unit.

Kay, D.W.K. (1991) The epidemiology of dementia: a review of recent work. *Reviews in Clinical Gerontology*, 1: 55–166.

Keating, G.C. (1991) Fashionable pride: An ageless concern, *International Journal of Aging and Human Development*, 33(3): 187–96.

Kehoe, M. (1988) The present: growing old (1950–1980). *Journal of Homosexuality*, 16(3/4): 53–62.

Kimble, M.A. (1990) Aging and the search for meaning. *Journal of Religious Gerontology*, 7(1/2): 111–29.

Kitwood, T. (1993) Frames of reference for an understanding of dementia. In J. Johnson and R. Slater (eds), *Ageing and Later Life*, pp. 100–7. London: Sage.

Koenig, H.G. (1990) Research on religion and mental health: A review and commentary. *Journal of Clinical Geriatric Psychiatry*, 23(1): 23–53.

Koenig, P. (1991) Money and the medicine men, *The Independent on Sunday*, 12 May: 2–5.

Lachman, M.E. (1991) Perceived control over memory aging: Developmental and intervention perspectives. *Journal of Social Issues*, 47(4): 159–75.

Laing, W. (1991) *Empowering the Elderly: Direct Consumer Funding of Care Services.* London: Institute of Economic Affairs, Health and Welfare Unit.

Langer, E.J. (1991). *Mindfulness: choice and control in everyday life.* London: Collins-Harville.

Leonard, P. (1984) *Personality and Ideology: Towards a Materialist Understanding of the Individual.* London: Macmillan.

Levy, B. and Langer, E. (1994) Aging free from negative stereotypes: Successful memory in China and among American deaf. *Journal of Personality and Social Psychology*, 66(6): 989–97.

Macnair, P. (1992) The beauty myth? *The Guardian*, 7 January, p. 16.

Manton, K.G. and Stallard, E. (1991) Cross-sectional estimates of active life expectancy for the US elderly and oldest-old populations. *Journal of Gerontology (Social Sciences)*, 46(3): 170–82.

Marmot, M.G. and Poulter, N.R. (1992) Primary prevention of stroke. *The Lancet*, 339(8789): 344–7.

Martin, P., Poon, L.W., Clayton, G.M., Lee, H.S., Fulks, J. and Johnson, M.A. (1992) Personality, life-events and coping in the oldest-old. *International Journal of Aging and Human Development*, 34(1): 19–30.

Mathews, D.D. (1992) Health care for older women. *The Lancet*, 340(8815): 357–8.

Maylor, E.A. (1993) Aging and forgetting in prospective and restrospective memory tasks. *Psychology and Aging*, 8(3): 420–8.

Maylor, E.A. (1994) Ageing and the retrieval of specialized and general knowledge: Performance of 'Masterminds'. *British Journal of Psychology*, 85(1): 105–14.

McCrae, R.R. and Costa, P.T. (1989) Reinterpreting the Myers–Briggs Type Indicator from the perspective of the five factor model of personality. *Journal of Personality*, 57(1): 17–40.

McCready, W.C. (1985) Styles of grandparenting among white ethnics. In V.L. Bengston and J.F. Robertson (eds), *Grandparenthood*, pp. 49–60. Beverly Hills, CA: Sage.

McEwen, E. (ed.) (1990) *Age: The unrecognized discrimination*. London: Age Concern England.

McGill, P. (1994) Thirsty for more, *The Guardian*, 10 May: 3.

Millar, B. (1992) Threescore years, and then? *Health Service Journal*, 102(5318): 10.

Milne, D., Pitt, I. and Sabin, N. (1993) Evaluation of a carer support scheme for elderly people: The importance of 'coping'. *British Journal of Social Work*, 23(2): 157–68.

Moberg, D.O. (1990a) Spiritual maturity and wholeness in the later years. *Journal of Religious Gerontology*, 7(1/2): 5–24.

Moberg, D.O. (1990b) Religion and aging. In K.F. Ferraro (ed.), *Gerontology: Perspectives and Issues*, pp. 179–205. New York: Springer.

Moody, H.R. (1988) Twenty-five years of the life review: Where did we come from? Where are we going? *Journal of Gerontological Social Work*, 12(3/4): 7–21.

Moore, S. (1993) A certain ageism. *The Guardian* (tabloid/women), 13 August, p. 11.

NAHAT (1990) Review of services for black and minority ethnic people. *Words About Action Bulletin No. 3*, October.

Nettlebeck, T. and Rabbitt, P.M.A. (1992) Aging, cognitive performance, and mental speed. *Intelligence*, 16: 189–205.

NHS Management Executive (1993) *Dementia*. London: Department of Health.

O'Brien, J. and Levy, R. (1992) Age associated memory impairment: too broad an entity to justify drug treatment yet. *British Medical Journal*, 304(6818): 5–6.

O'Connor, M. (1993) *Generation to Generation: Linking Schools with Older People*. London: Cassell.

Older Students' Research Group (1993) *A Brief History 1981–1993*. Milton Keynes: The Open University.

Orona, C.J. (1990) Temporality and identity loss in Alzheimer's disease. *Social Science and Medicine*, 30(11): 1247–56.

Parasuraman, R. and Nestor, P.G. (1991) Attention and driving skills in aging and Alzheimer's disease. *Human Factors*, 33(5): 539–57.

Peace, S.M. (ed.) (1990) *Researching Social Gerontology: Concepts, Methods and Issues*. London: Sage.

Peterson, D.A., Thornton, J.E. and Birren, J.E. (1986) *Education and Aging*. Englewood Cliffs, NJ: Prentice Hall.

Pollitt, P.A. and Anderson, I. (1991) Research methods in the study of carers of dementing people: Some problems encountered in the Hughs Hall project for later life. *PSIGE Newsletter*, 16: 29–32.

Quinn, M. (1990) Older sisters. *Social Work Today*, 22(10): 19–20.

Rabbitt, P.M.A. (1990a) Age, IQ and awareness and recall of errors. *Ergonomics*, 33(10/11): 1291–305.

Rabbitt, P.M.A. (1990b) Applied cognitive gerontology: Some problems, methodologies and data. *Applied Cognitive Psychology*, 4(4): 225–46.

Rabbitt, P.M.A. (1991) Management of the working population. *Ergonomics*, 34(6): 775–90.

Rabbitt, P.M.A. (1992) Memory. In J.G. Evans and T.F. Williams (eds), *Oxford Textbook of Geriatric Medicine*, pp. 463–79. Oxford: Oxford University Press.

Rabbitt, P.M.A. (1993) Conceptions of intelligence. *Ageing and Society*, 13(2): 270–3.

Rabbitt, P.M.A. and Abson, V. (1990) 'Lost and found': Some logical and methodological limitations of self-report questionnaires as tools to study cognitive ageing. *British Journal of Psychology*, 81: 1–16.

Rabbitt, P.M.A. and Abson, V. (1991) Do older people know how good they are? *British Journal of Psychology*, 82(2): 137–51.

Rabins, R.V. (1992) Cognition. In J.G. Evans and F.T. Williams (eds), *Oxford Textbook of Geriatric Medicine*, pp. 479–83. Oxford: Oxford University Press.

Rainey, N.A., McGuinness, C. and Trew, K. (1992) Old friends: The meaning and measurement of friendship for older adults. Paper presented at *The British Psychological Society (Northern Ireland Branch) Conference*, Virginia, Co. Cavan, May.

Rankin, G. (1991) Gilded age. *Good Housekeeping*, March, p. 15.

Reber, A.S. (1985). *The Penguin Dictionary of Psychology*. Harmondsworth: Penguin.

Reichard, S., Livson, F. and Peterson, P.G. (1962) *Aging and Personality*. New York: John Wiley

Reinharz, S. and Rowles, G.D. (1988) *Qualitative Gerontology*. New York: Springer.

Reker, G.T. (1991) Contextual and thematic analyses of sources of provisional meaning, Paper presented at the *Biennial Meeting of the International Society for the Study of Behavioural Development*, Minneapolis, MN, July.

Ritchie, K. and Ledesert, B. (1991) The measurement of capacity in the severely demented elderly: The validation of a behavioural assessment scale. *International Journal of Geriatric Psychiatry*, 6: 217–26.

Rinn, W.E. (1988) Mental decline in normal aging: A review. *Journal of Geriatric Psychiatry and Neurology*, 1(3): 144–58.

Robbert, R. (1990) The medicalization of senile dementia. Paper presented at the *2nd International Conference on the Future of Adult life*, Leeuwenhorst, The Netherlands, 4–8 July.

Robertson, A. (1990) The politics of Alzheimer's disease: A case study of apocalyptic demography. *International Journal of Health Services*, 20(3): 428–42.

Robinson, B. (1990) Why is suicide increasing among older Americans? *Ageing International*, 17(2): 37–8.

Rohling, M.L., Ellis, N.R. and Scogin, F. (1991) Automatic and effortful memory processes in elderly persons with organic brain pathology. *Journal of Gerontology (Psychological Sciences)*, 46(4): 137–43.

Ross, E.A. (1991) Wrinkle, wrinkle little star. *The Observer Review*, 7 July, p. 46.

Roth, M., Huppert, F.A., Tym, E. and Mountjoy. C.Q. (1988) *Camdex: The Cambridge Examination for Mental Disorders of the Elderly*. Cambridge: Cambridge University Press.

Rothenberg, R., Lentzner, H.R. and Parker, R.A. (1991) Population aging patterns: The expansion of mortality. *Journal of Gerontology (Social Sciences)*, 46(2): 66–70.

Rott, C. and Thomae, H. (1991) Coping in longitudinal perspective: findings from the Bonn Longitudinal Study on Aging. *Journal of Cross-Cultural Gerontology*, 6: 23–40.

Rubinstein, M. (1992) The realities of coffin dodging. *The Independent*, 4 September, p. 16.

Rykken, D.E. (1987) Sex in the later years. In P. Silverman (ed.), *The Elderly as Modern Pioneers*. Bloomington, IN: Indiana University Press.

Sabat, S.R. and Harré, R. (1992) The construction and deconstruction of self in Alzheimer's disease. *Ageing and Society*, 12(4): 443–61.

Salthouse, T. (1985). *A Theory of Cognitive Aging*. Oxford: North-Holland.

Salthouse, T. (1990) Influence of experience on age differences in cognitive functioning. *Human Factors*, 32(5): 551–69.

Sartre, J.-P. (1957) *Being and Nothingness*, trans. H.E. Barnes. London: Methuen.

Schaie, K.W. (1988) Some concluding comments. In K.W. Schaie, R.T. Campbell, W. Meredith and S.C. Rawlings (eds), *Methodological Issues in Aging Research*, pp. 249–53. New York: Springer.

Schulz, R. (1994) Introduction: Debate on generalised theories of slowing. *Journal of Gerontology (Psychological Sciences)*, 49(2): 59.

Schwarz, W. (1991) New centre aims to lift gloom and put ecstacy into dying. *The Guardian*, 6 April, p. 6.

Scrutton, S. (1992) *Ageing, Healthy and in Control: An Alternative Approach to Maintaining the Health of Older People.* London: Chapman and Hall.

Seale, C. (1995a) Dying. In B. Davey (ed.), *U205 Health and Disease: Book 5 – Birth to Old Age,* Ch. 12. Milton Keynes: Open University.

Seale, C. (1995b) Society and death. In B. Davey (ed.), *U205 Health and Disease: Book 5 – Birth to Old Age,* Ch. 13. Milton Keynes: Open University.

Selkoe, D.J. (1992) Aging brain, aging mind. *Scientific American,* 267(3): 97–103.

Shanan, J. (1991) Who and how: Some unanswered questions in adult development. *Journal of Gerontology (Psychological Sciences),* 46(6): 309–16.

Shapiro, J. (1989) *Ourselves Growing Older: Women Ageing with Knowledge and Power.* London: Fontana/Collins.

Sharrock, D. (1993) Anthony Quinn's lust for life results in 11th child at age of 78. *The Guardian,* 20 August, p. 1.

Sherman, E. (1991) Reminiscentia: Cherished objects as memorabilia in late-life reminiscence. *International Journal of Aging and Human Development,* 33(2): 89–100.

Short, I. (1991) Relating to the elderly. *Counselling News,* June, pp. 10–13.

Silverman, P. (ed.) (1987) *The Elderly as Modern Pioneers.* Bloomington, IN: Indiana University Press.

Simmons, H.C. (1990) Countering cultural metaphors of aging. *Journal of Religious Gerontology,* 7(1/2): 153–65.

Sixsmith, A. (1990) The meaning and experience of 'home' in later life. In W.R. Bytheway and J. Johnson (eds), *Welfare and the Ageing Experience: A Multidisciplinary Analysis,* pp. 172–92. Aldershot: Avebury.

Sixsmith, A. (1993) Philosophical perspectives on quality of life. In J. Johnson and R. Slater (eds), *Ageing and Later Life,* pp. 215–20. London: Sage.

Skinner, B.F. and Vaughan, M.E. (1983) *Enjoy Old Age: A Program of Self-management.* New York: W.W. Norton.

Smith, M. (1991) Costs of retiring. *Wales on Sunday,* 5 May, p. 16.

Spagnoli, A. (1991) Clinical relevance in drug trials for Alzheimer's disease and related disorders. *International Journal of Clinical Psychiatry,* 6: 265–7.

Spiro, H. (1991) A philosophic approach to aging. *Clinics in Geriatric Medicine,* 7(2): 387–93.

Sprinkart, P. (1988) Rediscovered lives: Work with older people in the search for time past. *Journal of Gerontological Social Work,* 12(3/4): 47–62.

Staudinger, U.M., Cornelius, S.W. and Baltes, P.B. (1989) The aging of intelligence: Potential and limits. *Annals of the American Academy of Political and Social Science,* 503: 43–59.

Stelmach, G.E. and Nahom, A. (1992) Cognitive–motor abilities of the elderly driver. *Human Factors,* 34(1): 53–65.

Sternberg, R.J. (ed.) (1990) *Wisdom: Its Nature, Origins and Development.* Cambridge: Cambridge University Press.

Stockton, P. (1991) The Alzheimer's disease epidemic: Mental status assessment of elderly people in the US. *Critical Public Health,* 2: 15–20.

Storandt, M. (1992) Memory-skills training for older adults. *Current Theory and Research in Motivation,* 39: 39–62. Nebraska Symposium on Motivation, 1991. Lincoln, NB: University of Nebraska Press.

Stott, M. (1981) *Ageing for Beginners.* Oxford: Blackwell.

Stroebe, W. and Insko, C.A. (1989) Stereotype, prejudice and discrimination: Changing patterns in theory and research. In D. Bar-Tal, C.F. Graumann, A.W. Kruglanski and W.Stroebe (eds), *Stereotyping and Prejudice: Changing Conceptions.* London: Springer.

Stuart-Hamilton, I. (1991) *The Psychology of Ageing: An Introduction.* London: Jessica Kingsley.

Sudgrove, J. (1993) Trading in old skin. *The Guardian (Tabloid),* 1 March, p. 10.

Sweeting, H. (1991) Caring for a relative with dementia: Anticipatory grief and social death. *Generations*, 16 Summer: 6.

Taylor, R. (1988) The elderly as members of society: An examination of social differences in an elderly population. In N. Wells and C. Freer (eds), *The Ageing Population: Burden or Challenge?*, pp. 105–29. Basingstoke: Macmillan/Stockton Press.

The Hen Co-op (1993) *Growing Old Disgracefully*. London: Piatkus.

The Samaritans (1992) *Reach Out . . . We'll Be There*. Slough: The Samaritans.

Third Age International (1991) *Third Age Typologies*. Milton Keynes: Third Age International Ltd.

Thomas, L.E. (1991) Dialogues with three religious renunciates and reflections on wisdom and maturity. *International Journal of Aging and Human Development*, 32(3): 211–27.

Thompson, P., Itzin, C. and Abendstern, M. (1991) *I Don't Feel Old*. Oxford: Oxford University Press.

Thorsheim, H. and Roberts, B. (1990) Empowerment through storysharing: communication and reciprocal social support among older persons. In H.Giles, N. Coupland and J.M. Wiemann (eds), *Communication, Health and the Elderly*, pp. 114–26. Manchester: Manchester University Press.

Tilak, S. (1989) *Religion and Aging in the Indian Tradition*. Albany, NY: State University of New York Press.

Tornstam, L. (1989) Gero-transcendance: A reformulation of the disengagement theory. *Aging*, 1(1): 55–63.

Troll, L.E. (1985) The contingencies of grandparenting. In V.L. Bengston and J.F. Robertson (eds), *Grandparenthood*, pp. 135–49. London: Sage.

Tuckett, A. (1994) Learning for life. *The Guardian (Education)*, 10 May, pp. 2–3.

Twigg, J. and Atkin, K. (1994) *Carers Perceived: Policy and Practice in Informal Care*. Buckingham: Open University Press.

Twigg, J., Atkin, K. and Perrin, C. (1990) *Carers and Services: A Review of Research*. London: HMSO.

Verhaeghen, P., Marcoen, A. and Goosens, L. (1993) Facts and fiction about memory aging: A quantitative integration of research findings. *Journal of Gerontology (Psychological Sciences)*, 48(4): 157–71.

Vincent, S. (1994) *Exits. The Guardian (Weekend)*, 19 February, pp. 6–10, 52.

Walker, A. (1990) The economic 'burden' of ageing and the prospect of intergenerational conflict. *Ageing and Society*, 10(4): 377–96.

Waller, P.F. (1991) The older driver. *Human Factors*, 35(5): 499–505.

Warr, P. (1994) Age and employment. In H.C. Triandis, M.D. Dunnette and L.M. Hough (eds), *Handbook of Industrial and Organizational Psychology*, pp. 485–550. Palo Alto, CA: Consulting Psychologists Press.

Weale, S. (1993) Why granny is down in the dumps. *The Guardian*, 19 May, p. 13.

Webb, L., Delaney, J.J. and Young, L.R. (1989) Age, interpersonal attraction, and social interaction. *Research on Aging*, 11(1): 107–23.

Welford, A. (1992) Psychological studies of aging: Their origins, development and present challenge. *International Journal of Aging and Human Development*, 34(3): 185–97.

Welsh Health Planning Forum (1992) *Protocol for Investment in Health Gain: Physical Disability and Discomfort*. Cardiff: Welsh Health Planning Forum.

Wenger, G.C. (1984) *The Supportive Network: Coping with Old Age*. London: George Allen and Unwin.

Whitehorn, K. (1991) You're as old as you feel. *The Observer*, 7 July, p. 47.

Wilkie, T. (1992) I would gain nothing by knowing. *The Independent*, 24 March, p. 17.

Woodward, K. (1988) Reminiscence, identity, sentimentality: Simone de Beauvoir and the life review. *Journal of Gerontological Social Work*, 12 (3/4): 25–46.

Woodward, K. (1991) *Aging and its Discontents: Freud and Other Fictions.* Bloomington, IN: Indiana University Press.

Woollacott, M. (1994) When people on the margins are pushed off the edge. *The Guardian*, 17 August, p. 16.

Young, M. and Schuller, T. (1991) *Life After Work: The Arrival of the Ageless Society.* London: HarperCollins.

Index

abuse,108
accentuation theory, 16
accuracy
  trade-off with speed, 60
adjustment, 134
age discrimination, 21, 22, 26, 27
ageism, 19, 20
alcohol consumption, 51
Alzheimer's disease
  beta-amyloid, 83
  differential diagnosis, 81
  histology, 84
  normal ageing, 78
  risk factors, 78
anxiety, 51–2
appearance, 21, 22–3
attention, 57, 64, 70, 74
attitudes
  to death, 30
  to health, 14
  to income, 14
  to life, 4
  to loneliness/isolation, 14
  to past vs. present, 31
  western, 39
attraction, 23

Baltes, P.B., 6, 131, 132
belief congruence theory, 16
beta-amyloid, 78, 82
biological ageing, 64

Birren, J.E., 61, 62, 63, 64, 117, 130–1,
  137
blood pressure, 66, 85
Bonn longitudinal study, 47–8
Bromley, D.B., 6, 8, 9, 21
Bytheway, B., 10, 13, 20

CAMDEX, 80, 89
cardio-vascular system, 65
caring
  care-mapping, 94
  community, 113
  dementia, 109–10
  family responsibility, 107
  formal, 40, 109
  gender patterns, 108
  hospice, 140–2
  informal, 37
  satisfaction in, 110
categorization, 13, 18, 27
centenarians, 2, 27, 46
cerebral blood flow, 65
Christianity, 133
chronic life syndrome, 2
class, 33, 37, 39
clubs, 34, 102–4
cohort effects, 48, 77
Coleman, P., 123, 124, 125
community care, 113
complementary medicine, 53–4
complex tasks, 58, 61

confidants, 98, 102
  gender differences, 103
control, 48–50, 129, 140, 143–6
coping
  active, 46, 50
  avoidance, 49, 50
  domains, 47
  emotion-focused, 48
  gender differences, 101
  religion, 138
  response variability, 47
cosmetics, 23
counselling, 52

daily hassles, 41–2
daily life, 40–1
death, 130, 139–43
de-differentiation, 62
dementia
  assessment protocols, 88–9
  care-mapping, 94
  carer support, 87, 94
  caring, 109–10
  compensatory behaviour, 113
  differential diagnosis, 80–1
  drugs, 95–6
  early detection, 80, 87
  experience of, 91–2
  imagery, 87
  labelling, 87
  malignant social psychology, 93
  memory, 79
  memory clinics, 87
  normal ageing, 78
  personhood in, 93, 94
  presentation, 90–1
  prevalence, 88
  reminiscence, 122
  responding to, 92–3
  risk factors, 88
  self in, 93, 94
  sub-clinical, 78
  therapy, 110
demography, 2–3
dependency, 32, 35, 50
depression, 52–3
  Alzheimer's, 90
  cognitive efficiency, 66, 68–9
  strokes, 86
despair, 130
disability, 21, 42–3, 51, 139
  dementia, 88
discourse, 20

discrimination, 12, 20–2
  in advertisements, 21
disengagement, 119, 137
  divorce, 105
driving, 57
  attention, 57
  awareness, 57–8
  cognitive-motor activities, 59
  identity, 58
DSM-III-R, 88
dying, 139–43

education, 116–19
electroconvulsive therapy, 53
electrophysiology, 62
emotionality, 30, 86
empowerment, 144
engagement, 119, 122, 138
Erikson, E.H., 6, 105, 120, 129, 130
ethnic minorities, 38–40
  health differentials, 39
ethnocentrism, 12
euthanasia, 20, 141, 143
exercise, 63
existentialism, 5

family
  contact, 101, 105–6
  relationships, 99–101
formal care, 40, 49
free radicals, 83
friends, 97–101
  functions of, 98
fulfilment, 115–16, 123, 133

gender patterns, 35–8, 105, 145
generativity, 105
gerontologists, 7, 13
gerontologization, 92
grandparents, 33–4, 104–6
Gray Panthers, 145
grieving, 142–3

health, 43
hearing, 50
Heim, A., 29–32
Hindu faith, 132–3
home, 111–13
homosexuals, 26
housing policy, 112–13
Huppert, F.A., 52, 74–5, 79, 81

illnesss
  cognitive change, 64–6
  demography, 37
illusory correlation theory, 16
informal care, 37
information-processing
  reduced capacity, 58
institutionalization, 49–50
integration, 27, 37, 123
  of human abilities, 131
integrity, 129
intelligence, 63, 67
  domains, 75
  drugs, 76
  pathology, 65
  physical fitness, 63
inter-generational relationships, 31
intimate relationships, 34
isolation, 101, 138

Kitwood, T., 93, 94

labelling, 87
language, 72–3
learned helplessness, 49
leisure, 33, 40–1, 116–19
lesbians, 26
Lewy Body disease, 83, 84
life expectancy, 2–3
  active, 2
life-histories, 145
life-reviews, 120–6
lipofuscin, 82
living wills, 140
loneliness, 101, 138

malignant social psychology, 93
meaning, 33, 34, 97, 111, 127–9
media, 15–16
medicalization, 92
memory
  aids, 74
  autobiographical, 71
  automatic, 79
  clinics, 87
  deep processing, 74
  dementia, 79
  depression, 52
  effortful, 79
  improvements, 73–4
  management, 31
  metamemory, 69, 71
  names, 70

pathological changes, 64
  prospective, 71
  remote, 70
  reserve capacity, 75
  semantic, 71
  subjective experience, 68–9
  testing acceptability, 79
  verbal speed, 63
  working, 70
metaphors
  of ageing, 8
  computer, 62, 77
  de-differentiation, 62
methodology, 9–10, 68, 78, 89
  health and illness, 64–5
  introspection, 138
  qualitative/quantitative, 67
migration, 112
mindlessness, 4
Mini-Mental State examination, 80
mortality compression, 3
MoT tests, 58, 59
multi-infarct dementia, 85

National Adult Reading Test, 81
nature/nurture, 7
neighbourhood, 111
neighbours, 102
neurofibrillary tangles, 82, 84

Open University, 5, 118, 119
oral history, 122–3

Parkinson's disease, 82, 83
pedestrians, 57
pensions, 36
performance monitoring, 58, 68
personal insights, 29–33, 34, 35
personality, 47, 48, 134–6
planning, 120
pleasures, 35
positivism, 134
poverty, 36, 38
prejudice, 12
  against women, 37
  racial, 39
prototypes, 17, 18, 28
psychodynamic theories, 16

quality of life, 32, 99, 113

Rabbitt, P.M.A., 11, 22, 58, 64–5, 67–8,
  74–6

reaction time, 61
realistic conflict theory, 15
reductionism, 8
relationships
    family, 99–101
    satisfaction from, 38
religion, 132–4, 138–9
reminiscence, 121–6
    orientation to, 124
repression, 125
residential homes, 113
resourcefulness, 33
retirement, 22, 114–15
    education for, 117
    policy, 115–16
role models, 5, 27–8, 118

Salthouse, T., 8, 58, 60, 67
self-confidence, 30
self-fulfilling prophecy, 17, 93
self-help, 104
self-interest, 128
self-knowledge, 10
self-management, 75–6
self-transcendence, 128
Selkoe, D.J., 82, 83, 84
senile plaques, 82
sex, 4, 24–6, 109
skills, 87
slowing
    experience of, 56
    general phenomenon, 62
social identity theory, 15
social learning theory, 15
spirituality, 129, 132–4, 137
stamina, 31
stereotypes, 13–14, 25, 34, 35, 75, 135
    cognitive theories, 16–17

of past life, 121
stress, 51, 63, 66, 138
    dementia care, 109–10
strokes, 85–6
    depression, 86
    emotionalism, 86
    incidence, 85
    national variations, 85
    rehabilitation, 85–6
students, 5, 118, 119
successful ageing, 6, 7, 74, 131
suicide, 54–5
support networks, 44–5
survivors, 32

terminology, 15, 18–19, 64–5, 77–8, 85
therapy, 110, 123, 124
Thompson, P., 1, 33, 34, 106, 108, 111
time, 56
tip-of-the-tongue, 69
tolerance, 30
transcendence, 138

University of the 3rd Age, 118–19
useful field of view, 59

variability, 22, 30, 32, 47, 59, 63
visibility, 27–8, 42, 95
volunteering, 104

Wenger, C., 44, 45, 105
wisdom, 62, 124, 129–32
Woodward, K., 120, 124–5, 132
world views, 8

Young, M., 114, 115, 116

AGEISM

Bill Bytheway

Ageism has appeared in the media increasingly over the last twenty years.

- What is it?
- How are we affected?
- How does it relate to services for older people?

This book builds bridges between the wider age-conscious culture within which people live their lives and the world of the caring professions. In the first part, the literature on age prejudice and ageism is reviewed and set in a historical context. A wide range of settings in which ageism is clearly apparent are considered and then, in the third part, the author identifies a series of issues that are basic in determining a theory of ageism. The book is written in a style intended to engage the reader's active involvement: how does ageism relate to the beliefs the reader might have about older generations, the ageing process and personal fears of the future? To what extent is chronological age used in social control? The book discusses these issues not just in relation to discrimination against 'the elderly' but right across the life course.

The book:

- is referenced to readily available material such as newspapers and biographies
- includes case studies to ensure that it relates to familiar, everyday aspects of age
- includes illustrations – examples of ageism in advertising, etc.

Contents
Part 1: The origins of ageism – Introduction: too old at 58 – Ugly and useless: the history of age prejudice – Another form of bigotry: ageism gets on to the agenda – Part 2: Aspects of ageism – The government of old age: ageism and power – The imbecility of old age: the impact of language – Get your knickers off, granny: interpersonal relations – Is it essential?: ageism and organizations – Part 3: Rethinking ageism – Theories of age – No more 'elderly', no more old age – References – Index.

158pp   0 335 19175 4 (Paperback)   0 335 19176 2 (Hardback)

HEALTH IN OLD AGE
MYTH, MYSTERY AND MANAGEMENT

Moyra Sidell

- Why do many older people rate their health as good when 'objective' evidence suggests that old age is a time of inevitable decline and disease?
- How do different perspectives on health inform our understanding of health in old age?
- What are the policy implications for ensuring a healthy future for old age?

This book addresses important questions which existing literature on health and old age has largely ignored. By juxtaposing detailed case histories and first person accounts from older people with 'official statistics' on the health of 'the elderly' it explores the myths and tries to unpick the mysteries which surround the subject of health in later life. It goes on to explore the implications of these myths and mysteries for the way individual older people manage their health. It looks at the resources and social support available to them as well as the implications for public policy provision. The book ends by exploring the problems and possibilities of ensuring a healthy future for old age. It will be essential reading for reflective practitioners and for anyone concerned with new developments in the fields of ageing, social policy and health.

Contents
Introduction – Part 1: The health context – The mirage of health – Lay logic – Patterns of health and illness among older people – Part 2: Experiencing health – Understanding chronic illness and disability – Maintaining health with physical illness and functional disability – Maintaining health with mental malaise – Part 3: Resources for health – Health care and the management of health – Personal resources and social support – A healthy future for old age – Bibliography – Index.

200pp   0 335 19136 3 (Paperback)   0 335 19336 6 (Hardback)

AGE, RACE AND ETHNICITY
A COMPARATIVE APPROACH

Ken Blakemore and Margaret Boneham

This is the first definitive study of ageing among black and Asian people in Britain. Until now, debates on race relations have tended to ignore the 'greying' of Britain's minority communities. Equally, ageing studies have lacked a focus on the challenging realities of a multi-racial society and of racial discrimination. In this wide-ranging and questioning book, the authors combine original research with the results of over a decade of community studies of age and race. They give a comprehensive overview of the British context of 'minority ageing', comparing it with that of other societies such as the USA and Australia. They show the range and variety of patterns of ageing in the Asian and Afro-Caribbean communities, illustrated by personal life histories, and there are substantial chapters on the challenges to be faced by the health and social services. This book will be essential reading, both for 'reflective practitioners' and for anyone concerned with new developments in the fields of ageing, race relations, sociology and social policy.

> This is an important reference book for practitioners, professionals, gerontologists and students who want to gain an understanding of the realities, complexities and implications of providing comprehensive quality services for black and ethnic minority elders . . . The authors present significant social and demographic background studies from a range of sources . . . Professionals and students will find this book valuable as a research tool and for general information and further exploration of the subject.

> I hope *Age, Race and Ethnicity: A Comparative Approach* finds its way into all good bookshops, social service libraries and every social policy and gerontology reading list. It is value for money.
>
> (*Care Weekly*)

Contents
Introduction – Research, understanding and action – Comparative perspectives – Double jeopardy? – The Afro-Caribbeans' experience – The Asians' experiences – Health, illness and health services – Welfare and social services – Conclusion – Bibliography – Index.

176pp   0 335 19086 3 (Paperback)   0 335 19234 3 (Hardback)